It has remained for our age to make problematic both God and man.

Neither the simple faith of Israel nor the theocentric universe of the medieval man seem viable in our century. Nor can modern man retain that optimistic view of himself which was possible to the man of the Enlightenment and after. Verdun, Buchenwald and Hiroshima have shown man that he is as much Mephistopheles as Prometheus.

This is the background against which the Rev. Robert W. Gleason has written *The Search for God*. Beginning with contemporary atheism, and tracing its roots into the nineteenth century, Father Gleason helps us to understand the widespread phenomenon of contemporary unbelief, and shows why "anguish" so scars modern man as he looks about for that God who, if not absent, at least seems silent. The author then takes us back in time to other ages when faith seemed an all but essential component in man's understanding of himself. By showing how the God of Israel fulfilled the dark intuitions of the nature religions and how Christianity fulfilled the revelations made to Israel, Father Gleason prepares the reader for a fresh understanding of that search for God conducted by the great Scholastic thinkers.

Finally, in a sequence of striking chapters, Father Gleason traces the reasons why the "God of Reason" had gradually seemed more and more remote to the modern mind; for this mind, alternately attracted and awed by scientism, increasingly apprehensive of the rational, a new approach to God seems called for—an approach which, without denying the legitimate claims of the head, would also give full response to the demands of the heart—an approach, in short, which has been fashioned, at least in inchoate form, by such contemporary thinkers as Gabriel Marcel and Henri de Lubac.

It has been repeatedly said that the basic problem confronting modern man is not the political nor psychological nor technological, but theological: the problem of God. One more readily appreciates the truth of this statement when he has, under the distinguished guidance of Father Gleason, seen how earlier cultures have answered this problem, and why our contemporary failure adequately to face the problem has rendered man mystery even to himself.

FATHER GLEASON, a native of White Plains, New York, is a professor in the Department of Theology at Fordham University. He attended Fordham, Woodstock College, and the Gregorian University in Rome, in addition to doing graduate theological work in Belgium, Austria, and Spain. He has travelled extensively in many sections of Europe, and for a time lectured at the Catholic University of Namur.

Father Gleason is an experienced retreat master, and has lectured and conducted numerous retreats for institutes for religious superiors, in addition to teaching ascetical theology to religious and clergy both here and abroad. He is also the author of *The World to Come*, *Christ and the Christian*, *To Live Is Christ* and *Grace*, which have been translated into many foreign languages, including Dutch, French, German, Italian, Spanish, and Portuguese. He is co-author of *Counselling the Catholic*.

THE SEARCH FOR GOD

THE SEARCH
FOR GOD

by *Robert W. Gleason*, S.J.

SHEED AND WARD : : NEW YORK

© *Sheed and Ward, Inc. 1964*

Library of Congress Catalog Card Number 64–19904

Manufactured in the United States of America

Contents

THE SEARCH FOR GOD

The Problem of God

1

The Modern World
and the Sense of God

To describe the modern era in a way that would be both accurate and adequate is an obvious impossibility, so complex and so changing is our present day world. For ours is a world in revolution, a time of political upheaval together with scientific, economic, social and intellectual innovations that are completely altering the structure of society. Pope John XXIII described our modern era as shot through with radical errors; torn and convulsed by deep disorders.

The same supreme Pontiff went on to say, however, that the age has also opened up immensely bright horizons, as amazing progress points toward new heights of human achievement, transforming, through scientific technology, our entire way of life.[1] But is this new world to be made Godless by the growth of certain modern ideas and values?

If there is any one feature of our contemporary crisis which distinguishes it from those of preceding civilizations, it would seem to be the chronic, almost universal loss of the sense of God. Men of former ages held one thing to be crucial: the religious question. In our day endless activities consume the time and energy of men: business, money, knowledge, power, work, the pursuit of pleasure. Engrossed in the conquest of the world around him, modern man seems interested in matter rather than spirit, in himself rather than God.

Today the universe appears to many to be a closed system in which God has no place. Envisaging himself as the center of a

world which he can exploit and dominate, man has lost interest
in the Sovereign Creator.[2] Forced to yield His place to man, God
has become the Absent One. As Leon Bloy noted, God is absent
even from the life of religion, for many of those who still wish to
be His friends do not feel the need of His Presence. That God has
little effect on their lives is evident, for many of their works simply
ignore Him.[3]

Statistics confirm the alarming fact that a very large part of the
modern world lives as if God were dead, or as if His absence were
a certitude. Various factors have led to this loss of the sense of
God's presence. Mouroux believes that at the root of this disease
there lies first a rupture: the temporal world divorced from God;
and then a perversion: human love given exclusively to the temporal. The rupture is the result of overemphasis on the transcendence of God, the perversion that of undue stress on His immanence.[4]
To some the transcendence of God is an intolerable thought since it
implies a diminution of human values, to others His immanence is
a direct threat to their passion for self-sufficiency.

This rebellion of the human spirit against its Creator is not a new
event in the history of mankind but is in fact as old as humanity
itself. The primeval temptation was towards self-deification, and
the insidious voice in paradise, "you shall be as gods," is still being
heard today. The original turning away from God to self is the
primary source of all refusals to submit, of all pride and arrogance
in the heart of man.

As a cultural phenomenon informing man's entire attitude
towards life, however, the loss of the sense of God seems to date
from the time when the ancient concept of a theocentric universe
was displaced by a vision in which man is the center and liberty
holds the highest position in the hierarchy of values. During the
thousands of years which saw man powerless before the forces of
nature, his spontaneous feelings of dependence predisposed him
towards a religious frame of reference. Not only did he admit the
existence of God but he attempted to live according to a God-
centered scale of values. In the time of Christian feudalism a change

of values became evident, but it was not until the Renaissance that the cry of satanic revolt was heard. This was the beginning of the great rebellion in which man assigned himself a role heretofore acknowledged as belonging to a Supreme Being. The Renaissance emphasis on the classics and the return to nature were not, of course, godless movements. But through them man found the way to a profane humanism which clearly had no need for the Divinity. Objected to as a hindrance on man's liberty, God was eventually dismissed as a useless, even absurd archaism.

Some two centuries later the revolt against God was made more pronounced through the rapid development of the scientific spirit. As a method, science was in no way contradictory to belief in the existence of a Supreme Being, but rationalistic philosophy soon made of it a tool for successful exploitation of the visible world. Man's power increased but so did his spirit of liberty and autonomy. With the development of his sense of superiority came the loss of his ancient feeling of subordination to a higher reality.[5]

Today, as science and technology dominate the scene, many things in nature which were once obscure and mysterious have been explained. Yet the sin of the world today, as Cardinal Suhard has pointed out, is once again the sin of the Old Testament: idolatry. God is denied and man is worshipped. In a world in which God has been reduced to nothing the man of science has become a god.[6]

Many men of science today are trying to transform a world which they see not as a mirror of God's presence but as a place wherein only science and technology can resolve the great questions concerning humanity's future. In their eyes, humanistic and religious approaches to these questions are merely secondary and auxiliary. Their belief in the salvific power of the natural sciences and technology is based on such triumphs as the increasing control over disease and death, the penetration of outer space, and the liberation of the forces of the unconscious through psychoanalysis and depth psychology. As a result they are convinced that the paths of scientific research are the only reliable avenues to truth. Preoccupied as they are with the physical sciences and a positivistic approach to

measurable realities, they have eliminated the hypothesis of God as
outside their field of interest; for them He no longer fulfills a vital
function.[7] The world of "I and Thou" is wholly excluded from
scientific activity, which, since it is exclusively concerned with the
world of observable objects and events, is necessarily confined to
the world of "I and It."[8]

As an antidote to such a philosophy of existence the work of the
late Jesuit anthropologist, Teilhard de Chardin, is of major importance. For a world fascinated by scientific technology his writings recall the sacral, sign value of nature, the fact that it points to
another existence, and the consequence that science can find its
true fulfillment only in a spiritual dimension. Moreover, the success
of Chardin's writings is an encouraging indication that he has
provided a scientific foundation for an idea which responds to widespread needs.

Since technical progress and the augmenting of man's powers are
obviously good things in themselves, it would be the sheerest folly
to associate the absence of God with the concept of human progress.
Nonetheless, the flat rejection of God as the principle of the intelligibility and explanation of the world is the characteristic of
modern man.[9]

The desire to eliminate God from existence is seen not only in
scientific milieux but in modern political philosophy as well.
Modern man is politically minded and his thought is pervaded
by the notion of establishing public order without God. This will
to disregard God, to view Him as irrelevant to the concerns of men,
is no cool rationalistic exposition on the philosophical level but a
determination, in the name of progress, to do away with the concept of a living, transcendent God Who intervenes in the affairs of
men. The God of history has become an obstacle to the goal of
a world without misery, and He must be done away with. To
many the living God of history is the real source of man's alienation from himself and his impotence to alter social and economic
conditions. In bitter resentment over what God has done to human
life, they attempt to free themselves from His dominance, not as

in the nineteenth century by asserting that He is dead but by arguing that "God has no right to be; it is necessary to destroy Him." Only when God has been suppressed will man himself be able to give meaning and direction to human history and be free to achieve the political liberation which he so ardently desires.[10]

At the root of this passionate rejection of a God Who intervenes in the affairs of men is, of course, modern man's exasperation with the problem of evil. It is here in the grim fact that evil exists and the innocent suffer that atheism finds its permanent, revitalizing bases. Today, more than ever before, there exists an obscure, often subrational resentment against God, to Whom man refuses forgiveness for the fact of evil in the world. In his grandiose plan to be the servant of history and the savior of the world, the modern God-opposed political philosopher aims at doing away with poverty, hunger, injustice and war.[11]

Yet another type of modern man who has lost the sense of God is the one for whom the sole value in human life is freedom, and for whom the affirmation of the liberty of man implies the negation of the existence of God. In order to give meaning and value to his own life this kind of person believes that he must remove God as an obstacle on the path to full self-mastery. If to act according to the will of a transcendent God of history is to be deprived of the freedom to choose one's own destiny, then to achieve autonomy one must oppose that hindering God. Man can become a human being in the full sense only by freely constructing the design of his existence. But to say that man is free is to affirm that he holds his being of himself, not by virtue of another. Therefore one must choose between the freedom of man and the existence of God. In spite of essential differences in many respects this is the common theme in Marxism and in atheistic existentialism. This refusal to recognize anything superior to man de Lubac has called "atheistic humanism," optimistic and quasi-triumphant with the Marxist, pessimistic and disillusioned in the case of the existentialist.[12]

The belief that man is self-subsistent automatically does away with the concept of norms received from the outside, antecedent to the action of man. What matters then is not acting according to any norm but acting freely. The result is the refusal to accept a universal moral law and the will to act independently at all costs, to be oneself the ultimate determinant of moral good and evil.

Whenever the sense of God's involvement in human history has been weakened or lost there has been little true morality. In our own times no surer signs exist that men have in large measure lost the sense of God than the widespread weakening of the sense of right and wrong, and the secularization of morality. Taking the human subject as the point of departure, a morality without obligation or sanction is constructed which, despite the intentions of its innovators, is but a caricature of authentic morality. Since sin presupposes a personal relationship to God, the very concept disappears and we arrive at a system of "morality without sin." As morality becomes more and more identified with the science of mores, a sociological morality develops in which society, represented by parental authority, teachers and companions, imposes certain norms of conduct. Insistence on the personal conscience is elevated to a law unto itself, while the widespread refusal to accept an objective moral standard culminates in so-called "situation ethics." Situation ethicians have, of course, some valid insights, but they lay such stress on the moral agent and the individual decision confronting him that universal laws can no longer be universally applicable.

With sin and guilt looked on as notions or as sources of mental anxiety, moral restrictions are considered a hindrance to the spontaneous unfolding of personality. Even religious leaders tend to settle moral questions without reference to God, as if morality could be detached from its foundation in Him. Looking to scientific appraisals of value as a guide to conduct, a naturalistic ethics searches for a factual ground of morality, but with a view of nature from which assent to God is excluded. That is why Pope Pius XII could say that the greatest sin today is that men have lost the sense of sin, no longer understanding it, or even taking it seriously. But the moral order, like everything else, has both its source and its object in God. Without a sense of His existence, any action can come to seem lawful.

Still another characteristic of our modern era is its pervasive secularism. The 1960 Pastoral Letter from the Italian bishops to their clergy isolated the phenomenon of secularism as the motivating spirit of modern man's erroneous positions in the religious and moral spheres. Even earlier the Catholic hierarchy of America had issued a pastoral on the danger of secularism in the national life. A twofold secularism can be distinguished. One in practice identifies itself with atheism, negating God, opposing religion, reducing all things to the merely human level; the other, less radical but more common, might be called "lived" or "practical" atheism. This modern phenomenon is a mitigated pragmatism of a bio-sociological character, based upon a psychology and ethics of conditioning. Although God's existence is acknowledged, natural values are so deified that, in effect, all transcendence is denied. Gabriel Marcel has asked if it is not the United States rather than Russia which breeds this concept of life. In it atheism is found as a corollary even though those who have adopted it retain membership in a church. Consequently, the secularist phenomenon is completely inimical to the religious sense of man, God having ceased to be seen as a personal Being truly concerned about His creatures.

The modern denial of God, together with the assertion of the self-sufficiency of man, has conjured up a spirit of universal disillusionment. Mankind today seems to be in the grip of fear and uncertainty. Lacking an absolute on which to depend, there is no solid base for inner peace and so man finds himself restless, anxious and insecure.[13]

The current cult of the individual seems only to have produced a continual inner frustration; inevitably so, for from the moment man attempts to make of himself an absolute he has begun to destroy himself. Since his innate religious sense is fundamentally a need for truth, to stifle it is to thwart his own nature. The godless man of our time is one who refuses to adore and who, as a result, is a man twisted and deformed. As certainly as God, the Author of nature, is integral to the concept of man, His presence is necessary to the structure of man's historical existence. The man who does not adore the Divinity has somehow lost his own humanity.

Today, by their actions, men manifest a feeling of rootlessness, a sense that existence is purposeless, that life is bereft of meaningful experience. Modern writers, obsessed with pessimism, accurately reflect the spiritual state of much of contemporary society. Mass media present frustration, failure, anguish and futility as symbolic of the crisis that comes to the man who thinks he has freed himself. In his desire to be rid of God modern man has handed himself over to the blankness of an idolatry which has as its object an empty abstraction in place of the living Ruler of all things.[14]

POSITIVE VALUES IN CONTEMPORARY THOUGHT

Although it would be naive to expect the world suddenly to recapture the meaning of God, it does not follow that there are no positive values in the contemporary situation. If we bring ourselves to face the modern mind objectively and with some degree of sympathy, it is possible at least to admit that current attitudes have revitalized the problem of God in our society.

The theme of God's existence and relationship with the world is not a mere peripheral adornment but a central theme in most of the great modern philosophies. Never before have so many books, articles, motion pictures and plays concerned the Absolute as they do at this precise moment, when the denial of God is most widespread. Surely this is to imply at least reluctant recognition of the very Reality which men pretend to deny. It might even be that the current rebellion against God could become the initial act in purifying our dialectic, the negative starting-point of a thought capable of orienting itself toward God in the end.[15] For there is absolutely no doubt that modern man is looking for a new way in which to grasp the meaning of human existence.

Modern systems which exclude all notion of God actually exploit authentic human values to which their devotees give a passionate commitment. Marxists, for example, are concerned about the contemporary sense of history, the mastery of matter and the collectivization of man. In their view the idea of the community as a corporate entity, the equality of all men, and the all-pervasive presence of poverty have assumed an importance implying a definite Christian failure in these matters.

The existentialists, reacting against Marxism, stress the value of the person—his freedom and his membership in the one great human family. To be so deeply aware of the value of human encounter may mean that they are actually "open" to the restoration of a sense of God.

Authentic value is also to be found in the destruction by modern science of the "God of explanation." The demolition of this concept is a gain, for scientific knowledge of the universe is utterly unable to lead us to a knowledge of God. If we "prove" God scientifically we merely make Him one more object among many others. Consequently, the denial of God on the level of science may simply be another way of rendering unwitting homage to the unique character of the Creator and so safeguarding the possibility of an authentic knowledge of God.[16]

Much of modern man's religious anguish arises out of his refusal to accept a God Whom Christianity has at times defined only in abstract, legalistic, non-temporal terms. But this can be of value for our times because the living God should not be presented as if He were a cold and lifeless category. In addition, the modern denial of God has been an efficacious criticism of outmoded, inadequate and anthropomorphic representations of the Deity. Current atheism, by contesting the classical theology of God, has put it on trial, forcing it to purify itself, highlighting the fundamental truth that faith is a gift, and reminding us that our knowledge of God is always precarious and obscure. Although, according to some, contemporary thought represents a serious threat to the traditional concept of God, examination of these new ideas discloses, mingled with error, gen-

uine values which can be assimilated without in any way weakening
or endangering faith.

The modern challenge thus provides an opportunity to do away
with a conception of God in which He plays a false and inferior
part. Centuries of bourgeois thought have tended to "compromise"
God, degrading Him to the position of a "jack-of-all-trades trouble-
shooter," waiting on the sidelines for the moment to rush in and
bolster man's ineptitudes, to intervene whenever man proves impotent to cope with life. In rejecting so false a concept of God contemporary minds are giving us the opportunity to affirm the transcendent Lord of history Who has been made known to us by
revelation. Curiously enough, the atheist is often a great help to the
believer, unintentionally cooperating in the necessary purification of
faith by providing the salt that prevents the believer's idea of God
from becoming corrupt. So it is possible that our profane civilization,
although it has lost the sense of God, may yet enable us to discover
Him at a deeper level.[17]

A primary requisite for restoring the lost sense of God is an
awareness of mystery. For God is a mystery in His very essence.
Although the human mind can discover many doors which lead to
Him, He is ultimately incomprehensible and there is no key which
can fully unlock His impenetrable mystery. To be sure, man can
know God with certitude through reason, but there is also a
rationalistic approach to Him which tends to dispel all sense of
mystery. The human mind is not the measure of God and the in-
clination to treat Him as one more intelligible object should be
firmly resisted.

In discussing the "problem of God" this distinction between
mystery and problem is crucial, setting before us, as it does, a central issue of our time. One confronts a problem; one lives a mystery.
A problem is an impersonal concern; a mystery involves us personally. A problem permits a number of solutions; a mystery permits only some form of acceptance. Moreover, a mystery relates
itself to what is most interior in us and stirs us to commitment.
Consequently, God should not take on the aspect of a problem. He

is a mystery confronting man with a basic option: either he belongs to himself or he does not belong to himself. If the latter is the case, then he is dependent upon a creative principle which transcends him.

All men, whether they realize it or not, depend upon God and are mysteriously drawn to Him. Yet in the very midst of this attraction, this strong movement of desire by which man is pulled out of himself toward an all-pervading Presence, there is another movement of regression by which man shrinks back in awe before the Wholly Other. On the one hand God seems approachable, familiar and intimately present to man. On the other He appears sovereignly transcendent, disconcerting and disturbing to the human being.

In the past the biblical notion of God as the cause of all things, the highest good, became little by little so emphasized as to lead to the view that God alone had value. So heavy a stress on the transcendent aspect of the Divine Being inevitably led to a reaction. In rejecting the idea of extreme transcendence, many ended up championing only God's immanence. Beginning by attributing to the world worth and power that never belonged to it, they came finally to a denial of God Himself. This was in fact a protest against a distorted notion of God as well as an attempt to preserve the greatness of the world and of man.[18]

In the minds of some, our own era has exalted immanence to the detriment of transcendence and therefore man must be brought back to a sense of God's transcendence. Actually, what is needed is a balance between the two. The mystery of God is a reality that is partly revealed and partly hidden; for the mysterious, hidden God is always the God Who is near. The paradoxical coexistence of these two traits is the heart of the contemporary crisis.

To restore the true notion of God it is important to return to the sources of Divine Revelation wherein we find united these two aspects of the living God. The God Who deigned to reveal Himself to men appears at some times transcendent and apart, at others present to man and immanent in the world. Incomparably lifted above every created form of being, He is nevertheless present in all creatures. It cannot be emphasized too often: the true idea of God demands not a choice between His immanence and His transcendence but a synthesis.

An analysis of all the reasons why our modern world is distinguishable from previous civilizations by its lack of a sense of God would involve a study of such highly complex movements as naturalism, secularism, atheism and existentialism. Although the human mind has been diverted by a many-faceted world revolution, its innate tendency to absolutize some value confirms the fact that man is irresistibly drawn to God even when the God of Revelation is not known.

The modern world must be reminded of the sovereignty and approachability, the presence and eternity, of the God Who "so loved the world as to send His only begotten Son" (John 3, 16). True knowledge of this personal, loving God will lead unerringly to an affirmation of the reality and meaningfulness of the world. Once created reality is accepted as an image of the Divine, men will realize that it is one and the same to give glory to God and to perfect man and the world. Far from entailing withdrawal of interest and energy, recognition of God awakens renewed concern for one's responsibility in the practical affairs of the natural world and human society.

Modern man has no reason to despair. The God of Whom he is ignorant "makes even the wrath of men to serve Him." Misshapen worlds are no problem to One Who will cause them to bear fruit in His own way. The eternal God, totally present to the totality of each epoch, is the Master of all, even when men try to proclaim His death. However bleak and forbidding our modern world may seem to be, this sterility is no impediment to the God Whose salvific designs for us remain marvelous beyond all understanding.

NOTES

1. Pope John XXIII, *Christianity and Social Progress,* New York, Paulist Press, 1961, p. 79.

2. J. Daniélou, "Presence et Transcendance," *Monde Moderne et Sens de Dieu,* Paris, Pierre Horay, 1954, p. 252.
3. E. Suhard, "The Meaning of God," *The Church Today,* Chicago, Fides, 1953, p. 173.
4. J. Mouroux, *The Meaning of Man,* New York, Sheed and Ward, 1948, p. 11.
5. H. Daniel-Rops, "Dieu dans le monde d'aujourd'hui," *Monde Moderne et Sens de Dieu,* p. 15.
6. Suhard, *op. cit.,* p. 178.
7. M. D. Chenu and F. Heer, "Is the Modern World Atheist?" *Cross Currents,* XI, 1961, p. 8.
8. H. Taylor, "Science and Religion: Towards Unity," *Perspectives,* V, 1960, p. 6.
9. J. C. Murray, "On the Structure of the Problem of God," *Theological Studies,* XXIII 1962, p. 19.
10. J. Lacroix, "The Meaning and Value of Atheism Today," *Cross Currents,* V 1955, p. 208.
11. G. Marcel, "Contemporary Atheism and the Religious Mind," *Philosophy Today,* IV 1960, p. 261.
12. J. LeBlond, "The Christian and Modern Atheism," *Theology Digest,* III 1955, p. 139.
13. S. A. Turienzo, "Absence of God and Man's Insecurity," *Philosophy Today,* III 1959, p. 136.
14. B. Vawter, *"Missing the Mark,"* The Way, II 1962, p. 27.
15. Marcel, *art. cit.,* p. 256.
16. La Croix, *art. cit.,* pp. 205–206, 215.
17. H. deLubac, *The Discovery of God,* New York, P. J. Kenedy and Sons, 1960, pp. 180–181.
18. H. Pfeil, "The Modern Denial of God: Its Origin and Tragedy," *Philosophy Today,* III 1959, p. 22.

2

The Sense of Sin
in the Modern World

IN addition to the loss of the sense of God, our age has a diminished sense of sin. The prime reason for this is modern man's diminished awareness of the transcendent majesty of God. Fortunately, in spite of its uncertainty about God and religious values, today's world still holds to some moral system which differentiates between ethical right and wrong. On the other hand, while Christianity has kept alive for her members the consciousness of sin, the Christian conscience is often blunted, especially in matters of charity, social justice and the more nuanced moral issues of interpersonal relations.[1]

Some notion of sin seems almost innate in every human being, for no man is without some god, some focal absolute around which his life revolves. This god determines a man's credal commitments, the values he accepts or rejects and the resulting conscious, or preconscious, implicit and obscure idea of sin. Since it is intrinsic to his nature, man bears an inescapable consciousness of responsibility, and thus a sense of guilt, both inherited and personal, is inseparable from the human condition. It is, in fact, one of man's gravest burdens and concerns, one that accounts in part for his anguish of existence, his sense of strangeness in the universe.

The problem of sin then is as important today as ever; if man is a moral animal, then no effort of his mind has lasting importance that is not somehow concerned with this problem. Renan may have believed his boast: "It is I who have abolished sin," but the sense of sin somehow remains; man guesses obscurely at a destiny missed,

experiences the distress of an existential catastrophe in his moral
failings. Sin may be a word that has grown tired with over-use, but
the reality it signifies remains both dynamic and destructive, its
effect far-reaching and comprehensive; all men are involved by
virtue of their human and supernatural solidarity.[2]

Our age is not anxious to hear about sin, in the ancient meaning
of that word. Yet some sincerely recognize it as a mortal anguish,
an estrangement from self and the world peculiar to humanity, and
agree that to deny to man the possibility of sin is to deny him his
humanity.

Paul Tillich has remarked that "Man's essential loneliness and
seclusion, his insecurity and feeling of strangeness, his temporality
and melancholy, are qualities which are felt even apart from their
transformation by guilt; they are his heritage of finitude" (*Shaking
of the Foundation,* New York. Charles Scribner's Sons, 1949, p.
170). But the existential anxiety that is rooted in contingency is only
part of the burden of man's ultimate anxiety. To it has been added
the failure of sin.

The story of sin is certainly the story of man's failure, but somehow implicit in this failure there is grandeur, for man can only fail
where he can succeed. Man is not easily freed from this dichotomy
of his existence: he transcends the laws of nature by his freedom
and yet is subject to them as an enfleshed spirit. While the rest of
creation is physically moved to its end, man is morally moved to
his. Sin is a betrayal of that finality because in sinning man twists
and bends his nature from what it was intended to be and to do.
Man's nature is a rational nature, and where reason should rule
supreme, the sinner upsets reason, seeking ends which reason would
not strive for. Hence, every sin is unnatural, a betrayal of the ultimate self, for every sin is against reason. Christianity weighs fully
the metaphysical gravity of sin, for it sees it not only as a social disorder, a psychic blunder, a fault, but as an event that is enacted, by
man's liberty, between man and God.[3]

A large part of mankind is losing the sense of sin, no longer
understanding what sin is or accepting it as a meaningful reality.

Past generations were as sinful as the people of today, but they did not attempt to evade, excuse, diminish the reality of sin. This distinctive fact of sin is after all the basic premise of any religion which proclaims salvation; that one is a sinner and has need of a Savior is what distinguishes religion from superstition. The reality of sin and the need for penance have always been preached by Christianity. Precisely because man has the freedom to choose evil or good he can be base or noble, sink to great depths or rise to great heights.

Some psychologists, failing to distinguish neurotic from genuine guilt, free-floating anxiety from rational regret, have held that it would be better to obliterate the notion of sin since the feeling of sinfulness causes man a needless anxiety which is a threat to self-development. While it is true that many labor under psychical defects that diminish human responsibility, no sane man fails to enjoy liberty in vast areas of his life, a liberty whose judicious employment greatly aids the expansion of authentic liberty in *all* areas of his life. While distressed psyches may not be held accountable for what they cannot control, Christians must not forget that there exists both a direct and an indirect control. Man is at least responsible to himself and God to seek his mental and spiritual health and to employ the necessary means. The human person is an incomplete, developing being, answerable for himself and expected to use his liberty to achieve fulfillment and to say "yes" to grace. The kleptomaniac is not freed from responsibility to seek charity and chastity, justice and spiritual freedom, whatever be his burden of irresponsibility concerning kleptomania. The alcoholic may not be free to choose or not to choose his daily spree. He is free to seek help. Sin is not, as some ancients thought, a sort of madness sent by jealous gods, inescapable, unavoidable, brutally *there*. Moral determinism is only relative and partial and the normal man is well aware of this. Man seems naturally to retain an obscure presentiment of sin.

Even in Christian circles there is today a weakening of the concept of sin as a personal affront to a personal God, a breach in an intensely personal relationship. Occasionally it is referred to as a social deviation or psychological abnormality. Actually it is a failure in one's personal relations with a personal God, a freely chosen estrangement. Because of the dignity of the person offended, sin is profoundly serious and for its forgiveness, for the resumption of the dialogue of love, God's utterly free, unpredictable initiative of pardon is an absolute imperative. Since Christ's reparation on the Cross is more than abundant for our sins, it is the Christian's duty to acknowledge his basic sinfulness and to ask God's bending forgiveness. Only He can pardon effectively; Only He can instill in us His peace which surpasses all understanding, can compel our rebel wills.

Sin is a deliberate act of disobedience to God in which we choose to forget that His Law orients us to our full development and that by sin we cripple our growth, limit our potentialities, retract our sphere of liberty. Wanting our happiness, God helps us to love Him, but we are required to take the final step. Aeschylus remarked that when mortal man labors at his self-destruction the immortal gods join hands to help him. Christianity sees things from another point. Respecting human liberty, God solicits and cajoles man's assistance in His effort to fulfill an individual destiny.

Sin is tragic because it is a waste of God's immense love, man's immense liberty. Modern man fails to see that God is a Person, Who loves and out of Whom love has come. We fully realize the tragic seriousness of sin only when we see God's love; love that endures, supports, perseveres even while we are sinning. Because of His love for us, because of His gracious action, we ourselves become lovable. Sin is man's unique personal achievement, his personal property. Awareness of its nature could easily tempt us to despair. Yet even after all our futile bravado and hatred is spent, God's love lives and seeks to pardon. Hell is the ultimate logic of sin, where isolated selves finally attain the wish expressed by selfish lives bent on self-destruction. We live one life and all the actions of that life are somehow connected. Each act alters it slightly, building our fundamental orientation either towards or away from God, so that at its end man's posture is fixed, bent either to acceptance or radical refusal of God's love.

The common element in every sin is its free, responsible transgression of the law of God. It is perhaps unfortunate that in the world of today recovery of the idea of collective responsibility has involved the risk of minimizing individual responsibility; to do so would attack the dignity of the human person itself. Often it seems too easy to say that everyone is at fault, hence that no one appears to be really at fault.

The dualism that exists in man between flesh and spirit involves the need for certain renunciations. In this world man must use created goods to attain to uncreated Good; life or eternal death will be the manifestation of man's free choice. As to who will be ultimately condemned, we submit the possibility, supported by the Pauline text, I Corinthians 6:9, that it will be the habitual, hardened sinner rather than the one who offends by a single act.

To be guilty of sin man does not need to reflect deeply on either the majesty of God or the eternity of Hell. Let him act contrary to the demands of his conscience; he sins. Formative influences—hereditary, sociological, bio-chemical—acting on the individual certainly lessen responsibility but they do not remove it completely. One should add that the common characteristic of every sin is a false self-love by which man refuses to give himself to the God Who would help him to that authentic greatness prepared for him by One who seeks the evolution of man's ultimate individuality.[4]

The sense of sin is an interior awareness of our state as sinners, a reflection on the inevitable fact of sin in man. It perceives the disruptive effect of sin upon his whole spiritual and physical being. Sin is the absence of life, it is sickness and shame, yet its very existence sketches an appeal for hope; for sin is a relationship between God and man. A proper concept of sin requires knowledge of the unspeakable grandeur of God, of His sovereignty over the world and of the bond of dependency between that which is created and the Creator. God should be seen as a Being Who inspires respect, gratitude and hope; there should be a friendship with Him in love, clinging trust; not terror. If to know God's holiness is to appreciate the gravity of our sins, an awareness of His paternity will provide the realization that God communicates His goodness to man for man's greater glory, as well as for God's.

Perhaps the ultimate dimension of sin is revealed in the mystery of Christ, for He it is Who made known the tragic nature of sin as a divisive force, with all its stupidity and meaninglessness, its shame and ignorance, its unhappiness and isolation. Yet the same Cross of Christ that unveils the ultimate threat and intention of sin also reveals the necessary and liberating action of God's salvation in Christ.[5]

Such an analysis of sin is not of course acceptable to moderns. For one reason or another, modern man has diluted or ignored the traditional concepts of sin, and in their place substituted various philosophies, implicit and explicit, which seek either to explain the situations actually wrought by sin (such as the feeling of guilt for wrongdoing) or to direct his life with some degree of reasonableness.

Foster sees the world today differing from that of other generations in terms of its symbols. Modern Christians have replaced the symbol of the scapegoat, characteristic of the Jewish law of holiness, with the less valid symbol of the underdog. But no matter what the symbol may be, a genuine sense of sin brings with it a sensitiveness to the divine, the habit of humility and dependency, a feeling for the community, the ability to value all things in the light of their intrinsic worth.[6]

In today's world, as we have seen, a diffuse sense of corporate guilt seems to have replaced the traditional feeling for sin. Yet not to seek complete abandonment in God, not to realize one's powerlessness outside of God, creates a false and illusory world. If one turns one's back on reality, one must replace it with illusion; in modern man this not infrequently takes the form of championing the cause of the socially underprivileged. The defense of this cause is concomitant with strong feelings of guilt and personal inadequacy. The worshippers at this shrine are sometimes characterized by a basic ambiguity; in point of fact do they sometimes seek to keep the underprivileged as they are, that they may continue to play God? The human situation is inseparable from sin and consequently man's frequent, piercing estrangement from God is the result of sin. It is only by accepting this difficult and often tragic plight of man that we are able justly to evaluate it. Christ is no humanitarian with a boundless heart and an endless capacity for service. It is not enough to give drink to the thirsty or food to the hungry; we must be aware that the person we are serving is one whom Christ has implicitly identified with Himself. To serve the people of this burdened world we must give of ourselves unselfishly and with all the power and knowledge of Christ wherein we share. Christianity calls for deep feelings and genuine service to all mankind.

Although in the world of today there has been a lessening of the sense of sin, it cannot be assumed that the modern world has nothing to contribute to the Christian notion of sin. Christians have a role to play in this world, too, and modern man's sense of sin may be so obscure because Christianity has not always been clear in presenting or in practicing its own morality. As in almost everything else in our complicated world, man's conception of sin is influenced by many contributing factors.

The sense of sin in the modern world is frequently identified, by Christian and non-Christian alike, with a type of guilt complex. This in turn is thought to revolve around the Sixth Commandment. Because of his preoccupation with sex, modern western man often equates sin with sex, relegating charity, justice, honesty, to roles of minor importance. Feelings of guilt frequently center around the area of sexual sins with a resultant deep sense of shame and inferiority, and the subconscious longing for an angelicized sanctity divorced from the body, the secular world and matter.

Psychoanalysts at times explain guilt feelings as coming from a person's superego rather than from his rational conscience. From a child's first moments of awareness, society, through parents and later through friends and institutions such as the school or church, authoritatively imposes certain norms, taboos or rules for specific ways of acting. When he internalizes irrational "don'ts" which he is incapable of understanding, the child may feel that the attainment of many of his autonomous drives and urges is forbidden. To these taboos are added threats of punishment or disapproval, with the result that the child develops lasting feelings of inferiority and rejection. Yet he still has the desire in spite of the fact that its satisfaction is denied him, and since he cannot comprehend why he is being deprived of this satisfaction, he cannot adequately or permanently resolve his situation. The subconscious memory of this conflict and its consequences of insecurity are forced into the child's unconscious, to return later in life in the form of a neurosis of irrational guilt over aggressive and bodily urges.

The human person is complex, his properly human life emerging from a dynamic interplay of forces within him, many of which he is unconscious of, and hence cannot consciously control. Sin might seem to be ever present to him, objectively speaking, but sin is sin only when it is a clear, conscious attitude, deliberate and truly personal, and when the sinner is able to judge and evaluate the inner, objective value of his actions. Nor must sin be confused with neurosis, which, although similar to sin, is not the same thing. For sin is a freely chosen breakdown in the sinner's personal relations with God or his neighbor, a step backwards in the personal development to which we are called by God. Neurosis is a non-free psychological step backwards to the level of infantile development to which our feelings seduce us. Depriving the person of certain dimensions at the emotional level, neurosis can have a damaging effect on his conscious life, but it is not sin.[7]

In the Freudian theory of the unconscious, the sense of sin is the expression of guilt feelings. Sin and the sentiment of sin are considered harmful because they involve a vicious circle; the sinner vindictively, mercilessly punishes himself because he has sinned against himself. To Christians, however, sin is a more serious thing than what is expressed by Freudian analysis, but it is also infinitely more curable. As a Christian, the sinner knows that he has not sinned against himself but against someone more powerful, infinitely more tolerant, than himself: God. Although the Christian cannot pardon his own sins, neither is he required to. Instead, if he confesses his sins to God, the One he has offended, he will be pardoned by One Who is graciously omnipotent and unambiguously just. Without the hope of pardon it is almost impossible to recognize sin. But once a sinner recognizes that he is loved even though he is guilty of offending God, he can in a sense afford to be a sinner, knowing that all he need do to be forgiven is to repent sincerely.

Another modern position, psychological determinism, does away with man's freedom, and hence responsibility, by explaining his acts as purely the results of inner tension, motivations, drives, urges, and the prodding of the unconscious. If he seeks goals exclusively because of sexual motivation, in the broadest sense of "sexual" as a drive to expansion, the highest forms of his activity, artistic, religious, and heroic, as well as all the lower forms, become merely unconscious efforts to achieve sexual satisfaction.

Against such determinism, existentialism has reacted strongly by elevating the undeniable liberty of man. In order to become fully human, man must freely construct the design and pattern of his existence. Opposing the usual notions of right and wrong, chiefly because they imply an external set of norms prior to man's action, existentialism holds that the fulfillment of man lies in the future and not in the past; it is the result of his free activity rather than of reliance on norms imposed from the outside. It is of sovereign importance that he act freely and be independent of pressures applied or imposed by state, church, or any other authority; and it does not matter whether or not he acts in accord with what society considers the right thing.

In spite of theories of determinism, modern man in general still seems aware that his great possession is his distinctive freedom, that his inescapable responsibility is to be true to whatever moral values or positions are imposed by his personal experiences and judgment. Sincerity is still valued, highly so in existentialism, which has no tolerance for inauthentic morality. Placing great stock in his personal commitments and philosophy instead of in some impersonal force, and refusing to become a slave to rules and the letter of the law, the existentialist's primary interest is to do what he personally judges the right thing. Above all things, he prefers to act in accordance with what his "heart" considers right.

The shattering individualism of years past has yielded to a philosophy of humanism in which all mankind is seen as a single family. National boundaries are slowly being dissolved—witness the Common Market in Europe—and the world is starting to become color-blind. Differences among the peoples of the world have not disappeared, but we are entering an era wherein we are anxious to make much of our similarities and to minimize our differences. Yet we still find ourselves, strangely enough, at an unreachable distance from others. The world itself has become depersonalized as it has advanced in progress; the accompanying awe and dread of marvels that overshadow man seem to have set him in frantic search of someone—we will call him "thou"—with whom he can establish truly personal relations. Man does not seem content to give just part of himself; wanting to give himself totally, he also hopes for a total reciprocity. Modern man is really seeking a relationship in which the absolute value of his being is acknowledged, but unfortunately he is seeking such a knowledge in a world from which all absolutes have been reluctantly or joyously dismissed. The collapse of his traditional values and point of view in the crisis situation of our times threatens him with meaninglessness and cosmic anxiety if he does not find some absolute.

Christianity would seem a logical step for modern man to take. If he does not turn in that direction it is perhaps because he feels that such a step would be to go backward into ritualism, legalism, conformism, bourgeois moralism. This conception of Christian morality, although exaggerated, is not entirely wrong, for in Christianity a deviant tendency to devaluate the body and to make the sense of sin similar to the guilt complex has not always been sufficiently distinguished from authentic Christian doctrine. The personal element, which modern man craves and which should be an essential part of any religion or morality, has often been de-emphasized in favor of the imposition of certain ritualistic practices and doctrinal exaggerations, with impersonal "law" replacing or seeming to replace the nuclear virtue of charity.

A non-Christian approach to the sense of sin usually follows a theology that sees sins primarily as a breaking of rules. When sin is thus conceived, God is no longer the intensely personal God of Christianity but a "lawgiver," although He is not so described in the New Testament. The resultant type of rigid, fearful moralism is deadly in its effect on the human spirit; men become misers of virtue. Carefully kept balance sheets mark the score; one's neighbor becomes a competitor for first place in the field of righteousness, charity is bypassed, neglected, its inner heart ignored. Legalism leads to hardness of heart and, when the good life is conceived of as merely an obedience to external law, the individual's Christian freedom is slowly forfeited.

Modern man's sense of sin is further perverted by the appearance of other competitors for his allegiance. Human reason is worshipped today as it has been in ages past. Yet whenever reason assumes a divine status, it nourishes the seeds of its own destruction. In the modern world such a worship is most explicit in that deification of science which denies man's freedom because it can not be discovered with instruments and reduces his perception of good and evil to appetites because that perception is incapable of being measured. Capable of magnifying the trivial and the tedious, science can turn men into machines run by conditioned reflexes. Whenever a value is displaced from its natural realm in the hierarchy of values and hyper-exalted, the opposite disvalue, by a strange rhythm of nature, appears to take its place. Deifying humanism dehumanizes man.

Besides reason, modern man flies to the banners of idealism. Since he cannot be sure that God exists but he can be sure of ideals, the man of today considers it more realistic to base his religion and its corresponding values on humanistic values. But virtues such as un-selfishness and humility turn into their opposites, when divorced from an absolute and sought for their own human sake. Tolerance, when made absolute, turns on itself because of its assumption that no belief is more right or wrong than another, a view basically intolerant. Humanism deifies man in an age that degrades him. His pride, his science, reduce him to the lot of an animal, capable of being studied under a microscope. Democracy, rapidly becoming a sacred cow in today's world, could also become an end in itself. When one is no longer free to dissent from the majority, then individualism will be contained and tyranny will set in. When a way of life is divorced from God, it decays into what it originally opposed.

SUMMARY

While trying futilely to eliminate sin man reveals an inextinguishable yearning that can only be satisfied within the framework of an authentic sense of sin and of pardon. Identifying sin with superstition or a form of religion satisfactory for the unenlightened, man grows apparently more and more self-sufficient, but his self-sufficiency is lonely. Material progress has made man feel that he is able to control his own destiny but he remains existentially and historically insecure. He now blames his feelings of insecurity on uncontrollable factors. Seemingly obsessed with freedom and the necessity to do what he personally thinks is right, he exalts his freedom and yet somehow forfeits it. In this dilemma the one thing that can help him is a just sense of the tragedy of sin, its significance and redemption.

Modern man starts with interior sincerity and seeks objective standards. The Church starts with the objective standards and seeks to have the people of God interiorize these. As long as sin is conceived as a human folly having only human significance, then sin will cause anguish and a sense of helplessness. It is God Who gives the proper perspective to the sense of sin for He is the cause of our sorrow and the cause of our rejoicing in penance.

The modern world fears the concept of sin because it does not know how to cope with it. It turns to ideals and philosophies, seeking a natural solution to a supernatural problem.

A true sense of sin must grow among men today, not only because it is the right thing but because it will answer many of modern man's longings. But first we must restore the true meaning of God, Christ and His Church as the Mystical Body, a solidarity expressing genuine love. We must restudy the relation of law as the remote norm of morality to conscience as its proximate norm. Free will must be examined in the light of the findings of such social sciences as sociology and psychology, and sin must be shown as a breach in one's personal relations to a personal God that results in the sinner's own destruction.

A healthy sense of sin will not shackle an individual, but will liberate him. Peace cannot be had on a basis of human or self-forgiveness; men forgive too partially, too defectively, too humanly. It is only the Eternal God, Transcendent Lord and also our Savior, Who forgives perfectly, with utter humanity and divine power.

NOTES

1. H. Rondet, *The Theology of Sin,* Notre Dame, Indiana, Fides, 1960, p. 1.
2. E. La B. Cherbonnier, *Hardness of Heart, a Contemporary Interpretation of the Doctrine of Sin,* New York, Doubleday, 1955, pp. 13–19.
3. M. Oraison, H. Niel, F. Coudreau, J. De Baciocchi, and G. Sieworth, *Sin,* New York, MacMillan, 1962, p. viii.
4. W. Farrell, *Sin,* New York, Sheed and Ward, 1960, pp. 9–11.
5. R. O'Connell, "The Sense of Sin," *The Way,* Vol. II 1962, pp. 16–19.
6. J. Foster, "The Scapegoat and the Underdog," *Life of the Spirit,* Vol. XVI 1962, pp. 433–443.
7. M. Oraison, et al., *op. cit.,* p. 12.

The Denial of God

3

Nineteenth-Century Atheism

THE nineteenth century witnessed the full development of a theoretical atheism which aimed at eliminating God from accepted belief. Most of this atheism derived from Hegel's philosophy, and even 20th century atheistic attacks upon the transcendence of God have depended largely upon his well-known argument against the "unhappy consciousness" supposedly induced by Christianity.

Hegel's influence was at its height during the last years of his life in Berlin, his system seeming to offer a philosophic framework wide enough to embrace the whole spiritual climate of his day. His discussions of Jewish and Christian theology characterize the Jewish conception of God as one in which God and man are totally foreign to each other. Man is declared to be worthless in himself, capable of only a servile relation with God. This transcendence of God generates the primal master-slave pattern which structures every type of theism in which the mind is inevitably tormented by an "unhappy consciousness," a sense of separation from the Infinite which, combined with an insatiable longing for perfect union, generates only misery and anguish.

For Hegel, authentic religion is man's aspiration to transcendence, that is to say, the expansion of the divine life which is contained in man's own nature. It follows that any view which assumes that God and man are irreducible beings will always result in an oppressive estrangement, a devaluation of humanity.[1]

Hegel also maintained that the State is the most important of the various ethical communities, for it unites in itself the essence of the family and of civic society and stands for God Himself. Being the progression of God in the world, it must be honored as something half earthly, half divine. The modern state should be the organization of freedom in which civic society, the family, and private individuals would find the satisfaction of their particular interests. But the state often demands as a duty that which is properly the right of the individual to give. To act thus is to forget that the state ought not, and in fact can not, be reached without the support of the smaller societies and individuals which it embraces. The world of ethics is thus given up to the contingency of subjective opinions and caprices, and the work on which reason has been engaged for more than a thousand years left to the mercy of personal feeling. History has proved the falsity of Hegel's doctrine that the state can grow only through the free cooperation of the people.[2]

Hegel further believed that the state is mind objectified. The individual mind, which is only partly free, subjects itself to the yoke of necessity, in order to attain a fuller realization of itself in the freedom of the citizen, the perfect social embodiment of which is focused in the state. The Constitution of a state is thus the collective spirit of the nation, and the government is the embodiment of that spirit. Each nation has its own individual spirit, and the greatest of crimes is the act by which the tyrant stifles it.

What are apparently contingent events of history are in reality progressive stages in the logical unfolding of the absolute spirit embodied in the state. Passion, impulse, interest, character, personality —all these are either the expression of reason or the instruments which reason constructs for its own use. Historical happenings are therefore to be understood as the stern, inevitable working of reason towards the full realization of itself in perfect freedom.

Hegel's philosophy is an attempt to unify the forms of transcendental idealism bequeathed to him by Kant, Fichte, and Schelling. According to Kant, theoretical experience teaches us that nothing exists except the appearances of things and the unknown and unknowable *noumena* behind these appearances. Hegel believed, however, that, if instead of Kant's destructive criticism of theoretical experience we make use of an incessantly progressive and productive immanent criticism, we shall find that reality is not an unknowable substrate of appearances, but an active process, which constantly passes into its opposite in order to return to a higher and richer form of itself. This process is being in its barest form; its fullest and richest form is spirit, absolute mind, the state, religion and philosophy.

The difference between religion and philosophy consists in this: that religion adorns its content with the forms of the imagination, so that what appear to the philosopher as ultimate relations, expressions of eternal truths valid for all times, are, to the religious mind, historical events. But all this external, pictorial, historical appearance will slough off when philosophy translates the content of religion into the form of thought.

All the various religions of the world can be arranged in a logical, graduated series, from the most elementary to the highest forms, the highest being that in which the concept of religion has attained to full development, since it embraces the serious conception of the deity as spirit. This religion is Christianity. According to Hegel, humanity did not have to wait for philosophy to become aware of truth, for religion contains truth, but truth wearing the clothes of the imagination.

The dogmas of creation and of the atonement, for example, are symbolic expressions of the infinite life which interpenetrates all things and from which we are never separated, however great the pain of limitation and finitude. Even the religious ideas of the past can be of value to us once we are able to see how in one way or another they express our own experiences and thoughts.

The influence of Hegel is far-reaching, partly because of the imaginative vastness of his philosophical synthesis. Typical of the spirit of collectivism which characterized the nineteenth century, his philosophy is also an application of the principle of process and development which dominated progressive nineteenth century thought in literature, science, and even theology. In theology, Hegel revolutionized the methods of inquiry because his notion of development was applied to biblical criticism and to historical investigation.

In science and literature, the substitution of the category of becoming for the category of being is today widely accepted, largely owing to the influence of Hegel's method. In political economy and political science Hegel's collectivistic conception of the state supplanted to a large extent the individualistic conception which the eighteenth century had handed on to the nineteenth.

Since "the rational alone is real" all reality is capable of being expressed in rational categories. Hence God, a reality, should be comprehensible by the finite mind. God *is* in fact only in so far as He is conceived under the category of becoming, for, to Hegel, God is process.

The years following Hegel's death in 1831 saw philosophical debates focus on the problem of God, and it was here that his followers broke up into the right and left wings of Hegelianism. Feuerbach assumed the leadership of the left, his purpose being parallel to that of his friend Friedrich Strauss, historian of the origins of Christianity. Strauss had tried to account historically for the Christian illusion; Feuerbach tried to account psychologically for the religious illusion, or, as he himself put it, to find in anthropology the secret of theology. For Strauss the Gospels are myths expressing the aspirations of the Jewish people; with Feuerbach God is a myth expressing the aspirations of the human consciousness.

In 1839, Feuerbach first revealed the flaws which he claimed to have discovered in the Hegelian framework. In his *Critique of the Hegelian Philosophy*, he announced that Hegel's theory of the Absolute Idea is not a logical deduction at all but simply an assumption which Hegel nowhere successfully establishes. Moreover, his effort to make the Absolute Idea appear plausible distorts the ordinary notion of sense perception by claiming that it can transcend the sensible world and function successfully in the idealistic realm of meaning.[3]

Maintaining that Hegel's starting point, Pure Being, is a meaningless abstraction and that the only meaningful being is determinate being, he argues the irrelevancy of sense perception in the pursuit of knowledge and the fact that sensory experience can be excluded from it. An object is real only when composed of a set of universals, since all reality is individual, and logical relations are only abstract forms of speech which serve to identify individual things.

In his later writings, Feuerbach concerns himself less with the difficulties immanent to Hegelian philosophy and more with the consequences of his own humanizing of the Hegelian Absolute, which he equates with the universal notion of God. He notices too that in theological circles, of no matter what religion or sect, the reduction of God to a merely human level, if not directly opted for, is at least the logical culmination of the tendencies of the times.

Feuerbach's fundamental insight is that all traditional religions arise out of man's unconscious deification of himself.[4] When religions begin, there is no essential distinction between God and man. When a religion grows in years and understanding, when consciousness arises of the identity between the human and the divine, then theology arises and religion begins to lose its initial vital force. Man's original and involuntary objectivation of himself, by which he unconsciously creates God as a separate being, becomes, at the theological stage, a reflective, conscious separation of identity. Consequently, the nearer religion is to its origin the truer and more genuine it is.

The first distinctive sign of the end of simple religion and the beginnings of theology is had when God and man are consciously separated, when the existence of God is made the object of formal proof. The aim of the proofs is to make the internal external, to divorce it from man; once this has been done God has become a "thing-in-itself."

Instead of studying the myths, legends or sacred truths which constitute the focal point of all religious feeling, Feuerbach probes the theoretical superstructure of theology to uncover the nerve of the process by which they arise. In spite of the absurdity of these revelations in the cold light of scientific analysis, it appears that the religious belief of which they are a constitutive element will remain, because religion is basically emotional rather than intellectual. The questions which we should put to religious beliefs, therefore, should have nothing to do with their "truth," but with their genesis. Why do they arise in this culture rather than in that? What role do they play in the lives of those who have embraced them?

Feuerbach attempted to prove that at the heart of religion was man, that its objects of worship and devotion were exalted expressions of his emotions. Viewing the religious phenomenon as the projection of some element of human experience into an object of worship, Feuerbach claimed that when man lived in the state of nature, his deities were the gods of nature, personifications of natural forces like rain, sun, fertility. When tribal life became dominant, henotheism prevailed. When man began to live in houses, his gods resided in the temples. As he moved farther along the way of social evolution, particularly as he developed culturally, man ascribed to his gods the distinction between what is fitting and what is not. Thus the gods of the Greeks were paragons of strength, knowing the art of love, while the dominant god of the war-loving Germans was the great and fearful Odin. Through the entire history of religion, man continued to fashion his gods in his own image and likeness.[5]

Traditional philosophy and theology manifest the same arbitrary isolation of a single feature of experience, often relatively the most important or desirable, from its context in social life, and its subsequent erection into an absolute principle whose validity is independent of all space, time and society.

Feuerbach submits to close analysis the various "mysteries" of the Christian religion, the Trinity, the Incarnation, the Resurrection, and so on, to demonstrate how human relationships are idealized, purified of elements judged to be unworthy and glorified into abstractions. For him the relation between the infinite and the finite becomes one of mutual rivalry, in which man enriches the divine nature at the cost of impoverishing his own human nature.

Since man's desires include his needs, as well as his ideals, he projects his earthly frustration along with his beatitudes. Although his frustrations may be material, they may also be psychological and sexual. Curiously Feuerbach has pages anticipatory of a much more modern psychological system in which he describes and evaluates the vicarious satisfactions achieved by the Christian nuns and monks from the denial of their sensual tendencies.

To explain the genesis of the idea of God, Feuerbach resorted to the Hegelian concept of "alienation." Hegel had applied it to absolute Spirit; Feuerbach applied it to man in his flesh and blood. Thus alienation became man's state of being dispossessed of his wisdom, will, justice and love for the benefit of an illusive reality.[6]

Wisdom, will, justice, and love, in Feuerbach's view, are attributes of man's own being which nevertheless affect him as if they belonged to another. So he spontaneously projects them beyond himself, objectifying them in a fantastic form, the product of his imagination, to which he gives the name of God. If the divinity of nature is the basis of all religions, including Christianity, then the divinity of man is religion's final term. The turning-point of history will be the supreme moment when man at last becomes aware that his only God is man himself.

Feuerbach thought that human nature with all its noble prerogatives was fully realized only in the community. But by substituting for that community the illusion of an external God, we generate a false religion which disintegrates mankind into a collection of isolated individuals, each one turned back upon himself. The basic principle of authentic religion results in practical actions rooted in love, which takes the individual out of himself and obliges him to discover himself in solidarity with the rest of mankind.

Feuerbach, of course, did not care to be called an atheist. For him, the true atheist is not the man who denies God, but the religious man for whom the attributes of divinity—love, wisdom and justice—are projected outward, elevated into a fiction whom he calls God.

Religion then would seem to be the process of projecting our essential being into the ideal sphere of divinity and then humbling ourselves before our own objectified essence. In worshipping God, man is really paying homage to his own essence, viewed at an ideal distance. Consequently, a fully self-conscious, religious mind must inevitably be atheistic. Man is the only true God for himself. As soon as he grasps the real significance of religion, he can dispense with God or the absolute spirit and devote himself to the cultivation of his own being. The wretchedness of actual existence leads him to yearn for a more perfect condition, to picture this condition as an ideal essence, and, finally to objectify that essence as an independent, infinite, personal God.

Although intending to destroy the idea of God, Feuerbach wished to retain the religious attitude, but fixed now upon the perfections of man. But this building of religion on an atheistic foundation depends on the soundness of his two preliminary assumptions: 1) that the Hegelian philosophy recapitulates all others and 2) that the Hegelian absolute spirit is the authentic and unique God. Acceptance of these two questionable premises enables Feuerbach to infer the impossibility of reconciling God with a developed humanism.

Feuerbach offered several reasons for applying infinity of a qualified sort to man. He repeated almost verbally the Aristotelian formula that the human mind can somehow become all things through a cognitive union and that man is potentially infinite and universal in knowledge, capable of endless increase in knowledge. In an attempt to wean us away from ordering our minds to an infinite reality distinct from ourselves, Feuerbach suggested that the only object of adoration worthy of the human mind is its own subjective nature, treated in objective fashion.

Feuerbach's emphasis on empiricism was significant for the spread of atheism. Seeking to shift the emphasis of philosophy from idealism and theology to empiricism and science, his atheistic arguments took on a psychological approach and a practical bent. Psychology becomes the final science, of which metaphysics is only a secret objectification. The whole problem of God is thus reduced to that of the genesis of the idea of God itself.

KARL MARX

Karl Marx, the most famous exponent of nineteenth century atheism, contributed almost nothing to its philosophical development. With little concern about religion, his writings only expand the fundamental doctrines previously laid down by Ludwig Feuerbach.

Reproaching Feuerbach for making religious alienation in some sense a metaphysical act, instead of a more positive sociological act, Marx attempted to replace the cult of abstract man, the center of Feuerbach's new religion, by the science of real men and their historical development. Once he had stripped from the human essence the halo with which Feuerbach had surrounded it, all else began to pale in his thought before the technique of economics and the tactics of class warfare. If he bothered hardly at all with religion after 1845, this was because it seemed to him settled once and for all, a starting point at which there was no further need to linger.

The consequences of Feuerbach's theory of God or the Absolute Idea as the pure and perfect synthesis of all man's desires and needs appeared to be hand-tailored for Marx's political and economic views. The foundation-stone of all religious belief—the alienation by man of his own essential attributes and their subsequent transferral to an illusive reality claiming *a priori* validity—might very well be extended to all the forms of society: politics, ethics, economics. The dualism which religion had introduced into the life of man under the form of the sacred and profane, the lay and the secular, found their counterpart in the dualism of the state which, separating the political function of the community from the social and economic, pretended in theory that all citizens were equal before the law but in practice recognized all sorts of irrelevant class distinctions. Thus Marx incorporated his master's religious criticism into his own social criticism, arriving at the conclusion that humanity must abolish the state as it had abolished religion; he also adapted the Feuerbachian conception of religion to all of social life.[7]

Just as Feuerbach's theoretical humanism was his answer to the religious and philosophical problem which confronted him, the followers of Marx posed a practical humanism as the answer to the socio-economic problem, the major determinant, as they thought, of all other problems.

So Feuerbach's conception of the process by which religions grow and die flows directly from Hegel, criticized by Feuerbach for hiding his insights in metaphysical trappings, to Marx, who in turn criticized Feuerbach for not developing and generalizing his own philosophical principles. Hegel reasoned that the development takes place through the necessary self-alienation of the Idea, which like God, generates the world out of itself by logical activity. Feuerbach humanized the necessary self-alienation of the Idea and made it the self-alienation of man, the unconscious projection of human nature in objects of worship. For Marx, man's self-alienation is traced to the processes of work and its influence upon the development of human nature. With Feuerbach, God is the image of man; with Marx, the sentiments and ideas of men reflect conditions of their existence. Feuerbach saw the history of the gods as merely the repetition of the earthly progress of men; Marx viewed human history as a reflection of the history of the conditions of production. What fundamentally separates Marx from Feuerbach is his historical approach and his concrete analysis of the factors of social life which to Feuerbach were merely abstractions. Even where he adopts Feuerbachian principles Marx differs by stressing the dialectical method and its concrete application.

Marx believed that the chief defect of those who had philosophized about materialism before his time was that they conceived of all reality only objectively, never subjectively as a form of human activity. Consistently ignoring the role of nature in the development of man, seeing him only as a product of his environment and education, materialism had failed to observe that, in the process of his development, man transforms the social situation in which he lives. The world does not exist independently of man; each acts always upon the other.

Attributing the projection which is God to recognition of the social contradictions which pervade man's life, Marx thought that Feuerbach failed to see that the religious sentiment is itself a social product, that the abstract individual whom he analyzes is himself a member of a particular type of society. The nature of society is essentially practical. It consists of the union of man with nature, a union realizable only by human activity, particularly that in the economic realm. Until we have understood the character of social life and human activity the problems which incline men towards religious and social illusions cannot be resolved. Only historical materialism, concludes Marx, considers the true nature of man as constituted by his social activity and it alone can transcend the notion of the isolated individual, as he exists in Hegel and Feuerbach, to arrive at the true conception of socialized humanity.

This is Marx's doctrine of historical materialism, in which human history is conceived as the gradual adaptation of man to his social environment, dominantly expressed by modes of production and of work. Here is contained the essential point of his synthesis of man and nature. With it his psychology of religion becomes clear, its connection with his political and social philosophy and with the awesome consequences which that union will bring, at last explicitly revealed. To Marx, religion is not the product of a natural dichotomy in all human thought. For the real forces impelling men to find satisfaction in some mystical empire where they may enjoy the uncontested power denied them in this life are not merely psychological but social. From the antagonisms between the way men actually produce, and the traditional, social and legal forms under which that production is carried on, result the fragmentation of experience, the absence of unified control of the collective lot, and the worship of meaningless abstractions—all of which are characteristic of religious belief. Religion then is a reflection, not of man's essence, but of the actual conditions of his empirical life.

Marxism also developed out of Hegelianism; Marx's thought was formed according to Hegel's dialectic, a vision of the past, of man and of the movement of history that determined the course of Marxism as a philosophy, as a code for man's dealings with man, and as the motivating principle of a totalitarian culture.

To understand the original lines of Marx's thought we must see them in the context of the Hegelian school from which they derive and which constituted the philosophic climate of Prussia in the years 1830–1845. Hegel's critics had discovered the weak points and the imperfections in the master's system and Marx and his followers were led in time to reject more than one of the master's positions.

Society and history are the main preoccupations of Hegel's reflections. There is a history of peoples and cultures, but permeating this history there is also one of universal dimension. The rise and fall of civilization and empires are so many manifestations of a deeper reality which Hegel identifies with God and which is universal history. Behind these changes world history pursues its inexorable course, the stream of life sustaining all living things. There is thus a progressive development of truth through the dialectical flux of life and death, and the accumulation of historical experience is progress. Therefore we must worship the State as the manifestation of the divine on earth, the Incarnation of God, the Creator of truth and law. Justice is nothing more than the powers of the State. Conflict and war are good things; by means of them the State triumphs.[8]

This historicism of Hegel's was taken over by Marx, who appeals to the dialectical development of history but applies it especially to the future. Epochs succeed one another necessarily and history is the story of man's alienation from himself, from nature and from his community. Capitalism is the extreme case of alienation. The State for Marx proclaimed liberty, equality and fraternity but in so doing disguised the tragic economic situation of liberal capitalism in which servitude, inequality and strife prevailed.

From Feuerbach and Hegel, Marx derived his basic postulate: the dynamic self-sufficiency of man-in-nature. He termed his standpoint either naturalistic humanism or a humanistic naturalism according to whether he wished to stress the restriction of human effort and aspiration to purely finite aims or the distinctive contribution of human intelligence and work to the natural order; Marx thus highlighted the function of labor as the chief means for humanizing nature and for fulfilling man. To Marx the transforming power of labor in history seemed proof of finite man's self-sufficiency; through it he becomes a social man. Consequently, society is the dynamic, essential unity of man with nature, the true resurrection and humanism of nature, the achieved naturalism of man. Since all social revolutions tend ultimately toward the realization of the social whole of man-laboring-in-nature, the dialectical meaning of history is a purely immanent one for which man in society is the new absolute in place of Hegel's absolute spirit.[9]

Obviously Marx would seek to eliminate God from philosophy and practical life, agreeing as he did with Feuerbach that the more a man attributes to God, the less he attributes to himself. The God thus indicated was, of course, the Hegelian absolute spirit. To Hegel man and nature were merely predicates of this unique, spiritual subject; the entire natural world of things and social relations was unessential in itself, an objective realm expressing absolute spirit in an alienated way. In order to remove the alienation, the absolute spirit would have to subvert the entire objective order. But Marx appealed to man's instinctive devotion to nature and his humanistic reverence for cultural achievements as sufficient reasons for the atheistic attitude, proclaiming that only the half-hearted naturalist or humanist could admit a divine actuality beyond nature and a spiritual principle distinct from human intelligence and labor.

Marx's criticism of God thus rests on two unspoken premises: that Hegel's God is the true God and that Feuerbach has reduced God to a mode of alienation of the human mind. In this twofold reduction is contained the sum total of Marx's denial of God. Marx often warns against wasting energy in attacking God and religion; since the demolition of God has been completed in principle by Feuerbach, there is no need for a fresh appraisal of the religious attitude.[10]

It is remarkable how few references are made by Marx to the proofs of God's existence. He considers them formally in only two places, both of which are in early manuscripts written before his attention turned completely toward the critique of political economy. Against the idealists who try to defend their acceptance of God on Hegelian grounds, Marx points out the weak features in the Hegelian proofs of God's existence, observing that they manifest only the existence of aspects of human consciousness and that therefore one should call them proofs of God's non-existence, since analysis reveals them to be only projections of man's ideas of himself. These criticisms afford considerable insight into how the problem of God presented itself to Marx's mind. With his principal objections directed against the ontological proof, since this had been given prominence in Hegel, Marx rightly rebelled against the notion that human self-consciousness is significant only as providing material for the realization of an absolute consciousness. In agreement with Feuerbach's appeal to the distance between the concept of absolute spirit and its actuality, his defense of the finite nature of the human mind and the integrity of sensible, contingent things was an effective argument against the ontological proof of absolute spirit, although it did not furnish Marx with a new perspective on a non-Hegelian God.

The only causal argument to prove God's existence which was familiar to Marx did nothing to clarify his position. For Marx any attempt to think away the finite universe by proceeding backwards over the generations until one reaches the first moment of producing nature and man, was bound to result in failure. But Marx failed to see that the realistic proofs from causality seek to explain not a series of events trailing away into the past but a presently real thing, in the sense that it is finitely existing, changing, or pro-

ducing change in another present thing. The here-and-now existence of the composite existent requires causes that are *presently*
acting, for they are dependent upon a completely actual and presently existing first cause. The causal inference that God is the
"first" cause concerns His independent existence and activity, not
an initial moment of a *time* series, as envisioned in the arguments
which Marx knew.

Marx's attacks on the proofs of God from causality are therefore
irrelevant for an approach which does not consist in transporting
oneself by imagination back to the dawn of creation. The individual concerned about the existence of God must ask this fundamental question, precisely because he maintains steadily before his mind
his own existence and that of other finite, limited, composite things.
But the question is possible only when the inquiring mind exists;
in fact, it is not only possible but unavoidable in view of the characteristics of existing man and other beings having limited existence. The truth of the proposition concerning God's existence depends upon preserving the finite existent in its own integrity of
being, while penetrating into the need for a first cause to explain
its existing, *present* actuality.

In claiming that the inquirer must be there at the creation of
man and the universe, Marx was led astray by Hegel's dialectic of
a beginning.

Concerning the theme of religious estrangement, Marx appropri-
ated much from Feuerbach but with a more critical spirit than that
shown in his handling of the question of God's existence. Because
Marx declared that every sort of religious attitude is an estrangement of some portion of human nature and hence detrimental to
mankind, it has been suggested that his philosophy is more properly
anti-religious than atheistic. But Marx is genuinely atheistic, since
he denies the real existence of a supremely perfect being distinct
from the finite world. He does, however, subsume his atheism
within the wider context of his opposition to religious estrangement; he is atheistic not only because God is unreal to him but also
because he thinks that acceptance of God alienates a man from him-

self and nature, rendering him weak, impotent, unhappy. Regarding belief in God as the most typical and extreme sort of religious estrangement, Marx singles it out for special attack.

Pondering over why men project their ideals into another world, Marx decided the basic reason to be the unjust social and economic conditions of life. Theism and other manifestations of the religious spirit are the result of the inhumane conditions of economic, social, and political existence, together with man's practical desire to shake them off and to find peace in a realm free from the miseries of everyday life. Thus religious estrangement and worship of God are a protest against social tyranny and the inhumane use of material power.

Drawing a strict parallel between religion and private property, Marx found the former to be the core of man's theoretical estrangement and the latter to constitute his practical estrangement. The complete abolition of God and religion cannot be achieved until there is a transformation of society so complete that the conditions which foster belief in a transcendent being will disappear. Progressive social change will render theism and the religious outlook both meaningless and useless in the future social order, when life will be humanely, naturally and equitably ordered.

In the social whole of men-laboring-in-nature—Marx's goal of historical change—religion will wither away and the question of theism versus atheism will be simply irrelevant. The critique of religion will end with the discovery of the truth that man is the supreme goal of man. The final forgetting of God will then be the sign that men have attained to perfect solidarity.

FRIEDRICH NIETZSCHE

The same year saw Feuerbach die and Nietzsche begin to publish. Like his two predecessors, he was convinced of the decline and ultimate disappearance of God as a necessary casualty of the development of science and culture. Having acquired most of his early philosophical orientation from the works of Arthur Schopenhauer, he also believed that the principle of sufficient reason, as used both by the rationalists and by Hegel, was unable to establish the existence of either God or of Absolute Idea. This was evident since the principle applied only to sensuous objects and to particular sorts of reason, whereas God was conceived of as non-sensuous being and as an absolute reason for things. Though denying the capacity of the finite mind of man to penetrate the infinite order of being and thus to employ the principle of causality to establish God's existence, Kant had retained his theory of the moral postulate, with God as a sanction for the moral order. But Schopenhauer denied this too, maintaining that the practical reason had the same limitations as the theoretical intellect with regard to the principle of sufficient reason. Even Schopenhauer, however, left open one path to a higher being: the undirected will-to-live, the result of our irrational intuition. This will-to-live, the font of all pain and striving, could be suppressed only through acts of charity and contemplation, in short, through the practice of an asceticism such as is called for by Christianity. To Schopenhauer, the essential message of Christianity is the denial of the world, both in its sensuous aspects and in its inner will toward the increase of life.

For Nietzsche the consequence of this will-to-live was utter nothingness and it is around this concept that much of his philosophy is based.

Like Feuerbach, Nietzsche conceived of religion as the result of a psychological duplication. Viewing the Christian ethos as a process of self-debasement to its logical, and theological consequences, he held that without the gift of grace nothing good could come from the actions of a debased personality. It is as if man, intent on lowering himself to the depths, invents another world—an amorphous mass populated only by "God"—that he might be permitted so to lower himself.

Unable to live in a transient, humanly unoriented cosmos, man must stabilize the flow of his passions and drives, somehow making them meaningful in his life by resorting to concepts like "law" and "value" as pragmatic tools for achieving this significance out of the mass of becoming. Knowledge, then, is not a relation of conformity but an evaluation by the will-to-power of whatever may enhance human value in the world.[11]

With Nietzsche, we cannot speak "the" truth but can speak only *about* humanly founded truths. No absolute truth corresponding to some region of permanent essence exists, because there is no evidence for it. Hence, it is meaningless to proclaim the absolute truth of God's transcendent reality. Human truths—perspectives taken on a particular situation for a particular purpose—remain many, open to revision, and confined to human projects. This applies also with equal rigor to moral truths. No universal moral world order or absolute good exists—only the plural goods of human aims with all their finite sanctions.

To understand Nietzsche's antitheistic position we must know his theory of historical refutation, the result of his views on Christianity's own character and history.

There are three elements to examine in Nietzsche's theory of world history: his awareness of the crisis of the present era; his argument that Christianity is the cause of the crisis; his view of world history as a whole and the position of Christianity within it.

The crisis of the present era results from the fact that God is dead. Others before him had proclaimed the death of God, but with Nietzsche it is not a mere statement of seeming fact, an expression of personal disbelief, or even a psychological statement about the rise of unbelief. He was simply observing a "fact": we were given a choice, and as a result of our preference God is dead.[12]

The vast majority, of course, are unaware of it, and would think any one mad who announced it. Men, therefore, fall into two categories: believers and common atheists. The first, failing to understand the fact, are not even disturbed. Blind and deaf in their faith, they continue to dream in the midst of a world that is waking. The second merely laugh at the news since they have never believed in anything beyond the life of sense perception. Towards believers, whom they think to be sincere and simple, they are circumspect, as if fearing to cause them suffering by making themselves too well understood.

Not satisfied with the mere fact of God's death, Nietzsche investigates the reasons for His death. Though there are several, the basic ingredient seems to be the very fact of Christianity, for Christianity destroyed all the truth by which man had been living in pre-Christian times—above all, the tragic truth of life as understood by the Greeks before Socrates. As a substitute, Christianity invented mere fictions: sin, grace, immortality. And once men see through these fictions, only nothingness can remain, for Nihilism is the logical end product of all great human values and ideals. Since the supports for the values offered by Christianity are mere fiction, the moment of their exposure must plunge men into a nothingness such as was never before experienced in all human history.[13]

Liberalism, socialism, democracy—not matter how anti-Christian they may appear—are all essentially the result of enervated Christianity. In them, Christianity lives on, and maintains a secular existence. Modern morality and humanism are simply Christian ideals in disguise. When men at last see through them, the result is the nihilism which no longer leaves anything, which holds nothing to be true and which is the essential consequence of a distorted Christianity.

Nietzsche thought, however, that the turning-point had been reached. Not only will it be possible to conquer nihilism, but also, for the first time, to plan on a grand scale for human nature. Our knowledge of human history will yield the design for breeding a superior man once it is carefully scrutinized to see how various events affect the human personality. Thus far, the exceptions, the examples of greatness, have been the result of a series of fortunate accidents; now their appearance is to be controlled by the human direction of history itself. Knowing what Christianity has done to man, we may ask what other potential man has. From history we learn the results of accidental breeding that in the future we may make direct and positive improvements.[14]

Since the God of Christianity is no longer believed or even believable, all the outgrowths of Christianity, all the modern ideals, must be rejected as inimical to human life. In their place must be substituted a new world-affirming outlook, which, instead of debasing him, will elevate man, enabling him to plan the future course of his history.

Nietzsche particularly admired Schopenhauer's bold acceptance of the godlessness of human existence as a fact needing no defense in our positivistic age. His hope was to persuade men to embrace atheism out of sheer honesty, to have the courage to face the truth about reality and to see the harsh but unavoidable implications of all the healthy advances in western culture.

Nietzsche's antitheistic program embraced two steps: an experimental revision of our view of being and knowledge, and a dramatic announcement of God's death. Following the usual pattern of modern atheism set by Feuerbach and Marx, he supplied also a prophetic image of the man of the future. The new philosopher is to be a blend of skeptic, critic and experimenter. Skeptical of all traditions and absolutes of the past, he will apply a fearless scalpel to all unexamined convictions about God. He will not, however, be paralyzed by the indecisiveness of the complete skeptic but will act as a critical moralist, using a scientific method and standard of values. Engaged in intellectual and moral experiments to support his belief concerning the total fluidity of all things, he will be prepared to take a radically new stand toward the world, himself and God.

The most significant achievement of biological science in the latter part of the nineteenth century had been the Darwinian theory of evolution, which offered clear testimony to the universal struggle and transiency of structures. Despite some sharp criticism of the Darwinians, Nietzsche sees in evolution a general metaphysical significance providing scientific backing for change in the universe. He also invokes the sciences of history and philology as added witness to this constant fluidity in the realm of human institutions, concepts and languages. Since man is caught up in the evolutionary flow of life, the evidence is overwhelming for a monism of becoming as the fundamental datum of reality.

In announcing the death of God, Nietzsche goes beyond Hegel, for instead of seeing it as the prelude to the birth of absolute spirit, he makes it the outcome of the error about absolute spirit. To Hegel, God's death had been an act of becoming already precontained within the absolute; to Nietzsche, the idea of becoming is withdrawn from the context of absolute spirit and God is then taken as a synonym for the illusion about the absolute. God is dead precisely because the infinite and eternal spirit is exposed as a deadly creation of a human mind. Consequently we must raise the essential question of whether or not worldly existence has any intrinsic meaning. Using the figure of the madman who tries to spread the news of God's death, Nietzsche criticizes those who receive the news passively. The death of God means the deliberate eradication of the idea of God and the downfall of the entire system of standards and conduct which centered on that idea. Men who no longer adhere to it are murderers of God, and must bear personal responsibility for deicide and all its consequences for human culture.

Nietzsche thought of religion as the result of a kind of psychological projection. In certain intense, exceptional states man becomes aware of a great power that is in him. Taken by surprise, he cannot account for these sensations and, not daring to ascribe them to himself, he attributes them to a transcendent God Who is wholly other. He thus divides the two aspects of his own nature between two spheres, the weak and pitiable aspect belonging to "man," the rare, strong and surprising aspect belonging to "God." By his own absurdity man defrauds himself of all that is best within him.

Every form of religion debases men, but Christianity carries the process of self-despoilment and self-debasement to its utmost limit. In Christianity, it seems, there is nothing good, great or true that is not bestowed by the grace of God. Man thus perversely seeks a principle in the name of which he can despise man; he invents another world so as to belittle this one; he makes of nothingness a God, and calls upon Him to judge and condemn this present existence. Since

Nietzsche assumes that God cannot exist anywhere but as a figment of the human mind, to rid ourselves of Him there is no need to refute the proofs of His existence but merely to show how such an idea arose and came to be formed in the human mind. In the phrase, "the death of God," Nietzsche is expressing a choice as well as a conviction. It is a preference that decides against Christianity. For Nietzsche the death of God is not merely a terrible fact; it is a liberating human option.

Nietzsche's positive doctrines of the superman and the eternal recurrence of the same events were his deliberate substitutes for theism. By making a godless existence human and meaningful through a new appreciation of temporal existence he would divert our human tendency to transcend nature. In his myth about temporal becoming there can be gods or particular manifestations of the will-to-power, but no transcendent God; there can be a cycle of recurring events, but no personal and eternal God; there can be self-legislating supermen, who stand above the herd of common mortals, but there is no opportunity for all men to share in the eternal life of God. The result is a situation in which Nietzsche willed passionately that the great cosmos of natural becoming should support all our significance and all our human values.[15]

The other great nineteenth-century atheist, Auguste Comte, traces his ancestry back to the eighteenth century, to people like Diderot, Hume, Kant and those of the Scotch School. He was convinced that only by the consistent application of positivism within the sphere of religion can we hope to regain that harmony of spiritual and social life which modern criticism and revolution have destroyed, and he made a mighty attempt to accomplish this.

Comte believed that knowledge passed through three stages of development: 1) the theological stage, in which the imagination plays the greatest part in explaining reality; 2) the metaphysical stage, where abstract principles replace the deities of theology; 3) the positive stage, where both imagination and argumentation are subordinated to science, and facts become the ultimate criterion.

Since facts arrange themselves in as many irreducible groupings as there are distinct sciences, the unity of knowledge is subjective, not objective. Comte's hope was to unite the treatment of the emotional and intellectual needs of man. But for this a new religion was necessary: the "Religion of Humanity."

Comte considered the metaphysical stage, at which Christianity had arrived, as an intermediate one. In it the mind links facts together in accordance with ideas which are no longer wholly supernatural but not yet entirely natural, for metaphysical conceptions are really only theological conceptions modified by physics.

Associating religion with sentiment, he came to distinguish more and more clearly between religion and theology. Without denying the law which relegates theology to a dead past, he rediscovered religion in his own way, deciding that the history of mankind is a development from primitive religion (fetishism) through theism to definitive religion (positivism). The three states constitute a universal rule which provides positivism with its basis as method and as doctrine.

With the appearance of the positive age, theology would necessarily wither away, as physics would advance, and the great synthetic function previously performed by theology would fall to positive science. Having placed sociology at the apex of his classification of the sciences, Comte had completed the structure. Positivism was able to bring all things into harmony, and could show how the old religions were spontaneous institutions by which mankind created imaginary guides because it could not find any in the real order. Monotheism, however, introduced the most dangerous fanaticism, causing disturbances both in society and in the individual mind. Monotheism opens the door for ontology, which can only put all things into disorder since it preserves the unity of theology while eliminating its necessary corrective.

Moreover, in the positive state, the understanding no longer perplexes itself with curious and useless "whys"; no longer speculates on the causes of phenomena but strives instead to ascertain the laws according to which they happen. Having reached its final state the human mind abandons its quest of the absolute and indulges in the systematic neglect of causes.

Having once decided that the problem of God cannot be solved, Comte turned his energies to the positive organizations of this world. Strictly speaking, however, he is not an atheist, since he does not formally deny God. For him, God is simply unknowable.[16]

Today atheism takes the form of refusing God as the ultimate principle of explanation for reality. The aristocratic atheism of the eighteenth century had aimed only at a liberation of intelligence, but its direction changed during the nineteenth century. It was especially owing to Marxism that atheism, from being aristocratic and intellectual, became democratic and social. To Marxists the intellectual criticism of the idea of God and of the Christian religion had emerged from the whole materialistic movement as a valid and even definitive acquisition for the human mind. Nietzsche himself never wished to kill the idea of God; he merely claimed to have observed its death and reproached men for not having the courage to accept it.

There is also another discontinuity with the past in the Marxist development of atheism. Through the analysis of social forms and of economic alienation, Marxists believe that they have discovered the last sources of the theist error. Thus nineteenth century atheism appears as an immense effort of man to liberate man, an extraordinary attempt at the total recovery of man by man.

The word *atheism* in the nineteenth century covers many different realities. There is the rejection of false gods and the continual purification of our representation of God, the remains of idolatry and of all that is too human in our conceptions of God. There are methodological atheisms which result from rejecting God as an explanation even while retaining Him as meaning and presence. There is also the radical and mysterious atheism of the man who, in some degree, knows the true God and nevertheless refuses to accept Him voluntarily and consciously.[17]

The Christian should always bear in mind that both faith and experience teach him the existence of this latter atheism, the absolute and radical denial of God. Confusion arises from the fact that the various forms of atheism interrelate in the lived situation. While methodological denial can easily harden into dogmatic denial, an apparently dogmatic denial may conceal an implicit affirmation of God, for false gods are always possible and the true God is always present.

Spirit, reason, liberty, truth, brotherhood, justice—these great realities without which there is no true humanity, these realities which ancient paganism had half perceived and Christianity had fully blessed, quickly become unreal when no longer seen as a radiation from God, when faith in the living God no longer provides their vital substance. Without God they inevitably fade into empty forms.

Many feel the attraction of these revolutionary systems without grasping their full import. Viewing only the programs for temporal organization, they either refuse to consider the religious problem, or solve it for themselves in quite a different way. The denial of God is a very real and fundamental threat to today's life and as long as it persists man himself is in grave danger.[18]

The philosophers whom we have been discussing were all protesting against the same thing: the emphasis upon God's transcendence at the expense of His immanence. Both Feuerbach and Nietzsche were reacting to philosophical concepts that were becoming part of the intellectual heritage of Europe: Feuerbach against Hegel's Absolute Idea and Nietzsche against Schopenhauer's will-to-live. Hegel had tried to divinize nature itself; Feuerbach, finding that unacceptable, thought he had no recourse but to humanize the Absolute and so to exclude the divine entirely. Schopenhauer, having created the will-to-live as source of the world's pain and striving, had then cautioned all Christians not to fall victim to it; Nietzsche discovered that, in denying the will-to-live, he was denying all reality, leaving only utter nothingness. Faced with an alternative that was not really an alternative, each man built a defense of the natural world against the encroachments of an absolute spirit, and in so doing constructed a case, if not precisely for atheism, certainly for anti-theism.

What these philosophies failed to see is that life is at its highest where it participates most fully in the infinite life of God, and hence is divested of all that is a sign of imperfection. Since every human person has an absolute value and in this respect is nobler than the life of the species and social life, the whole purpose of society should be to make it possible for each human being to develop fully his life as a person. Because the human person is called to enter into communion with the Absolute, he is sacred, an inviolable sanctuary whose horizon is not limited by history or an epoch. His only measure is the divine, which is imperishable, and his vocation to share in it rests on no other title than personality itself.

The question today is: shall we revert to barbarism, no doubt very different from the old one, but surely more centralized, technically efficient and inhuman, or shall we, through deeper knowledge and a freer, more magnificent impetus, succeed in rediscovering the living God Who made us in His own image?

NOTES

1. J. Collins, *God in Modern Philosophy*, Chicago, Regnery, 1959, p. 207.
2. H. Hoffding, *A History of Modern Philosophy*, London, Macmillan, 1924, p. 179.
3. S. Hook, *From Hegel to Marx*, New York, John Day, 1936, p. 226.
4. "He who says no more of me than that I am an atheist, says and knows nothing of me. The question as to the existence or non-existence of God, the opposition between theism and atheism belongs to the sixteenth and seventeenth centuries but not to the nineteenth. I deny God. But that means for me that I deny the negation of man." Ludwig Feuerbach, *Sammtliche Werke*, 1846, Preface to Vol. I, pp. xiv–xv, cited in *Hook.*, p. 222.
5. W. B. Chamberlain, *Heaven Wasn't His Destination: The Philosophy of Ludwig Feuerbach*, London, Allen and Unwin, 1941, p. 54.
6. Collins, *op. cit.*, p. 243.
7. Hook, *op. cit.*, p. 249.
8. M. M. Cottier, "The Romantic Conception of Life and the Marxist Conception of History," *Blackfriars*, Vol. XL, No. 477, 1959, pp. 498–502.
9. Collins, *op. cit.*, pp. 249–257.

10. E. Borne, *Atheism,* New York, Hawthorn Books, 1961, p. 66.
11. Collins, *op. cit.,* pp. 259–264.
12. H. deLubac, *The Drama of Atheist Humanism,* New York, Sheed and Ward, 1950, p. 18.
13. W. Kaufmann, *Nietzsche: Philosopher, Psychologist, Anti-Christ,* Princeton University Press, 1950, p. 125.
14. K. Jaspers, *Nietzsche and Christianity,* New York, Regnery, 1961, p. 13.
15. Collins, *op. cit.,* pp. 267–268.
16. deLubac, *op. cit.,* pp. 79–93.
17. J. Lacroix, "The Meaning and Value of Atheism Today," *Cross Currents,* Vol. V., No. 3, 1955, pp. 203–219.
18. deLubac, *op. cit.,* pp. 33–34.

4

Contemporary Atheism

CENTURIES ago St. Thomas Aquinas indicated two perennial sources of atheism: the presence of evil in the world, its undisputable dominion over vast areas of human activities, which seems contrary to the idea of an omnipotent and good God, and the self-sufficiency of human knowledge in its own limits. Since scientific investigation does not of itself lead to the knowledge of God, the conviction can arise that God is an unnecessary hypothesis, improbable from the moral standpoint and scientifically superfluous.

Practical atheism, of course, can exist in many forms since man can deny the existence of God in as many ways as he can sin. The most common form is a simple turning of one's whole power of attention to the relations between man and the world. No explicit denial is made of the existence of an Absolute, for in this view, no end would be served by such a denial.

One may also proclaim oneself a believer in God but in practice divorce completely this so-called belief from the well-springs of moral action. In church on Sunday one satisfies the exigencies of the transcendent Being, while the remainder of the week is devoted to the aggrandizement of self in relation to the real or imaginary needs created by the world we see. This is a truly blasphemous conception of a Supreme Being: a God who demands only an hour's service a week and is scarcely concerned with man's relations with his fellow man. The convenience of such a conception for the interests of modern bourgeois capitalists is clear. Attention is riveted on the world because it seems able to yield, to those who know best how to manipulate it, an ever-increasing flood of happiness-producing riches.[1]

For Christianity to accept such a caricature of God would be to identify itself with a culture committed to the destruction of Bolshevism, an identification which could compound the already unfortunate association between Christianity and capitalism. Christianity is in a very real sense at war with Communism but it cannot risk having its cause misinterpreted as a defense of another brand of materialism. Such misinterpretation could hinder the reunion of separated Christendom itself. It was Vladimir Soloviev, the eminent theologian and philosopher of the Russian Church, who saw the mission of the Church to lie in the reunion of Eastern and Western Christianity.[2]

Contemporary atheism may serve to help prepare the Church for fuller conformation to Christ Crucified.

In its atheistic accusers the Christian consciousness faces its ultimate trial, a trial of strength of mind and heart in which victory will go to the one who truly comprehends the other.[3] The Christian must seek to understand the atheist of the twentieth century, to appreciate that he is often a man in revolt against a caricature of God, presented by a defective Christian witness. Just as it is undeniable that the failures of contemporary Christian civilization aid the growth of militant atheism, it is also conceivable that the West has borne such poor witness to the Judeo-Christian vision of man that God may abandon it to its own devices. Some new culture of the non-Western world may well prove a better instrument for a spiritually richer incarnation of His image.[4] The Protestant theologian, Karl Barth, among many others, has challenged the presumptuous alliance between God and the makers of Western civilization, not because he opposes Western culture, "but because man has no right to 'domesticate' God in the name of progress."[5]

Atheism may also prove to have been a time of purification for the sincere man who has substituted the cosmic dynamism of nature for the supra-temporal life of the soul. In the sincerity of some such atheists lies a hidden germ of questioning that is in reality an obscure appeal for the grace of faith. Their nakedness of spirit, often their anguish, leave them with no pretences to sufficiency and their experience of emptiness may dispose them ultimately for the Divine plenitude.

It is in keeping with Christian tradition not to reject out of hand even the aberrations of reason but, appreciating their contribution to human history, to complete, to rectify, and to fulfill them. Despite their errors, a Luther or a Voltaire belongs to the cultural universe of the Christian, honored respectively for their nonconformism and civil tolerance. The Christian will in the same tradition honor Marx for his profound intuition, which Jacques Maritain has called "the great lightning-flash of truth which traverses all his work," i. e., the understanding of the sad consequences of wage-slavery in a capitalist world, of how the conditions of heteronomy dehumanize not only the proletariat but the possessing classes as well.[6] This intuition is pregnant with Christian values, but the task remains for a Christian critique to free it of the errors which underlie its Marxian formulation.

The materialism of Marx is more profound than that of the eighteenth century French materialists or of mechanist materialism. It is, in a sense, a reaction to an idealist or "angel-minded" misunderstanding of a material world. For Marx, the source of all activity is material causality as it is integrated with the historical process. Owing to his monist metaphysic he was to confuse materialism with realism. Thus his Communism did not originate in his economics; its origin is philosophical and metaphysical.[7] Before he was a Communist, he was an atheist. Transferred from the sphere of religion to that of social criticism, the atheism of Feuerbach became the sponsor for Marx's adherence to Communism. At a second stage in his thought, in contradistinction to Feuerbach, he came to regard the alienation of man through private property as giving rise to the alienation of man from himself by God. Communism would end man's alienation from his work and with the triumph of atheism the alienation of man from himself would cease. The assertion that religion diminished the combative efficiency of the pro-

letariat and the assertion of the non-existence of God are intimately
connected in Marx's mind because he set out from the materialist
conception of the world. To know whether or not atheism is at the
root of this conception of the world, we must understand the part
played by metaphysics in the origin of his system, and its ultimate
rejection.

Atheistic Communism professes to return man to human life.
Here, in its claim to authentic humanism, is the powerful attraction
of modern atheism. "It is easy," said Marx, "to be a saint if you
have no wish to be human." The truth, of course, is that no social
technique or system of re-education can automatically bring about
the transformation of beings born to tend to that perfection of love
which is sanctity.[8]

When we ask ourselves how the Russians were led to accept
Marx's humanism, we must remember that that country never
knew a Middle Ages or had a Renaissance. Nature and reason were
never properly appreciated for themselves. An extreme supernatural-
ism, "whose tendency is to despise reason and regard nature as a
process of corruption," said Soloviev, made religion all too vulnerable a target. It is even possible that modern atheism, an anthropocentric humanism, is the antithesis in a historical dialectic which
will eventually restore an authentic humanism in Russian thought.

Social injustice was another condition in Russia that disposed the
people for the pseudo-justice of atheistic Communism. Despite all
the arguments against it, atheism retains its permanent bases in the
existence of evil and in the suffering of the innocent. A theology or
a philosophy that indulges in logical manipulation to discount the
tragic, that substitutes some abstract effigy for the reality of suffering and evil, serves only to reinforce atheism.[9] The results of evil are
often so pitiful "that even the most ludicrous wishful unthinking is
preferable to having to remind ourselves of it all, by thinking out
the theological explanations."[10] It is easy for a textbook to show how
the argument for atheism drawn from the existence of evil can be
dissolved in the framework of punishment and reward after death.
But the argument becomes less convincing in the hands of witnesses

whose chill faith renders them more suitable for the role of prosecutors of God. Truth must be incarnate to be appreciated by the human mind and one of the best proofs of the existence of God remains the existence of genuine human, Christian charity in His witnesses.

Only a perversion of the Christian conscience could explain the peaceful coexistence of Christian belief with economic exploitation of the poor. Such a conscience, having failed at certain periods to see that charity without justice leads to the distortion of reality, gave substance to the criticism of Marx when he described charity as a hypocritical attempt to keep the festering wounds of the underprivileged from becoming gangrenous. In his efforts to make injustice less intolerable, the Marxist insists that charity today is an evasion of the issue. The real world, he says, can be transformed only through justice.[11] But this supposed rivalry between charity and justice only means that Christianity has not been successful in promoting justice in the political, social and economic spheres. At times its critics claim that Christianity has been almost exclusively concerned for two thousand years with private morality, chiefly with matters pertaining to sex, paying small attention the while to crimes against humanity. Moreover, to disengage himself from public life the Christian has sometimes used the pretext of concern with his interior life. All of which attests to the believer's unawareness of the dynamic dimensions of charity and his consequent failure to bear witness to present-day life.

To assert that humanity develops and perfects itself in proportion to the degree of its love is to recognize the identity between being and love. For, strictly speaking, love is cosmic and universal, not merely individual and social. As he loves others, man deepens in being and more truly exists. This is the meaning of the intimate relationship between the first and second Commandments. Since being is ultimately love, the Christian who disassociates himself from the building up of society is neglecting his proper work, that is, social union. And if he fails to make any effort to transform the temporal world, he will be detested for his too tranquil acceptance of the misery of others. The moderate pessimism of Christianity should not be that of inertia. While it knows that the creature comes from nothingness, the strong optimism of Christianity also knows that the creature comes from God and is returning to Him. But the temptation of the Christian will always be to take his rest too soon.

Scientific though Marxist atheism may appear, it denies God more on the grounds of ethics than of metaphysics. It refuses to forgive Him the existence of evil in the world, as it refuses to forgive Him the creation of an imperfect world. In its efforts to divinize human society, it effects "the paradox of taking an irreligious humanity as a religion."[12] And an anthropocentric religion is always contemptuous of the mystery of the imperfections of human liberty. The immense cosmic struggle with evil in which man is continually engaged is not only comprehensible but re-creative in the Christian perspective. But once man's metaphysical center is sought outside of God, the mysteries of life become agonizing problems that aggravate and agitate him to rebel against his human situation.

The communist state, in its search for liberty and its indignation against individualism, has profaned the mystery of the freedom of the person and perpetrated greater evils than those it sought to remedy. In its destruction of liberty of thought and in its socialization of both the person and the mind, it has brought to a peak the fearful risks inherent in any collective organization.

Atheist Communism and atheist Existentialism, denying as they do the reality of a Supreme Being, also dislocate the nature of created being. For the communist all being is material, but for the radical existentialist it is existence without essence. By robbing being of its essence, radical Existentialism leaves it unintelligible. This is why it is a phenomenology rather than a philosophy; unable to understand being, it can only describe the phenomena of an existent. But such a disturbance of the delicate balance within being of existence and essence results in a philosophical tragedy.

A challenging type of atheism prevalent today is that of the man who claims to have examined without prejudice things as they are and to have found that the Christian concept of God is impossible.[13] Atheism such as this raises problems about the meaning of man and of the universe which do not have easy answers. Whereas practical atheism exists outside of any logical relation to a specific doctrine, true atheism bears a relationship to the God it denies. This is why, in periods of decadence, when superstition usurps the place of true religion, the polemical position of the just man may, in the language of the time, be termed atheist. Atheism directed against a contemporary deformation of the idea of God may however perform the function of a catalyst, causing Christians to purify or enlarge their conception of the Divine Being. Atheists of this sort do not thereby establish the truth of atheism but they do make their Christian brothers aware of guilt.

One form of atheism, common enough today, is reductivist. The scientist decides that the physical universe is enough to keep him satisfied. He makes no real attempt at argument against the possibility of God since such argumentation, so prevalent in past centuries, is now seen to be unnecessary. Actually, the accumulation of scientific facts cannot challenge the basis for God's existence for no one claims to prove His existence on this level of fact. But science, preferring to ignore whatever does not pertain to the realm of efficient cause, has discovered that its method works amazingly well for the achievement of the ends it has set for itself. It has in fact found that it can reach these ends with a sort of finality unattainable in other fields. Because of this many of its devotees have decided that the ends of science are the only true ends of rational man.

Marcel notes that the fundamental claim of scientific atheism seems to be that it possesses decisive facts unknown to the believer which, if they were known, would force him to proclaim the nonreality of God; his only alternatives would be bad faith: to contest the facts arbitrarily or to refuse to draw their consequences.[14] Such a position, however, is philosophically untenable. The intrinsic character of the affirmation of God deprives us of every right to place His reality on the level of scientifically observable facts. Moreover, there are scientists who are also believers: does the nonbelieving scientist claim that he has access to facts denied to the believing ones? The affirmation of the reality of God is an act belonging to a completely different dimension of knowledge, inseparable from the commitment of the whole human person. We are "interested," and we have right to be, in affirming the existence of God, our ultimate concern.

Scientific atheism has much in common with the practical variety. In each, the pursuit to which one has devoted one's life becomes the only matter really deserving of attention. Moreover the explicitly reductivist approach of the atheist-scientist constricts the possibilities of human life quite as much as does the implicit denial-by-inattention of the "business is business" mentality.

A third choice open to the scientist is to aggrandize science by claiming that it can explain all of human activity. The logical consequence, perhaps, of positivist reductivism, this is clearly unsatisfying in its designation of religion as "mythological."

Another obstacle to man's grasp of God's self-revelation lies deep in his own desires. Whereas those forms of atheism that stem from a positivist outlook see the world as quite sufficient for man, this source of denial looks on it as absurdly out of proportion to the greatness of human desires. Here the solution is not to do away with God as no longer necessary, but to see Him as inherently impossible, the poor excuse that mankind has dishonestly offered throughout the ages for the obvious insufficiencies of the world.[15]

This, of course, is a far more honorable attitude than that of the positivist. It is the sort of atheism which Pascal had in mind when he described the phenomenon in his *Pensées* as "an indication of spiritual vigor, but only to certain degree." True spiritual vigor is indeed present in such a denial, because it manifests a vital concern with the question what man can ultimately hope for. Not many believers have conducted as strenuous a spiritual inquiry as have such men as Camus and Malraux, who pose this problem of man's desires and hopes in relation to God.

Since the explanation for this kind of atheism must be sought on a more profound level of human experience, the question might be asked: can the whole matter be considered a refusal to accept the problem of evil as *a* mystery, but not the central one?

Owing to the pervading atmosphere of a scientific age, the hiddenness of God seems to be subconsciously conceived of as an evil. If God is something good for man, why is He not made manifest to him instead of remaining a hidden God in contemporary life?

This is the malaise against which Rousseau argues in his *Discourse on the Arts and Sciences*: a state in which man does not think but his age thinks in him. Here is one more proof of that fact that we cannot fully escape the tyranny of the presuppositions of our era.

The very people who wish to eliminate God in order that the individual may at last be free, pride themselves on having refuted Christianity by describing how their God does not compel assent. But it must be asked, what freedom would man possess if the hidden God were to reveal Himself in His glory on earth? The existentialists seek the liberty to choose, to say yes or no. But God evidently wanted man to have this choice, since He has, in fact, remained hidden. Existentialists fail to consider that if the demand which they make upon Christianity were fulfilled, man, by their own definition of him as a free being, would lose his humanity. In point of fact, the actual human condition envisaged by Christianity does meet the existential demand. For man can "create" himself by his liberty although he must decide whether or not to do so in accordance with the Divine Will.

Although the existentialist systems proclaim their "discovery" of the primacy of existence over essence, this primacy is not a new revelation but a well-known fact whose source lies in the "Judeo-Christian revelation of God as the transcendent self-existent Being Who confers upon His creatures all that they have and are."[16] From this revelation St. Thomas derived the principle of existence with which he transformed the philosophy of Aristotle, not by plastering over it a façade of Christian ornamentation, but by providing it with a guiding principle hitherto lacking but essential to his thought if it was to achieve a real unity and coherence. Unless Thomist philosophy was to be fundamentally existential, no analogical transition from finite beings to God could be validly made. In an essentialist system, analogical discourse would be doomed to either sterile agnosticism or clumsy anthropomorphism. Sertillanges' description of Thomism as "an agnosticism of definition" is justified by the fact that a finite mind can form no adequate concept of the essence of God. Analogical knowledge of God is possible only because an inherently existential element is present in all our affirmations about God.[17]

While the existentialism of St. Thomas affirms God, that of Jean-Paul Sartre denies Him. For St. Thomas the Absolute Existent *is* God, but for Sartre finite being is absolutized in defiance of God. In the Thomistic view, creatures receive their being from a subsistent Act of Existing. Man's being is thus limited because his existence is received in an essence, whereas to Sartre man creates himself by acts of unconditioned decision. By distinguishing between ontology and metaphysics Sartre is able to offer a description of human existence while avoiding embarrassing questions about God and the soul.[18] If, however, we make a distinction between the metaphysical and moral meaning of "essence" as Marcel did a decade before Sartre began writing, then it is true to say that, in the moral sense, man creates his own essence throughout a lifetime of free decision. Sartre's special brand of existentialism rests forever upon an ambiguity since it fails to make the necessary distinction between these two meanings of "essence."

Sartre's thesis stands on shaky ground when he opposes it to a typical theistic position which he assumes must assign the primacy of essence over existence. Such an assumption is wholly invalid with regard to St. Thomas's philosophy, for the exemplary idea which Aquinas sees as present in God's mind, even before the production of a particular creature, is not a kind of master die for the production of finite individuals. What Aquinas holds is that the entire being of the creature is present to God's mind both in its unique existential act and individual traits, as well as in its essential nature. Since essence and existence are co-principles in finite being, they require each other simultaneously, although the act of existing enjoys primacy within the being. Consequently, Sartre's thesis loses its distinctive character when a clarification of terms reveals the existential orientation of the philosophy he is opposing.

The one unique thing in contemporary atheistic existentialism is its special brand of atheism, which denies God far more explicitly than did the negative agnosticism that flourished in the second half of the nineteenth century. Thus an obvious characteristic of Sartrean existentialism is its absolute atheism. Because Sartre is really preoccupied with God, his denial of Him results more in a privation than an absence.[19] The postulate of the non-existence of God is to Sartre one of his regulative ideas. His existentialism is nothing else than an attempt to draw all the consequences of a coherent atheistic position. Charging theists with making the gratuitous assumption that God exists, he justifies his atheism as simply a contrary postulate, ignoring the traditional claim that knowledge of God is a consequence of a previous analysis of finite existents.

Only *a priori* and postulatory methods are considered by Sartre and so he reviews the ontological argument of Descartes and the dialectical proofs of Hegel. Having once demolished these dubious proofs for the existence of God, Sartre tries to make a reasonable defense of the atheistic principle based on three arguments. The first is that there is an intrinsic contradiction in the notion of God. In point of fact, however, it is in the Sartrean theory of the modes of being that the contradiction lies, not in the idea of God or in the religious conception of God. The second argument asserts the impossibility of creation, because to Sartre causal activity cannot communicate being. His third argument, a genetic one, is a psychological explanation of the origin of the idea of God in the course of which, owing to his commitments about the general structure of being, he dismisses or distorts the constant testimony of the religious mind.

This last argument against the existence of God involves a caricature of God as an absolute third party, a transcendent starer whose gaze would make of society a squirrel-cage.[20] Such a parody is the result of attempts to deal problematically with God. Kierkegaard had long ago protested against any philosophy that makes of God an aloof observer never entering into communal relation with His creatures as a personal subject. Philosophy had reduced God to a problem; Sartre, aided by the Nietzschean view of the world as a chaos of becoming in which there are no inherently inscribed meanings, makes a further reduction of God to a mere idea.[21] Man must face the contradiction involved in the idea lest he be consumed by a useless passion for God.

Traditional proofs for God's existence undergo curious changes in the framework of atheistic existentialism. For example, the doctrine of the contingency of the world becomes that of the absurdity of the world. Rather than suffer the delusion that the world is a self-contained rational system, the atheist prefers to see it as nonsensical. Granted that God does not exist, he is right, of course, in asserting that the world is unintelligible and existence absurd. The discovery that all things are completely contingent is the key to the nausea of Roquentin, the hero of Sartre's novel, *Nausea* (1938), which contains the background for his theory of the In-itself.* The contingency of the In-itself is identified with its absurdity and lack of causal origin. Sartre's device for avoiding the force of the principle of causality is to make the being of the In-itself unamenable to intelligent explanation. As he puts it: "the In-itself. . . . escapes contingency in being its own foundation: the *Ens causa sui,* which the religions call God."

Although Jean-Paul Sartre has often been linked to Marxist causes, his approach to atheism is quite different from that of Marx. Far from making an act of faith, Sartre in his *Being and Nothingness* purports to give a highly technical proof that God cannot possibly exist. The basic doctrine in his case is one of absolute freedom, which is in absolute contradiction to the notion of man's creation by another being. To be free in the Sartrean sense means to owe nothing to anyone. Each time I am forced to make a free action, I

---

* The theory of the In-itself is examined at greater length in chapter VI.

am forced to escape myself. This is an immediate consequence of the definition of man's freedom, and it is, in the last analysis, self-creation *ex nihilo*. Each time he exercises his will man leaves behind the self previously knowable by himself and by others, and takes on a new self. To overcome this constant frustration, man has invented the idea of God in Whom this flight from self is halted. Through bad faith, man now persuades himself to ignore the fact that this flight is the essence of life and that such a being as God is therefore clearly impossible. Through dishonest belief in a creating absolute, he has rejected strenuous freedom for subhuman repose.

This whole development follows once one accepts Sartre's prejudicial idea that freedom is the identification of every free agent as a first cause. The political absurdity of his doctrine would seem to appear in the logical conclusion that one should take no action in the State lest he deprive its other members of the right to total self-creation. But Sartre's affiliation with the Marxists in political life is the best possible refutation of his doctrine.

The religious aspirations of men are mere caricatures in Sartre's system. Moral activity that attempts to realize, in a finite way, some likeness to God and to have a creaturely share in eternal life proves too profound a concept, and because of his notions on being and consciousness, he fails to distinguish between the attitude of seeking to *be God* and that of seeking to become *like* God, through participation in His holiness.

The signs that point to God are always open to perversion and mis-interpretation but this only proves that God reveals Himself in signs which are to a certain extent ambiguous and equivocal. His use of such signs is in order to preserve man's freedom. For the response which He wants is a free response of love. Should the sign that fails to communicate God effectively be a human being, one who has a commission to be the light of the world, then the response of his brother, the unbeliever, is conditioned by the very one upon whom God counts to cooperate with Him in the work of salvation. Were the Christian to witness effectively to the vital relationship that grace effects between God and himself, then the sincere unbeliever would be less ready to identify the desire to be God with the desire to be like God. Love does not seek to be the "other"; this would only destroy the relation of opposition, the rapport between the "I and thou." Love yearns for the union of personality, not identity. Sartre's idea of Christianity seems to be that of merely another Hellenistic mysticism in search of a blending of the creature with the divine. In point of fact, the kind of union that the Christian desires and believes in could only be brought about through divine ingenuity, since it is a union that is at once most intimate yet maintains a radical distinction between man and God.

Perhaps the success of the modern arguments for the nonexistence of God is somewhat owing to the Christian's own misunderstanding of the nature of faith and his consequent failure to confront his existential situation. The egoist seeks himself in the faith; the indolent man seeks dogmatic slumber; the timid man seeks a panacea; only the authentic Christian discovers that faith is total, loving adherence to a Person.

It is this deficient and immature image of the faith that enables Albert Camus to look on Christianity as merely an excuse for an intolerable postponement of happiness for the masses. An atheistic moralist, he is not so metaphysically handicapped in his existentialism as is Sartre. In developing the moral side of atheistic humanism, he substitutes for the metaphysical determinism of Sartre a cultural determination of the mass mind against the acceptance of God. His sympathy is with the masses of people whose sufferings have left them to feel God-forsaken and finally Godless in the crushing atmosphere of their present existence. This indictment of the social order bears all too sad testimony as to how Christians have neglected the social doctrine of the Church. Pope Leo XIII liked to think that if those outside the faith did not know of the supernatural goal of Christianity, it would seem to them to have been founded for the temporal happiness of society, because of the way in which it has leavened that society. The communist and existential revolts of the present century are a direct challenge which Christians must answer by changing the social and intellectual circumstances so conducive to an atheistic outlook. A Christian critique of the humanism of Camus, who agrees with Nietzsche that the rebellion against the idea of God is not a complete nihilism but "the beginning of an absolute affirmation of the earth and all things finite," would require an honest and searching examination of the Christian affirmation concerning the earth and all finite things.

Unlike Sartre, Albert Camus guided his entire life with a remarkable singleness of purpose. His hope was to bring a modicum of justice into the world by preventing tyranny and violence as far as he could. Seeing the world as essentially unjust—and therefore nonsensical—he yet believed that man's reason is able to distinguish between what is just and what is not, and therefore he is obliged to do that which is just. Since the absurdity of the world is entirely opposed to man's efforts to order the world, he is condemned to a life of absurdity in which he is tortured as was Sisyphus.[22]

The appeal to the absolute, which so intrigues men, is merely an excuse for dropping on other men's heads the load which they should be carrying up the mountain. But it is not only the theists whom Camus condemns for rock-dropping. Contemporary events convinced him that those (including Sartre) who establish any kind of an absolute are as dangerous to Camusian peace and quiet as is the religious fanatic. Blood is bound to flow unjustly in the service of any absolute—a fact which derives from the very essence of absolutism. For the absolutist is induced to turn his main attention away from the struggle against the world's injustice and to fix his gaze on some imaginary transcendence that can magically justify any action.

Camus's atheism springs from experience. Granted that the world is meaningless, there is still no reason for making an active denial of God except for the fact that this fiction appears to cause more violence than would occur if it did not exist. Yet Camus admits in his *Lettre à un ami allemand* (1942) that Nazism has as its basis the same doctrine of radical absurdity as his own. Inasmuch as the Nazis killed six million Jews in a few years within his own lifetime whereas Christianity has apparently broken the habit since the days of the Inquisition, it seems impolitic for a philosopher of non-violence to opt for absurdity. Even in a world of nonsense, fictions should be handled with care, and, after all, perhaps it is Christianity which keeps violence at a minimum.

At bottom, Camus's atheism is, also, an act of faith.[23] Through an act of the will he puts his faith in man, trusting that the absurd individual will prefer Camus to Hitler. The absolute is the scape-goat whose death may allow man to perform his absurd tasks in serenity. Although the absurd man appears to stand a great distance away from Nietzsche's superman, who must become a god in order to seem worthy of God's murder, actually they are alike. Both philosophers address themselves to a small band of elite, to an intellectual and ethical aristocracy.[24] The difficulty in accepting Camus's responsibility without guilt is as great as that of swallow-ing Nietzsche's transvaluation of all values. How is the absurd man to act vis-à-vis the unenlightened multitude? Should he not try to find through political means a way to uproot the destructive mythology of the absolute? Camus attempts to avoid this difficulty by elevating non-violence into a universal value. Absolutism, then, the cause of all violence, can only be destroyed through the discreet use of violence by the Camusian elite.

But Camus halts before reaching this revolutionary conclusion because he realizes that the end of all revolutions is absolutism. Some voice within man cries out against absurdity and will not let him rest in it. Nor was Camus himself really an absurd man. In point of fact he cherished his personal absolute, one which was as unconditional as any other absolute, and firmly believed that his ideal of non-violence could be meaningfully furthered by his own efforts.

The intuitions of Camus and Sartre, like those of Luther, Voltaire and Marx, are good and are not to be rejected. In reality they are an attempt to rediscover values which were once revealed but have grown somewhat distorted in the course of time. In particular they have grasped the truth that man will grow in freedom to the degree that he learns to affirm his selfhood, assume his own attitudes, and take responsibility for what he does.

Much is made of man facing up to his existential situation—that of a being-unto-death. The man in revolt, realizing the absurdity of his situation, can either assert his autonomy by taking his own life, or like Sisyphus, who despised the gods, can, by embracing his human condition, find recompense in the meaningless struggle toward the summit.

The existentialist intuition about death is less an intuition than an image of the primary imagination, an isolated phantasm and feeling of initial disgust. Artists, philosophers and theologians are all needed to complete and integrate this image.[25] One of the facets of this image, particularly nauseous to Sartre, is passivity. The passivity that is death is not so much feared as the form of passivity within man during life. To receive is incompatible with being free, is demeaning. Even though to receive is half of life and half of our nature as well, Sartre will not have it. This repudiation deprives him of the source of all man's energies and action, the gift of receiving. The sharpest, deepest form of activity, the ability to say "yes," the act of receiving, seems to him to be death.

Sartre's existentialism is but the other polarity of that puritanism which denies freedom and life, a prostitution of existence, for he defines it as a "disease of being."

The man in revolt actually sets up shadow enemies instead of standing up to his existential situation. Having depreciated reality to a sadistic image of existence devoid of metaphysical content, he has failed to take up his proper task of working out a "phenomenology of existence" and therefore has fallen into error.

Nevertheless, this type of atheism, rooted in revolt against the fact of evil, can also be the starting-point of a dialectic that can lead a sincere man to a purer recognition of God.

In his refutation of existentialist atheism, Gabriel Marcel examines the nature of opinion and finds a general tendency to confuse it with faith. Formed as if at a distance from its object, opinion wavers between mere impression and affirmation, a fact clearly seen in the case of the militant atheist who maintains without proof that God does not exist.

But God, says Marcel, simply cannot be judged from a distance. For God concerns me in the most fundamental sense, and the more something concerns me the less valid is opinion about it, since involvement (*engagement*) and opinion naturally exclude each other. The unbeliever has expressly placed himself outside of God, Whom he ignores, and outside of the universe, in which he sees evil and suffering. At the same time he renders himself radically incapable of understanding that evil is the consequence of sin, permitted, although not willed, by the God he denies. Consequently, the idea of sin loses its meaning and becomes merely an imperfection or an error which can be eliminated.

Atheism that results from this type of intellectual approach is at best only a philosophy of that lived atheism which is rooted in satisfaction. The masses of today, surfeited with the glories of technical achievements, appear to need nothing beyond the visible or beyond that which is manageable by technical devices. Such a way of living and of conceiving life leads directly toward spiritual death, for it is pragmatism of a bio-sociological character, ruled by a psychology and an ethics of conditioning. All psychic disturbances and especially anguish are seen as psychosomatic disorder, states of mind which psychoanalysis and related techniques are present to remedy. But this is a degradation of belief more offensive to the religious consciousness than a declared atheism. In the latter there is at least a negative reference to God, whereas the atheism based on satisfaction implies a denial of all transcendence.

It would appear then that atheism today is not sufficient for a certain type of modern mind. Though a negative thing, atheism is still a theology. Even if we try to prove that there is no God we are still asking the fundamental questions about the ultimate origin of the world and the nature of man. It is Auguste Comte, after all, who is perhaps the true prophet of our post-modern era. His law of three stages manages, by relating religion to a past state of human development, to render it useless. The new man, the man of the positive age, does not even know what religion is: God has been simply forgotten in today's "atheism by oblivion."

It is well to consider the implications of this unique situation in the history of godlessness and to ask if we are in the presence of an entirely new type of man.

On the premise that a radical atheism emerged out of Western Civilization only because this civilization inherited from the Jews the idea of a radical monotheism, it follows that the further development of the same ideas in Christianity will result in a new development of atheism. In Christ the one God became man, and thus manifested a radical proximity of man to God in a wholly unique way. With the advent of Christ man acquired a new dimension, whose consequences have only begun to appear. Significantly, in accordance with the latest trends in existentialist thinking, man's being is no longer conceived in terms of his abstract nature only, but in relation to the future to which he is directed. Similarly, modern theology tends to conceive of man in terms of this future as revealed in Christ; seeing in Christ the revelation of what man really is.

To deny God is to dislocate man. Mistaken about his metaphysical situation, the existentialist compounds his error by his defiant stance toward his existential situation. If he would look, the contemporary atheist could find the values with which he is obsessed in an authentic Christianity; but he rejects all dependence on God in his frenzied desire to be free. If he could only be brought to a knowledge of the triune God, Whose intimate life unfolds not in isolation, but in the interrelationship of Persons, his own dependence on God and on others might appear to him less a servility than a new dimension of liberty.[26] Actually, in the sense in which the existential revolt understands autonomy, God Himself is not autonomous, much less alone. If the Son, in His eternity and existence, is totally uttered by the Father without His divinity or absolute character suffering thereby, why should man, whose condition He took without loss, refuse to depend on God? Through Christ the Christian knows that God is personal, absolute, triune. The three subsistent Relations, Who are the Persons in God, are open to one another. The Son receives, without dependence or inferiority, all that He is, even His divinity, from another, the Father, Who is only Father in regard to His Son, while the Holy Spirit proceeds from the Father and Son, and exists for them.

To the Christian, man is made in the image and likeness of God. If the pattern of the Trinity were to be realized in his life, true freedom would be manifest, not in terms of alienation from God and every sort of absolute, as Sartre's Orestes defines the authentic man, but in total dependence on God and in total self-donation.[27] The liberty of man is no more a solipsism and egoism than is the freedom of God. The authentic situation of man is made comprehensible by the "situation" of the Trinitarian God in His being and in His action.

The question of human freedom is the test case upon which Sartre is willing to base his claims for the liberating effect of atheism. Having accepted Dostoyevsky's challenge that, if there be no God, all things are permitted, he maintains that the denial of God is the beginning of man's self-development. Only after God has been banished as a living belief does man become really free, for by this banishment the bond of dependency is dissolved. But Sartre is in error and divine dialectic in the Trinity, if accepted in faith, renders his test case invalid by proving false its basic assumption that "to receive is incompatible with being free."

The choice between the freedom of man and the existence of God is a theme common to Marxism and atheist existentialism. In seeking to drive out the notion of creation from the popular consciousness, Marx was well aware of the consequences of owing to another not only one's existence but its conservation as well. "No one is independent in his own eyes unless he is sufficient to himself and this condition is reached if he owes his existence only to himself." Both forms of atheism make the mistake of considering the problem of freedom in a framework of independence. But to do this is to be unrealistic. The metaphysical situation of man is always that of a relative being. In so far as he is related to his Creator, it is impossible for him ever to be independent.[28]

If ever they could agree on the meaning of freedom, Christian and existentialist would find themselves in possession of a common ground for discussion. Perhaps a working definition might be: to have the power to fulfill one's nature. The Christian could agree with the atheist that freedom, defined this way, is the end of personal and social life. Actually, the entire theology of the Christian, and especially of the Catholic, is a passion for complete freedom. Religion itself is the communication of freedom, for man is free to the extent that he can love people and things. A loving bond makes for perfect freedom and this is what Christianity offers when it brings to man the supreme love.

It is not the idea of freedom itself, however, which is the crucial issue. The real difference lies in the way in which liberty can be achieved. The Christian seeks to fulfill his nature in accordance with the interior law of freedom, for the eternal law of God does no more than command man to be himself, to be free. Illumined by grace the Christian experiences the interiority and suavity of the law; animated by the Spirit he spontaneously obeys it out of love for reality. But the man in revolt pursues only a phantom freedom when he attempts to develop his nature in accordance with his arbitrary will; in his futile efforts to control finite reality, he is crushed by the law that governs reality. And that which is hateful restraint for the rebellious man, is liberation for the Christian. Law frees man to be a man, "to live the inner life of reason and love, the classic life of wisdom, the Christian life of faith."[29]

That all men desire to be free is to say that all men seek to fulfill their nature, to be truly human. But only a humanism genuine enough to reveal the tragic flaws of pseudo-humanism can replace one that is atheistic. The reason why man is attracted by such pseudo-realism is that he "cannot stand too much reality."

Marx became obsessed with the material image, mistaking it for the whole of reality, but Marxist humanism is not so naive as to accept the position of classical materialism. Instead it claims for itself a dialectical materialism that conceives of a nature essentially mobile, dynamic, and which engenders life and progress. Its monist hypothesis about the nature of the "real" leaves man the creature of economic and social factors. Even though economic conditions play a supreme and decisive role in his life, communist man is obliged to act according to the "meaning of history," seeking his fulfillment in the task of fashioning his monolithic world into a Utopia for a future classless society. Human nature then becomes absorbed into the marvelous complexity of the universe revealed to it by science, and the spiritual operations of man become valuable only in so far as they serve the state and the humanity it is producing.

The result is a society of four-legged bourgeoisie, much resembling the animals on George Orwell's farm after their barnyard revolt. But the aspirations of humanity will not be satisfied in a classless society, for mankind will always strain to be what it was created to be: a "royal people."

The existential humanist is anxious, distressed and often nauseous in face of the responsibility placed upon him by his absolute freedom. Having no norm for evaluating his actions, since there are no transcendent values, he is *a fortiori* without an authority to impose them. What matters is that his purpose be sincere and lived up to intensely. Consequently, self-ability or "calculated responsibility" is something in which the existential humanist revels. The consciousness of his freedom destroys all the barriers; he cannot take refuge in any value since it is he himself who creates values. "Nothing can give me assurance against myself; cut off from the world and my essence by the nothing which I am, I have to realize the meaning of the world and my essence; I make that decision . . . with justification and without excuse."[30] This atheistic declaration of Sartre has its Christian counterpart in the words of St. Paul, who experiences a freedom from the law born of his love for Christ. "Who will rescue me from this body doomed to the grace of God through Jesus Christ Our Lord" (Rom. 7:24–25). "For me to live means Christ and to die means gain" (Phil. 1:21). St. Paul realizes in himself the Christian existential situation, when he writes to the Galatians: "With Christ I am nailed to the Cross" (Gal. 2:19).

Any humanism which fails to consider the total situation of man is embarrassed when man experiences the very thing it has denied (often out of fear) to be part of reality. Finite man is desperately in need of revelation to fill in the total image of reality; it is the task of the Christian to interpret reality meaningfully for his brother, the unbeliever. Since love is the way to faith, only in the Christian school of love can the atheist open his eyes to the reality of faith. For the reality that so often haunts the atheist, even to the point of disgust, is the revelation of God's love for man.

Ignorance and consequent fear of reality are often the real bases of infidelity, which is nothing less than man's failure to recognize God's love and to live up to its demands maturely.

Christians, too, are often dull and slow to accept the things which they must suffer before they may enter into their glory. Like the modern atheist, the modern Christian fears the *kenosis* involved in love. In spite of Sartre's objections to man having to lose himself in order that an impossible God may be born, man retains always his capacity for God.

Christian humanism, in its awareness of man's obediential potency, by which his nature is capable of responding to the touch of God's grace, is both optimistic and realistic about human nature. Enlightened by revelation, it sees deep into the meaning of man and his possibilities. An abundance of life rather than a catalog of legal prescriptions, it is committed to the whole man, sacrificing no facet to resolve the human paradox that the body and soul constitute. The material and the spiritual, the natural and the supernatural, the personal and the social, all are retained in order of hierarchy for man's greater "mystification" and glory. Christian humanism accepts man for what he ultimately is—a "mystery." And the most mysterious thing about him is that he is the sole being that realizes itself only by surpassing itself. His longing for plentitude is really an attraction for the divine and he keeps his dignity only by realizing all his dimensions and even by extending himself beyond them.

Through the wonders of science, new perspectives have opened up for modern man which the Christian humanist can harmonize and develop through the deeper perspectives of faith. For unless the Christian is wholly aware and appreciative of his "human" situation, he is not qualified to grasp God's revelation. Only in so far as he deeply understands and effectively lives truth, will he make credible the suavity and strength of God's answer to mankind. Teilhard de Chardin has brilliantly interpreted for his scientific peers the spiritual implications of the new dimension in reality. In his theory of evolutionary convergence, man realizes his mystical dimension by transcending himself in Christ. Even the communist and existential revolts fulfill their parts in bringing mankind to its omega point in the Mystical Body. Although a lethargic Christianity may have allowed them to usurp her mission to society by default, the progressive formation of Christ's Mystical Body is assisted by human growth towards collective organization and development of freedom, both of which are wholesome conditions for the reception of charity.

The denial of community, which is living in social justice and love, has led to the opposite polarity of atheistic communism. The denial of freedom and of the fullness of Christian life has led to the opposite polarity of atheistic existentialism. The denial of Christ has occasioned the death of God. It is not "the man in revolt" who will rise triumphantly from the tomb, but the repentant one who witnesses the crucifixion with Christ and is raised in Christ.

NOTES

1. E. Borne, *Atheism*, New York, Hawthorn Books, 1961, p. 124 ff.
2. K. Lagermissen, *Christian Denominations,* St. Louis, B. Herder, 1945, p. 619.
3. Borne, *op. cit.,* p. 9.
4. Norris Clarke, S. J., "Is the West God's Civilization?", *America,* March 31, 1962, p. 856.

5. "Witness to an Ancient Truth," *Time Magazine,* April 20, 1962, p. 61.
6. J. Maritain, *True Humanism,* New York, Scribners, 1938, p. 39.
7. M. A. Cornu, *Karl Marx,* de l'hegelianisme au materialisme historique, Paris, Alcan, 1934, cited in Maritain, *True Humanism,* p. 28.
8. Maritain, *True Humanism,* p. 83.
9. G. Marcel, "Contemporary Atheism and the Religious Mind," *Philosophy Today,* Winter 1960, p. 261.
10. C. Houselander, *The Risen Christ,* New York, Sheed and Ward, 1957, p. 92.
11. J. Lacroix, "Justice and Charity," *Theology Digest,* vols. I & II, 1953–54, pp. 182–183.
12. O. Dudley, *Will Men be Like Gods?* pp. IVf. in H. S. Box, *God and the Modern Mind,* London, Macmillan, 1937, p. 27.
13. Borne, *op. cit.,* p. 124.
14. G. Marcel, "L'Athéisme philosophique et la dialectique de la conscience religieuse," in *Athéisme Contemporain,* ed. E. Mauris, Geneva, Labor et Fides, 1956, p. 70.
15. Borne, *op. cit.,* p. 39.
16. E. L. Mascall, *Existence & Analogy,* London, Longmans Green and Co., 1949, p. 63.
17. Mascall, *op. cit.,* p. 119.
18. J. Collins, *The Existentialists,* Chicago, Regnery, 1952, p. 44.
19. H. Paissac, *Le Dieu de Sartre,* Paris, Arthaud, 1950, p. 9.
20. J. Collins, *God in Modern Philosophy,* Chicago, Regnery, 1959, p. 375.
21. *Ibid.,* p. 370.
22. G. Marcel, *art, cit.,* p. 54.
23. J. Maritain, *La Signification de l'Athéisme Contemporain,* Paris, Desclee de Brouwer, 1949, p. 17.
24. Borne, *op. cit.,* p. 56 ff.
25. W. Lynch, S.J., "Reality & Realism," *Critic,* April, May, 1962, p. 45.
26. P. Henry, "Sens et Valeur de L'Athéisme Contemporain," *Monde Moderne et Sens de Dieu,* Paris, Horay, 1954, p. 75.
27. S. Turienzo, "Absence of God and Man's Insecurity," *Philosophy Today,* Summer 1959, p. 138.
28. *Christianity and Freedom,* various authors, London, Hollis & Carter, 1959, p. 4.
29. J. C. Murray, S.J., "Literature and Censorship," *Catholic Mind,* December 1956, p. 665.
30. J. P. Sartre, *L'Etre et le néant,* Paris, Gallimard, 1943, p. 77.

The Ambiguity of God

5

Anguish

THE Middle Ages have often been called the "Ages of Faith," because of the universal freedom from preoccupation with the anguish of existence based on trust in the Providence of God. But when the splendid synthesis began to disintegrate, a general *malaise* set in, new currents of thought swept through the West, and the simplicity of faith gave place to a more questioning attitude.

Luther felt it necessary to oppose a growing casualness of attitude in Christianity and, in proclaiming the primary role of committed faith, evoked a certain anxious spirit in Christendom. For Luther, faith became an accepted risk, an agonized leap across the abyss of sin and despair which separated man from God, and in this he was a forerunner of Kierkegaard.[1]

John Calvin's doctrine of positive predestination made the abyss still wider, and man moved from anxiety to near-despair. Descartes and Kant, cleaving still further the natural from the supernatural, created an even stronger sense of isolation of man from God, and man's security was once again shaken by words of questioning anguish.[2] In the 18th century man had attempted to find a measure of security in the myth of the inevitable progress of material creation, but he failed to quell his perturbation of soul. Perhaps as a result, the late 19th and the 20th century have made the mystery of human existence a focal point for a philosophical treatment of man's anguish. Not that this anguish of man in the face of existence is anything peculiar to the 20th century. As children of Adam we have suffered from a division of nature and person, and concupiscence has pointed us away from God. Although objectively redeemed, subjective salvation is by no means assured. Consequently, man has always experienced anguish because of his precarious position in life. Still, one may wonder if anguish has not been stressed so much in our own day that we have lost perspective on the problem.

The concept of anguish and its role in man's relationship with God had never been treated systematically until in 1844 Kierkegaard published *The Concept of Dread*.

Here, for the first time, there is not only a description of the experience of anguish, but an attempt to penetrate its causes and effects, its relation to Christian theology. For Kierkegaard, anguish arises when man's finite spirit succumbs to terror before the infinite. Despite the fact that the Christian notions of God and Christ are implied, when not explicitly named, Kierkegaard's reflections left room for a double secular interpretation of his Christian-oriented thought.[3] Thus, the philosophy of existentialism finds its point of departure in Kierkegaard, and much of modern psychoanalysis can also trace its origin to the Danish philosopher.[4]

While it is true that before Kierkegaard there was no really serious theology of anguish, in the sense of a complete theological system, it is not true that no one before him had seriously treated anguish from the theological point of view. In point of fact, a fairly lengthy tradition exists, in both Catholic and Protestant thought, of interpretations of anguish.

The word anguish has been accepted for the translation of the Danish word *angest* as used by Soren Kierkegaard. Yet this is not completely correct. *Angest* has no precise English counterpart, although anguish seemed to have the closest etymological meaning.[5] Today the English word *dread* appears to be a better translation, since dread is great fear, especially in view of impending danger. Again, *angest* has been translated by "anguished anxiety" or "anguished dread" in an attempt to suggest the apprehensive element of *angest*.[6]

Anguish, or dread, is different from fear and anxiety, which are milder forms of anguish. The common psychological definition of anxiety is a "fusion of fear with an anticipation of future evil." Fear is "an emotion of violent agitation or fright in the presence (actual or anticipated) of danger or pain."

From these brief definitions, it would appear that anguish is a form of anxiety or fear, but much more intense and much more difficult to cope with. We experience it in the death of a loved one, in the collapse of very important plans, in the state of sin.[7]

Much of the semantic chaos seems to have resulted from combining the concepts of fear and anguish into one. Masso, for instance, hardly distinguishes between them. For him, fear is instinctive and unconscious while anguish is a sense of the unknown and the mysterious.[8] A more precise explanation is that fear always concerns a determined object; it is a reaction of the instinct of self-preservation. Anguish, however, is caused by the unknown, or at least by an incompletely determined object. To put it even more exactly, one might say that fear is caused by an external object or by the thought of it; whereas the object of anguish has a certain air of vagueness and indefiniteness about it. In religious anguish, for example, one must differentiate between the fear of hell and the vague unease of the individual before the simple uncertainty of his fate at the hands of a just God.

Anguish, as we have defined it, is a perfectly normal human experience, becoming morbid only in pathological cases.[9] Scripture testifies to its universality and we know that its experience is not limited to mystics. For all men share in anguish.

A difficulty arises from the fact that the German word "angst" can signify both "anguish" and "anxiety." Brissaud maintained that anxiety was fundamentally a psychic trouble, a sentiment of indefinable insecurity, physically evidenced by a sensation of constriction and suffocation.[10]

Anguish, however, is primarily a state, not a sickness. Janet maintains a distinction between anxiety and anguish while establishing it on different grounds.[11] In both states, the person is confronted with a continued interrogation among alternatives, ending up in ambivalence. In the state of anguish, it is the person himself who offers the alternatives to himself; forcing himself to choose, he breaks his internal unity. In the state of anxiety, the ambivalence is due to the structure of the object confronting the person, that is, it is due to events, circumstances, and so on. With anguish, however, the internal ambivalence resulting from the personality of the subject himself produces a more intense emotional state and often gives the impression of mental emptiness or nothingness. There is usually also an immense disproportion between the poverty of definite images in the mind of the subject and the overwhelming intensity of the emotion. One lives anguish more than one thinks of it, but the contrary is true of anxiety.

Freud's analysis of the experience of anguish and anxiety throws further light upon the subject. According to him there are two basic elements in anguish and anxiety: an unsatisfied longing and a conscious awareness of some danger, some threat to inner security. With anguish, the longing arises from within the subject; consequently, these internal desires are the source of the threat of which the subject is conscious. Moreover, the greatest fear, the prime root of anguish, is fear of the loss of the desired object. A polarity exists between the desire of the object and the fear of its loss, and the anguished individual, torn by internal ambivalence, experiences a dialectical movement between both emotions. This polarity is the psychological base of the experience of anguish. On the religious level, it is manifested in man's natural movement toward God with a simultaneous fear of the loss of God.[12]

The experience of anguish, in its fullest expression, varies widely, occurring not only among the religiously oriented but even among atheists, and having frequent concern with man's confrontation of the Absolute.

Perhaps the prime example of anguish has to do with death. Seneca labels the "meditation upon death" the most common cause of human anguish. Even in the Old Testament there are many examples among the Jews; for example, in Ecclesiastes: "A living dog is better than a dead lion. For the living know that they shall die, but the dead know nothing more . . ." Oates calls this "eschatological anguish," for it deals with the uncertainty of man's future after death.[13]

In later Christian thought, there are many references to the anguish in the face of death. According to Aquinas, the subject must not be very far away from death (otherwise he would not consider it) nor must he be close enough to have it certain. Aquinas, however, was concerned only with the death of the body; the question of the total destruction of the very being of man obviously did not arise, for the Christian mind did not conceive the possibility of the "nothingness"[14] of being which preoccupies the moderns. In fact, throughout the Christian era until the latter part of the nineteenth century and the beginning of the twentieth century, man's anguish before death never involved the possibility of the complete annihilation of his self; it was left for the existentialists to discover this concept of "nothingness."

A more universal type of anguish is that of the finite individual before the Infinite. Again there are many examples in Sacred Scripture, for instance, the meeting of Zachary with the angel who announced the coming birth of John the Baptist. Perhaps the most vivid instance of such a confrontation is the Transfiguration of Christ on Mount Thabor ". . . the disciples fell on their faces and were exceedingly afraid." And in the Old Testament we have the experience of Isaiah.

This kind of experience is not, of course, limited to Christians; there are many allusions to similar experiences in the major religions. It is Rudolf Otto who has best described and analyzed this type of anguish in his *Idea of the Holy*. Examining the *mysterium tremendum* before which the individual experiences "awfulness" and "awe," he finds that this *mysterium tremendum* arouses conflicting emotions of fascination, horror, and repugnance, the accompanying anguish and dread then paralyzing the subject. Overwhelmed and drawn by God's love, man is profoundly troubled by his own unworthiness. Such an experience is not limited to the strictly mystical plane, but exists on all levels of religious experi-

ence. It is still true, however, that the nature of such anguish has
not been clearly delineated. There is, in fact, some question as to
whether the anguish is not purged in the more complete manifestations of the experience of God's approach.[15] Thus Schleiermacher
asserts that in the most pure religious experiences, there can be no
anguish but only joy. In any case, this anguish of the individual
before the Absolute can be shown quite conclusively to exist. Consequently, any study of the relationship between God and anguish
must take it into account.

A third common form of anguish is that before the justice of
God, an excellent example of which is found in the Psalms: "Let
death rush upon them, and let them go down alive into the abode
of the dead, for there is wickedness in their dwellings, in their
midst. But I will cry unto the Lord and He will save me. Evening
and morning and at noon I will lament and groan, and He will
hear my voice" (Ps. LIV). This anguish is intensified for the believers in an Infinite God Whose power of punishment is infinite.
And this is commonly called the anguish of the sinner.

Finally, there is the common experience of human anguish before the misfortunes and apparent absurdities of the world. The
most famous examplar of such anguish is Job. But it is the existentialists who, in bewailing the seeming absurdity of the human condition, have made the anguish of the unintelligibility of the world,
and of man's fruitless attempts to determine his place in it, the one
basic theme of their movement.

Since anguish is so universal a characteristic of the human condition, philosophers have sought to solve it, and have even developed systems to explain its existence and character.

There are two opposed schools of thought concerning the nature
and causes of human anguish and its role in man's life. The existentialists, notably Heidegger and Sartre, propose a negative understanding of the problem, while the Christian school offers a more
positive approach. Bridging the two, but leaning more towards the
Christian one, stands Kierkegaard.

For Heidegger man is essentially a "being-in-the-world," the

world being understood as all those things with which man is concerned. Because he is interested in the things which form his world, they are all in order and each is useful to him. Man is at peace with the world and this is the sphere in which he puts his trust.[16]
Dasein is being, interested in itself, because it is in existence. Man is such a being who realizes he has a task to be done. Although not generally aware of this characteristic of his being, the "mood" unveils his true essence and purposes. ". . . through the mood and in the mood it is revealed to us that we find ourselves in a world without having previously known, chosen, loved, or willed it."

Fear grips the *Dasein* because it is threatened in its most important concern, its existence. Man may try to escape by losing himself in the society of the impersonal *das Man,* where, to forget his fears, he forgets his freedom and the tasks confronting him. But such a person is unfaithful to his vocation.[17]

Man fears, although we might ask: why should he fear those things in the world which he has put together and organized for his benefit? The basis for all fear is dread. Fear is directed toward some objects: pain, sorrow, death. But dread has no object, for Heidegger says: "the 'what' of dread is not something existing in our world."

Dread changes man's outlook on the world. In the lived experiences of dread the world becomes threatening, things in it become unimportant, life itself becomes trivial, useless, and beset with problems.

Because "beings-in-the-world" are now unimportant and to be like them in the impersonal, unauthentic existence of *das Man* is useless, man is eventually confronted with himself. The essence of dread is that it shows the "nothing" of existent, external beings. Dread purifies, for it turns "the *Dasein* back upon that for which it is in dread—namely its own potentiality of being-in-the-world." This statement is closely allied to Kierkegaard's idea of anguish as an education of man according to possibility, but the end result of the purification of dread in Heidegger varies markedly from that of Kierkegaard for whom it is salvation with God.

For Heidegger, dread has changed the atmosphere of the world for man, now no longer at home in a world which was once the center of his trust. Dread causes man to reject "what is" and to consider the interconnections of all things in the world as trivial. Capable of transcending the existent through dread, man can accomplish this by being projected into "nothingness," thus being enabled to see the framework of the existent world. This action is necessary, otherwise man would have no relationship to "what-is" and, hence, no connection with himself.

This transcending of the worldly, the limited, leads the *Dasein* to the "infinite," which, however, is not God, for Heidegger argues that since the notion of the infinite was arrived at only through a contempt of the finite world, the infinite is really derived from the finite.

It must be admitted that the concept of dread in Heidegger is not very well defined. The roots of dread are never made clear. According to Strasser, this dread appears as an "evil fairy" who turns everything that was once trusted into a world of menacing demons—a perspective which leaves much to be desired by way of explanation.

Man, in Heidegger's thought, is bound by the limiting conditions of his past (facticity) and the circumstances of the present; he is thrown into the world without ever having been consulted. But man is free to choose what he wills to do in these conditions. Basically he has two alternatives: the choice of a free acceptance of his being under the conditions in which this being is given—such a decision Heidegger calls "authentic existence." On the other hand, the individual can escape into an autonomous and anonymous living or, "inauthentic existence."[18]

If the individual chooses "authentic existence," he faces the challenge of his own uniqueness and that of being-in-the-world. Man must realize that he is limited by his facticity; although thrown into the world, he must continue to project himself, to act. "Authentic existence" is then the recognition on the part of the individual of the tragedy of man in a hostile world which threatens the growth of that existence.

But if man is constituted by his possibilities, death ends all becoming and hence all further possibilities. The man who is in "authentic existence" faces death openly; for him it is the final project and he must accept the fact that it reveals the ultimate nothingness of all existence, including "authentic existence." The person who is in "inauthentic existence," like the Christian, will place the guilt and hopelessness of man's condition on some extrinsic object or idea such as original sin. However, the individual who is really existing is conscious that the true nature of his guilt or inadequacy lies in his own finiteness and the limitations imposed by his proper facticity.

Death reveals to man the nothingness and consequently the meaninglessness of all existence. Naturally, the individual confronting this nothingness is filled with deep anguish and dread. It is in this sense that Heidegger must be understood when he states that anguish is a reaction to an object which is nothing and nowhere. This "object which is nothing and nowhere" is none other than the being-in-the-world determined ultimately by the nothingness of existence. Yet Heidegger goes on to assert that although man flees nothingness, he feels anguish even in his fleeing. What he must do is to return and accept the ultimate nothingness of authentic existence, which, however, has no power in the face of anguish.

On the psychological level, Heidegger's interpretation of human anguish adds little to the empirical facts which he observed. On the philosophical level, however, his explanation deserves a more careful examination. Heidegger himself denies a nihilistic interpretation of his concept of anguish in *Existence and Being*. Anguish is not a purely negative phenomenon; nothingness is not a blank. Rather, anguish is the positive consciousness of Being and of the individual's possibility of authentic existence. By making ourselves more aware of our contingency, we increase our awareness of Being itself. Therefore, anguish enables man to draw himself toward this Being (which for Heidegger always remains without content). In accepting the anguish which he experiences before nothingness, man is led to a better understanding of Being itself.

Such a passive acceptance of the nothingness of the world is obviously unacceptable to Christian thought. It is, in fact, explicitly forbidden in the New Testament. The existentialists, however, assert that man is dominated by such anguish and that this can be empirically proved. Admittedly, such anguish exists on a large scale in the contemporary world, and can be considered as one of the roots of modern man's *malaise*. But when existentialism insists that man can surmount anguish only by enduring it, this solution, reminiscent of the Stoic position, is rejected by the Christian.

The existential and Christian solutions to the problem of human anguish are incompatible on the ethical level. But the source for the incompatibility is to be found on the deeper level of philosophy.

In his doctrine, Heidegger combines the anguish of death, the anguish of nothingness, and the anguish of the world. But there are no references to the anguish experienced by the individual before God or to the anguish of the sinner. Consequently, it is wrong to compare Otto's dread before the *"mysterium tremendum"* with Heidegger's anguish before nothingness. In the first place, the *"mysterium tremendum,"* though it has an air of mystery and strangeness, possesses a definite content, whereas the nothingness of Heidegger does not. Secondly, the "mysterium tremendum" is an end in itself, while the nothingness is an active power which directs the individual toward another object, namely Being itself. But this Being is not God, for Heidegger is indifferent to the possibility of His existence, neither affirming nor denying it.

The French existentialist, Sartre, gives us another interpretation of the nature and the role of anguish which can properly be understood only against the background of his total thought.

Sartre makes an initial basic distinction between *"l'être-en-soi"* and *"l'être-pour-soi."* The former is an unconscious being, while the latter is the conscious being. In the *"l'être-en-soi"* there is neither negation nor nothingness. The latter is possible only in the conscious being, for it can *not* know, *not* exist, and such a possibility haunts it. "Non-being" is found in the heart of being, for being must precede it. Nothingness is produced in and by the being, a process called "nihilation" or "noughtening."

Man brings this nothingness into the world by asking questions, for although he cannot modify Being itself he can alter his relation to it. But this requires freedom, which is not a property or characteristic of man but is man himself; freedom is man who abrogates the past (his facticity) and creates nothingness.

The human consciousness is aware of its own freedom and it is here that Sartre interposes his concept of anguish. Anguish is precisely the consciousness of man's freedom. The fact that he is forced to make decisions among many possibilities confronting him is the root of anguish.

Sartre sees anguish as the essence of man, finding existence insipid and nauseous, ordered to nothing, and finding anguish a weight, experienced each time man uses his freedom of choice. The decision of a man "involves himself" in existence, affecting not only himself, but all mankind, and the feeling of deep and communal responsibility is anguish. But man, to be man, must carry his freedom to its ultimate limits. Since this involves anguish, to be human is to be discontented. But to avoid anguish by "material or moral activity" is cowardice.

If Sartre's concept of anguish is accepted, then all men should be continually suffering from it, for men are always being forced to make decisions. Sartre's solution is that the "slobs" are not in anguish because they rarely have their freedom of choice; like those persons of Heidegger who are in "inauthentic existence," Sartre's "slobs" flee anguish in febrile entertainment and anonymous living. Because anguish is a disagreeable thing to man, he tries to "noughten" it. But such an attempt Sartre terms "bad faith," insincerity. Nevertheless, almost all men live in "bad faith," for they cannot sincerely state what they are, and are continually "noughtening" their present state.

Sartre's solution to anguish is somewhat like that of Heidegger, although they differ in their interpretations of its nature and role. Sartre proposes that man accept the anguish of being forced to make decisions, act in good faith, try to maintain his freedom (and his anguish) in every new action boldly and hopelessly. Man cannot be sincere, yet he must attempt to act sincerely.

Although Sartre bases his solution of anguish upon the value of sincerity he offers no demonstration of the validity of such a norm.

Sartre's conclusions reveal yet a further narrowing of the concept of anguish from that of Heidegger, for he omits all references to the anguish of sin, of the individual before God, even of death.[20] Moreover, his interpretation of anguish is invalid both on the philosophical and on the psychological level. Having been greatly influenced by the phenomenological methods of Husserl, he holds that all philosophy must begin with the individual; every value is the creation of an individual, in individual, unique circumstances. But this subjectivism leads to the rejection of all forms of anguish which have as their object a being extrinsic to the subject, and invalidates many of his conclusions.

The failure of such a restricted view of anguish can be more clearly seen if one examines the views of Kierkegaard. In his theory, anguish is the reality of freedom as a possibility before the possible. Knowing that he can choose to do this or that and foreseeing the consequences of both actions, man is a source of anguish to himself. Moreover, various forms of anguish exist which correspond to the various stages in a man's life.

In *The Concept of Dread,* Kierkegaard discusses Adam and his first sin. Denying that Adam is different from us in supernatural endowment before his Fall, he states that the command of God not to eat of the fruit in the Garden of Eden awakened the first experience of anguish. Having seen the possibility of incurring guilt by his free choice to disobey God's command, Adam experienced the anguish that is a pre-supposition of sin. Although the transition from innocence to guilt is difficult for Kierkegaard to fathom, he notes a "qualitative leap" from innocence to guilt. Adam's sin has now placed him in a new state, or quality of existence: guilt. The transition from the possibility of disobedience to the actuality is accomplished in anguish. The role of anguish here seems one of motivation, urging Adam to actuate the possibility.

As Adam's sin was born in anguish and brought anguish with it, every descendant of his passes through the same "qualitative leap" from innocence to guilt in committing his first sin and renewing this anguish.

Kierkegaard also discussed the anguish of those who have yet to commit their first sin. Anguish is the quality of a dreaming spirit, a spirit which has not exercised its power of freedom. In this state, anguish is not a burden, but a search for the adventurous and the immense. This is a special anguish, for it attracts one to an object while at the same time showing that the object is forbidden.

Since anguish is synonymous with possibility, does anguish cease after the possibility has given place to actuality in the act of sin? No, answers Kierkegaard; anguish is now related to present sin and to the future. There is now open the possibility of greater sin or repentance. Consequently, man is in constant anguish because there are always other possible states which may be reached by the exercise of freedom.

Anguish will affect various individuals in different ways. Some, of course, will try to forget it by indulging in outward distractions and activities, but they will never find contentment, for they will have failed to resolve the "true psychological ambiguity" of anguish. To misunderstand anguish, to diminish it by the superficial life, is to move away from faith and ultimately toward damnation.

Kierkegaard saw anguish as having an educative value. Anyone who is educated by anguish is educated by possibility, and only he who has been educated by possibility is educated according to his infinity. Kierkegaard's evaluation of anguish thus holds possibility as more difficult to face than reality. Possibilities for good, as well as for evil, teach man the heights to which he can climb, his infinity, and the depths to which he can fall. To those who face it for the first time anguish will be deceptive. But he who is educated by anguish will not run from it but will use it as "ministering spirit which against its (anguish) will must lead it where he wants to go." By using anguish properly, man knows that created reality has little to offer that is lasting, and so detaches himself from the illusions of the finite. Faith then enters to point man to his goal: God. Anguish and faith, hand in hand, lead a man to accept his destiny from Providence and to put his guilt in the hands of God. Obviously, Kierkegaard preferred to treat this problem from a theological and psychological point of view.

In his *Concept of Dread* Kierkegaard defines anguish for us as: "sympathetic antipathy and an antipathetic sympathy."[21] This polarity is found in the "spirit" of man, "spirit" being the third factor in man's nature; that is to say, man is composed essentially of body and soul, and the relation between these two is the "spirit." Man is torn between soul and body and this tension in the spirit produces anguish. But the origin of anguish is sin; and it is found in the inherently evil nature of man. Kierkegaard also declares that anguish arises from man's freedom to choose from among the possibilities confronting him. But there is no contradiction here, for if, as Kierkegaard maintains, sin hinders man in the proper choosing of alternatives, then strictly speaking, sin is the cause of anguish.

The later existentialists were to strip Kierkegaard's philosophy of its theological premises and to retain only the secondary psychological causes, the existential position losing much of its cogency in the process.

Asserting that sin entered man with the Fall, Kierkegaard distinguishes between subjective and objective anguish. Subjective anguish resides in the individual as a consequence of his personal sins (which have been made possible by the Fall), while objective anguish is in man's nature and is the effect of sin in the world after the Fall.[22] Since sensuousness became sinful after the Fall, sensuousness is a necessary condition of anguish. According to Kierkegaard women are more prone to anguish than men because they are more sensuous. He blends the "spiritual" cause of anguish to this latter assertion by declaring that both concepts are mutually inclusive and that in the blissful state of "spirit-lessness," there can be no anguish. For anguish resides in the spirit which is the violent (and tenebrous) relation between soul and body.

One type of anguish has as its object "nothing." But the "nothing" of Kierkegaard is not the same as the nothingness of the existentialists. Fate is the "nothing" of anguish, the spiritual relation of the human spirit to the external world which confronts it. It is this anguish which is akin to the anguish of the world mentioned in the Scriptures.

Another form of anguish is that of guilt, or the anguish of the sinner whose attitude toward guilt is both sympathetic and antipathetic, drawn as he is both away from sin and toward it at the same time. Such anguish is the result of the fear of God's justice. In this sense, Judaism is basically a religion of the anguish of guilt.

Kierkegaard correlates this type of anguish with that of freedom of choice. Man, reflecting upon himself, finds both guilt and freedom. To Kierkegaard, freedom is the liberty of a man to know of himself that he is free. But freedom and guilt are opposites and man fears being guilty, for only guilt can deprive him of his freedom. Although anguish is the relation between guilt and freedom, the ambiguity of the relation must be noted, for man is attracted to each of its terms, finding therein the same polarity, the same tension which exists on the empirical level of the psychology of anguish.

Kierkegaard also notes a third type, which he calls the "anguish of evil," and this is the anguish of falling deeper into sin. Even though a man is in the state of sin, the fact that he does not wish to fall further implies that he is still attracted to the good (aside from the possibility that his hesitation may arise from the fear of a greater punishment). Consequently, there is a continual ambivalence within the structure of the subject, which produces anguish.

Finally, Kierkegaard calls attention to demoniacal anguish, by which he means the anguish of the good.[23] In this state, the individual closes the door on the outside world, particularly the transcendent world. According to Kierkegaard, he may do this in two ways: somatic-psychically and pneumatically. In the former state, he casts himself into a spirit of rebellion, thus removing himself from all that is exterior to him. In his description of the "pneumatic," Kierkegaard introduces a new form of anguish, much resembling eschatological anguish, but still to be distinguished from it, and that is the anguish of eternity. Man feels anguish before the fact of eternity because it is alien to him. The acceptance of an eternal reward would mean that finite man would have to change his temporal ideas. But such a change produces anguish.

Kierkegaard thinks of the two demoniacal forms of anguish as perversions and propounds no solutions to them as such. However, a solution is hinted at in his analysis of the final and most important type of anguish—that of the individual before God. Man, a free spirit with a basic relationship to God, attempts to project himself to the level of the Deity. But when as a *self*, a free center of interiority, he faces God alone in his individuality, an anguish results, which is more than Otto's awe and wonder before the *mysterium tremendum*. This anguish involves two elements: longing for God and a fear of God at the same time. It is, in other words, the longing of the finite for the infinite, with a corresponding sense of fear. This inner conflict, lying at the center of anguish, comes from inhibitions of man's love for God. But Kierkegaard does not follow the logical path to the role of faith in overcoming these natural obstacles between man and God. Although he is correct in affirming the transcendence of the spirit and in showing that anguish results from the limitations imposed by the sensual on the spirit, he errs in his solution to the problem.

This problem is of primary importance to man's salvation. According to Kierkegaard, the deepest form of anguish is that of the self before God and it is a result of his natural yearning. Man is hindered in this confrontation by sin; but if he gives up his quest for God, through despair, succumbing to the allurements of sin, he contracts the "sickness unto death." So long as he continues to struggle, however, he will continue to feel anguish. Conversely, this dread feeling of anguish may be the sign of his election and redemption.[24] It is not a question of acceptance or prohibition;

anguish is inevitable and its absence signifies despair and the loss of the soul.

The role of anguish is more complex than that of being a mere sign of redemption. Anguish can show the errant Christian the way back to faith and to his ultimate salvation, by revealing to him the deceptions of all finite aims. Anguish is "possibility" of freedom and the man educated through the experience of anguish is educated by "possibility." He is, therefore, educated in accordance with the possibility of the infinite. In all of this, faith is a necessary corollary, for it is the inward certainty which anticipates infinity. Discovering fate and discounting it, anguish reveals to man his infinite guilt before God. Such a recognition strengthens his faith and ultimately assures his salvation, for in the eyes of Kierkegaard, awareness of guilt creates the pious and Christian individual.

This interpretation of the role of anguish and its significance further clarified for Kierkegaard the Sacrifice of the Cross. To him the Cross was senseless, absurd, and the Incarnation a barrier to the love of God, a guarantee that men do not approach too close to God. The love of Christ was *not* self-sacrificing, nor did Christ endure suffering to make men less miserable. The Crucifixion took place in order that men be made equally unhappy with God. Instead of the sacrifice of the Cross being an Atonement for man's sins, anguish is the sign of redemption. Man does not love God as the Being Who sacrificed Himself out of love for man, but shudders before Him from the consciousness of his own infinite guilt. For Kierkegaard, Christianity is a religion of despair more than one of faith, for faith follows despair and presupposes it.

Three centuries before Kierkegaard, Luther had written that anguish is man's awareness of the assault of Satan upon the human subject. Calling it the strange work of God, he said that in showing man the false security of the finite and forcing him to seek shelter in God, anguish might become a means of salvation for him.

In discussing the anguish of death, Luther asserts that it is caused by the fear of Hell; for the heathen who do not know God die peacefully, and anguish presupposes that awareness of God and His justice which can only be known by faith. Luther is in error here, of course, for there are many examples of the anguish of death in those without the faith. Anguish of this sort, with its corollary of fear of Hell, was greatly emphasized in the Old Testament, and emphasis on it is, in fact, more Judaic than Christian. In the former tradition, the anguish of the sinner before God must be overcome primarily through sacrifice and atonement, while Jesus preached an imperative of love. The emphasis of Judaism is upon the salvific justice of God, while Christianity emphasizes God's love for man and His mercy.[25]

The Protestant view of anguish is founded upon the assertion of the depravity of man. From Luther to Barth it gives to anguish the beneficial role of forcing upon men the recognition of the horror and insecurity of ordinary human life, thus strengthening their faith in God, increasing their fear of Hell, and indirectly leading to salvation.[26] The origin of anguish, however, is not only in sin, as the Protestant tradition claims. A necessary condition of anguish is the liberty to choose among alternatives; man is drawn toward God but he can also reject Him. This polarity of action existed before the Fall, for even then man had the possibility of sinning. Anguish, then, is not only the result of original sin, but also of man's essential separation from God as a creature before his Creator. Anguish is not the nothingness of finiteness as such nor only the transcendence of the spirit and its contingence. Anguish *is* immanent to the spirit, but this immanence has a transcendental condition which is man's separation from God. But this nothingness of separation is inherent in man's nature and consequently is not caused exclusively by original sin, although sin can worsen the anguish by placing more obstacles in the path of the one reaching out to God.

Anguish presupposes a natural desire for God which is accomplished through a natural striving for perfection. The whole tradition of Catholic thought affirms also that this natural desire continues to exist even after the Fall. Man is called to God because he retains that "image of God" which Adam knew. He has, however, lost his own supernatural "likeness to God," so that divine grace is necessary to restore the image and to attain the goal. Anguish then is the result of the difficulties which man encounters on his way to his natural and supernatural perfection. Existing always in a state of ambivalence within the individual, anguish is the witness to the struggle of his yearning for God.[27]

The Catholic solution to the problem of anguish differs from the existential and the Protestant solutions as much as does its explanation of the nature of anguish. The solution is not one of stoic acceptance, but of seeing anguish against the dark background of the Cross. The Incarnation took place in order that men might see that God understood and accepted responsibility for anguish, for He is the Creator of man's nature. On the Cross there is maximum anguish, only the Son of God being able to know fully the significance of man's separation from God. The Cross becomes the measure of all anguish, and, thereafter, all human anguish can be a participation in the anguish of the Cross. Because the Cross defeated forever the various forms of human anguish, there is no more reason to fear the world Christ has conquered; the anguish of persecutions and calamities ends in the heavenly reward and the faithful can take joy in their woes. Although the separation between man and God is closed by the Incarnation on the objective level, subjectively, the individual must have the fruits of the redemption applied to him by Baptism before the separation can be removed.

Furthermore, the anguish of the sinner before God is transmuted by the anguish of the Cross. The Cross, having taken away the sinner's fear, gives an entirely different perspective to anguish, that of grace, for now man has the possibility of sharing in the anguish of the Cross. Purely human anguish is a turning-in of the individual, a loss of communication, accompanied by feelings of sterility and imprisonment. The anguish of the Cross results in a turning-out and a gain of communication, for God's love is its base. Through the self-sacrifice of the Cross, Christ wishes to free man from the anguish of sin, and can free him, if only he opens himself to the Redemption. In place of anguish, man attains God in faith, hope and charity.

As a result of the Cross, however, a new form of anguish appears, distinctly Christian. Once the Redemption has taken place, the limits of the individual are surpassed, for the Cross has resolved each individual sin. No more are penitence and sinners isolated; the Cross has universalized penitence and made stronger Christian solidarity. We now desire the salvation of all, but we see that some, enmeshed in perplexity and sin, may not reach God. From this arises "Christian anguish," and its continuance, if not tempered by faith, could lead to a doubt in the Redemption. Such anguish, the gift of grace and the result of Christian solidarity, must be patiently endured through faith, hope and charity.[28]

The Christian anguish of the Cross must not be confused with the Lutheran and Kierkegaardian anguish of sin. For the Christian anguish of the Cross, there is a remedy—total commitment on the part of man to God through a union of faith, hope and charity. The acts which make up the commitment must always be a sudden "jump," a risked action. Once one has given up all to God in a total surrender of faith, anguish departs.

While the resolution of Christian anguish advances man along the road to perfection, paradoxically it can introduce him to the "highest anguish" of the Christian. This is the mystical anguish so vividly described by St. John of the Cross as accompanying the various stages of mysticism in the ascent to God.

To achieve the goal of mysticism, the highest union with God, the soul must almost be "annihilated in the most profound abasement . . . only in a death on the Cross while living in the body, in the sensual as well as in the spiritual sphere, outwardly as much as inwardly."

St. John, speaking as a poet, makes constant use of the symbols of the Cross and the night. The Cross is the death of Christ. The night is the time when the senses do not function and the mind must be given a guide. In this mystical night, the role of the senses becomes less and less dominant, and the soul seeks a new guide. As in the night of nature, various degrees of darkness surround the soul entering the mystical night, but they end in the dawn of resurrection.

The way of the mystics is a very difficult path, which St. John of the Cross does not speak of as filled with anguish, but which is obviously just that.

The first step in the ascent to God is the "dark night of the senses." Here, in the dusk of the mystical night, the sensual nature is purified. God at first fills the soul with consolation, but eventually withdraws His delights. The things of God lose their attractiveness, and He lets His servant suffer until he has sufficiently disengaged himself from worldly attachments.

A further, more painful next step is the "dark night of the spirit." To the few who advance so far, God, wishing to communicate Himself most fully, allows a painful purgation of faith. Well might the soul in this state speak the words: "In the desert land, waterless, dry and pathless, I appeared before thee, that I might see thy glory."

The soul is now in midnight darkness and naked faith, stripped of almost all human or divine consolation. While faith reveals that God is great, human reason is reduced to its nothingness before Him. The theological virtues of hope and charity help to prepare the mystic to receive God, but the soul experiences, on the level of consciousness, a deep suffering that purifies faith. To advance is to deny oneself, to suffer mental agony, and to remain in the dark night with only faith as a guide. This is anguish of body and soul.

The mystic must experience within himself the desolation of his own impotence in order to advance closer to Christ and to experience His words: ". . . he who is an enemy to his own life in this world will keep it, so as to live eternally."

So painful is this purification of body and soul as the soul is thrown into a sea of contraries that, realizing its misery and wickedness, it almost believes that God cannot love it. St. John says that the soul feels as if God has abandoned it and thrown it away in disgust. As a result, it suffers something akin to the pains of hell, to which is added the "fearful dread" that it will always be estranged from God, that the night will never end.

Since man, through his natural power of comprehension, is unable to perceive the divine light, he must be led in darkness until such time as he is purified and so able to know God through pure spirit. The night darkens the spirit only to enlighten it in all things. Like a wound that feels the painful but healing rays of the sun, the soul is purified, suffering all the while great pain because of its imperfections. This spiritual fire, which "burns" the soul, is like that of purgatory in the next world.

The "dark night" of the senses and that of the soul reveal the depth of the anguish of the mystic, who is like one torn from his roots in the world, and planted in God. This is the "narrow road" that leads to life everlasting. Few are called to it, and to those who are chosen, the way is agonizing. But the suffering, the anguish, are in proportion to the gift: the infused contemplation of God and the joy of His presence. In this final type of anguish all else is submerged, as the mystic concentrates upon the one goal: union with God. In this sense, anguish becomes the inner awareness which accompanies the agonizing movement from self-reliance to complete and total God-reliance.

But the fullest understanding of anguish and its role in human existence is provided for us in Sacred Scripture. Here we find a consistently growing understanding of the meaning of suffering in human life. The attitude changes from the Old to the New Testament, the problem receiving fuller treatment in the New.

In the fortieth chapter of the *Book of Ecclesiasticus,* we have a picture of anguish which affects man from birth to death, afflicts both the mighty and the lowly, disturbs man during sleep, and torments the sinner "seven times more." Anguish is seen here as universal, part of the curse of original sin.

The Israelites were constantly disturbed by the fact that the evil people of the world prospered just as much as the good, and, in many cases, even more so. In addition, the vague, often non-existent ideas about the judgment in the life-after-death, when God will put down the evil, contributed to their sense of oppression in misfortune.

Yet in all His dealings with His chosen nation, God tried to make them realize that He was the only God, ruling the universe without any rival and protecting those that feared Him. He covers the Egyptians with darkness, terrifying them with "apparitions" and "crashing sounds." But to His chosen people He gives light, promising aid from on high in their battles.

To remain faithful to God and His commandments will bring peace to Israel, He assures them. But to disobey will bring curses, and fear—although it actually happened that fear seized the good too.

This was Israel's glorious beginning. By His external and visible signs of power, God wanted to teach His people to fear no earthly might. But He was a jealous God and would punish those who turned against Him.

It is in the Sapiential books that we find God's perspective on anguish, reflecting, as these books do, the life of man who has been called to worship God.

Man should not be afraid, for God is near. Nor should he be dismayed, although surrounded by destruction or darkness, but put his trust in the powerful God. Isaias declares that God alone is to be feared: "let him be your fear, and let him be your dread." To him who possesses this wisdom of the fear of God is given the promise: ". . . with no fear of stumbling, fearlessly thou shalt lie down to enjoy untroubled sleep. . . ."

The fruit of fearing God and obeying His law is not present prosperity, but peace of soul. Although the sinner may externally prosper, his conscience troubles him and leaves him no rest. He is ever in anguish because he knows he will be called to justice.

If God punishes a sinner in this life, it is to bring him back to repentance and the fear of the Lord.

The anguish spoken of in the Sapiential books is three-fold: fear of the Lord, which is the beginning of divine wisdom; fear of poverty, of enslavement to great worldly power, which turns man from

God; and fear of damnation, which is an invitation to repentance.

One final insight given to us in the Old Testament concerning anguish is to be found in the *Book of Job*. There we read of a just man, severely afflicted by God, in darkness concerning the cause of this affliction, yet knowing that he has not been unfaithful to Him. Job wishes to plead his cause before God, but in the end comes to realize that man cannot argue with God, Whose majesty and wisdom are unsearchable. Him alone does Job fear: "It is God that melts my heart with fear . . . not the surrounding darkness. . . ." After his tribulations are over, and because of his faithfulness to God, Job is given back all his former possessions. This theme, of the just being afflicted with anguish in order to draw them closer to God, is developed at great length in the revelation of the New Testament.

NEW TESTAMENT

When the Son of God became man, He took on a complete human nature and experienced all the human frailties compatible with His divine nature and mission. Among them was anguish. St. Paul writes that Christ pleaded with His Father to save Him from death ". . . not without a piercing cry, not without tears. . . ." He wept at the tomb of His friend Lazarus, and in His final discourse to the Jews in the Temple He exclaimed: "And now my soul is distressed." During His public life He had been assailed by men, and always before Him were the future desertion and denial of His own twelve Apostles. At the Last Supper, "Jesus bore witness to the distress that He felt in His heart . . ." by telling His Apostles that one of them would betray Him and that Peter would deny Him three times.

In the Agony of the Garden Christ anticipated the heavy penalty that He must undergo to accomplish the redemption of man. His mental anguish became so great that He began as it were to sweat blood, and He asked the Eternal Father to take away the chalice of His future sufferings, if that were His will. No man's desperation, anguish or sorrow but Christ shared it in the hours of His agony.

Finally, on the Cross, Christ suffered fearful torment in fulfilling the mandate of His Father. In and through this anguish, Christ accomplished His appointed work, our redemption, and so transformed suffering, not as experience but in meaning, by making it also redemptive.[29]

At the Last Supper Christ told His apostles: "In the world, you will only find tribulation; but take courage, I have overcome the world." Clearly, His followers were to know suffering, not the anguish which is the result of sin, but association with the sufferings of Christ. In fact, Christ has demanded that everyone who wishes to be worthy of Him take up His Cross, that Cross which, while representing all that is difficult to nature, is also the key to eternal life, as it was for Christ: "Was it not to be expected that the Christ should undergo these sufferings, and enter so into His glory?"

There is also another important message in Christ's statement at the Last Supper. Although the Apostles would be required to suffer severely for the sake of Christ, they were to have courage, for He has overcome the world. Its terrors and threats should no more frighten them. These are Christ's consoling words to the anguished world. But it was not the first time that Christ had told His Apostles not to fear. We have the account of how He calmed the storm at sea and upbraided His Apostles for the lack of faith shown in their fear of perishing. Faith is the antidote to that darkness of anguish which can destroy those who succumb to it. After His Resurrection, Christ brought His Apostles the fruit of His Resurrection: peace. Man is re-established in God's friendship, and this new relationship should cause man to fear only Him Who is the source of salvation. The truly Christian fear, then, should be the obverse of love, namely, fear of offending the Beloved.

The wicked will be called to justice at the end of the world, when there will be "distress of nations" at the universal destruction. Sinners will know terror, for they will no longer be able to hide their sins. Then they will call on the hills to bury them and hide them "from the vengeance of the Lamb," and while all will fear on that terrible day, the lot of the sinner will be most terrifying, for "He (Christ) will put men to a test fierce as the crucible, searching as the lye that fullers use."

The perspective on anguish in the New Testament is a major development on the Old Testament perspective. The example of Christ, especially during His passion and death, is now the guiding light for those who take up their Crosses daily that they may enter into their glory.

Since it is the revelation of God in Christ which gives us the correct notion on anguish, all explanations of it are valid as they reflect the image of man given in Holy Scripture.

Anguish is a fact of human experience, as the existentialists have clearly seen. Its affects on mankind are universal, yet its effects are varied. The anguish of a St. John of the Cross, at the sight of his lowliness when compared to God, is quite different from that of the man of the world who sees that his material possessions are in danger of theft or that death might separate him from them. There is the anguish of a mother bringing a child into the world, of a father who seeks work to support his family, of a child who awaits the punishment of his parents for an evil deed. There is the anguish of a sinner, and there is the anguish of a saint. The cause of all this anguish is original sin.

Sacred Scripture reminds us that God should be the only final object of fear and that all other fears should be met with Him, and with faith in His assistance. This view is obviously impossible for men like Sartre who claim that there is no God. For them, anguish is indeed without meaning and life is senseless. Granted their major premise, that God does not exist, their conclusions are logical enough. Life can be and often is absurd when we fail to see God working in our lives. This is the plight of the "practicing atheist."

Anguish is indeed associated with possibility. The sinner knows the possibility of greater sin and desolation; the patient foresees the possibility of greater pain; the saint fears the possibility of being rejected by God because of his unworthiness. All this is proper to the intellect. Because anguish is often so intense, the intellect is in darkness: that is, it cannot see the purpose of anguish or how to handle it. From the revelation of the Bible, however, we know that faith serves as the guide in this darkness. Faith shows man the eternal truths and causes him to put his hope in God, Who orders all things to his salvation. Since anguish is associated with possibility, Urs von Balthazar, following the lead of Aquinas, states that the Christian hope can be joined with anguish, and that it enables man to bear the present agony. Sartre and Heidegger cannot see hope being coupled with anguish because, for them, anguish is simply part of man's condition, and all ends in death. Since death is certain, what can man hope for? Here again, the viewpoint determines the conclusion.

As Kierkegaard pointed out, anguish educates. The anguish of the mystic is his awareness that he is nothing in comparison to God. The anguish of a Gabriel Marcel or of a Soren Keirkegaard is in part the realization of the heights to which man is called. The anguish of a sinner is in learning the pain of choosing darkness.

Anguish is an instrument employed by God. For His faithful servants, God uses the "fire of anguish" to burn away imperfections and to draw them closer to Himself. For the sinner, God uses anguish to strike him with remorse and discontentment in order to bring about his conversion.

Anguish, whether it be physical or mental suffering, never goes unchallenged. Man wants to know: why this present suffering? But only faith can provide him with a satisfactory answer. It is the part of anguish to fill up our self-awareness so that we become more and more present to ourselves. Here we see a reason why suffering is a penalty for sin: it is "that being-in-himself that the sinner has willed."[30]

The Christian Church has been called a Church which glorifies suffering in itself. The Cross, claim our adversaries, is a symbol that is almost worshipped.

This interpretation of the role of anguish within the Church arises from a misunderstanding of the meaning of the Cross in the life of a Catholic. Although truly a symbol of suffering, it is also a means of salvation. St. Paul writes: "To those who court their own ruin, the message of the Cross is but folly; to us, who are on the way of salvation, it is the evidence of God's power."

Christ predicted suffering, and even demanded a "losing" of one's natural life in order to follow Him. His Redemption has conquered the power of anguish, but it has not removed its cause.

For every Catholic there still remains a void between himself and God. To make any effective movement towards closing the gap there must be some purification, some physical or mental anguish. God takes the initiative, causing us to be afflicted by petty things at first and later by true anguish. Different ones are called to different degrees of the "dark night of the spirit," but as the higher powers of man are purified by more intense mental anguish, God provides His graces. To St. Paul who complained about "a sting to distress . . . nature," God answered: "My grace is enough for thee; my strength finds its full scope in thy weakness."

Christ forbids His followers to give in supinely to anguish. To His Apostles on Easter Sunday, He says: "Peace be upon you. . . ." This is the fulfillment of His promise at the Last Supper: ". . . your distress will be turned into joy . . . and your gladness will be one which nobody can take away from you." It is still the final word on anguish.

NOTES

1. J. S. Whale, *The Protestant Tradition*, New York, Cambridge University Press, 1955, p. 18.
2. S. A. Turienzo, O.S.A., "Absence of God and Man's Insecurity," *Philosophy Today*, Vol. 3, Carthagena, Messenger Press, Summer, 1959; p. 136.
3. H. von Balthazar, *Le Chrétien et l'Angoisse*, Bruges, Les Presses Saint Augustin, 1954, p. 9.

4. Cf. M. deFleury, *L'Angoisse Humaine,* Paris, Editions de France, 1924, passim, see also R. May, *The Meaning of Anxiety,* New York, Ronald Press, 1950.

5. H. B. English and A. C. English, *A Comprehensive Dictionary of Psychological and Psychoanalytical Terms,* New York, Longmans Green and Co., 1958, p. 31.

6. D. G. M. Patrick, *Pascal and Kierkegaard,* London, Lutterworth Press, 1947, Vol. 2, p. 60.

7. Etienne Borne, "The Meaning and Meaninglessness of Suffering," *Philosophy Today,* Vol. 1, Carthegena, Messenger Press, June, 1957, pp. 98-99.

8. A. Mosso, *La Peur,* Paris, Alcan (n.d.), p. 142.

9. J. Boutonier, *L'Angoisse,* Paris, Presses Universitaires de France, 1945, p. 15.

10. E. Brissaud, "Compte Rendu du XII e Congrès des Médecins Aliénistes et Neurologistes, 1902, vol. II, pp. 762-3.

11. P. Janet, *De L'Angoisse à l'Exstase,* Paris, Alcan, 1926-1928, vol. III, p. 308.

12. S. Freud, *The Problem of Anxiety,* New York, Norton, 1936, p. 866.

13. W. Oates, *Anxiety in Christian Experience,* London, George Allen and Unwin Ltd., 1958, p. 47.

14. Balthazar, *op. cit.,* p. 115.

15. R. Otto, *The Idea of the Holy,* Oxford University Press, London, 1946, p. 14.

16. See J. Collins, *The Existentialists,* Chicago, Regnery, 1952, ch. IV, pp. 115-147.

17. This presentation of Heidegger's concept of dread depends upon that of Stephen Strasser in his article "The Concept of Dread in the Philosophy of Heidegger," *The Modern Schoolman,* Vol. 35, St. Louis, St. Louis University Press, November, 1957, pp. 1-20.

18. M. Heidegger, *Sein und Zeit,* Halle, Verlag Max, 1927, pp. 42-43.

19. J. P. Sartre, *L'Etre et le Néant,* Paris, Gallimard, 1943, p. 245 and *passim.*

20. R. Troisfontaines, *Existentialisme et Pensée Chrétienne,* Louvain, E. Nauwelaerts, 1948, p. 17.

21. S. Kierkegaard, *The Concept of Dread,* Princeton, Princeton University Press, 1946, p. 38.

22. *Ibid.,* p. 53.

23. *Ibid.,* p. 120.

24. S. Kierkegaard, *Fear and Trembling,* Princeton, Princeton University Press, 1941, p. 27.

25. A. Ussher, *Journey Through Dread,* New York, Devin-Adair, 1955, p. 34.

26. O. Pfister, *Christianity and Fear,* London, George Allen and Unwin Ltd., 1948, p. 245.

27. F. Berthold, *The Fear of God,* New York, Harper and Bros. 1959, p. 86.
28. Balthazar, *op. cit.,* p. 137–138.
29. *Ibid.,* p. 85.
30. St. John of the Cross, *Ascent of Mount Carmel,* as cited in: E. Stein, *The Science of the Cross,* edited by Dr. L. Gelber and Father Romaeus Leuven, O.C.D., Chicago, H. Regnery, 1960, p. 20.

6

Existentialism

THE existentialist approach to God today is wide and varied, ranging from atheism to Christianity. Since there is considerable agreement that, while the existence of God cannot be proved, neither can His non-existence, atheism comes to be as much a committed position as theism. That a commitment to one of these positions must be made is the position of the existentialist. Consequently, the problem of God is very much the concern of existentialist philosophy.[1]

The question as to whether or not human existence is meaningful depends ultimately upon the existence or the non-existence of God. The existentialist answers are varied and conflicting, some holding that, since God exists, all meaning comes from Him; and others arguing that, since He does not exist, there can be no permanent values in the world. It will be helpful, then, to consider the opinions of some of the better-known existentialist philosophers.

Seriously concerned with the phenomenon, now over a hundred years old, of the continued rejection of God and religion by intelligent men, existentialists have considered, but found wanting, the explanations usually adduced: economic materialism, social democracy and evolutionary naturalism. Because they are interested in the human condition of the particular individual, they find such explanations wanting, and so turn to more philosophical questions pertaining to man and transcendence. What touches on God and religion is accordingly regarded as having high practical importance

121

and is, as a matter of fact, part of the existentialist interest in the practical results of their philosophizing.

To begin with, we might ask: what exactly is existentialism—a word wide enough to include the atheism of Sartre and Camus as well as the Christianity of Kierkegaard and Marcel? Although, indeed, these philosophers differ greatly in their concepts of God, man and the world, they do agree on certain basic elements of approach, and so the common term may be applied to them.

Existentialism is a way of looking at things in which the irreducible, primary *datum,* or "given," is existence. So fundamental is it that it cannot be deduced from any other empirical data or from any other concept. Philosophical speculation about its nature is futile, since it is already implied in every attempt to consider it and in every manifestation of the mind. Existence, then, is so basic as to be utterly impossible of proof.[2]

The existentialist philosopher immerses himself in the concrete and complex world of reality. Beginning with existence, in all its fullness, he is interested in experience, not just of the senses, but of all the mystery of being, man included. Since the world and God cannot be considered apart from man, existential subjectivity is no sickly turning in upon itself, but a being-in-the-world, a relationship to all things else. For the existentialist, purely conceptual knowledge is not a matter of interest, since such knowledge can be only a mode of a manifestation of the first given—existence. This does not, however, imply subjectivism, but simply the fact that the concept cannot adequately grasp existence.

Arising out of the need to solve personal problems, existentialism moves not on the theoretical but on the existential level. Existence rather than essence is its ontological *point de départ* and it moves along the paths of the human situation, including such elements as personal involvement and commitment, human freedom and its implications, the uniqueness of the existing individual, and encounter with other persons. In the act of committing oneself to life, and actively accepting one's destiny, existence itself is encountered, often in anguish, at other times in the joy of intersubjective experience. In many ways the movement is a reaction against collectivism, determinism, the abstract idealism of a generation ago. Personal responsibility is its concern and the full burden is set squarely upon the individual.

The existential thinker is by no means indifferent to God, although each has his own concept of the Supreme Being. For Kierkegaard He is pure Being or eternity, for Jaspers impersonal transcendent Being, for Heidegger Being and non-Being, for Sartre the Absolute which is the Nothing. But all are in agreement that a new look at the nature of God must be taken and that it is of the highest importance to do so. Rejecting the traditional objective philosophical approach, all agree, too, that we can only find God in "encounter."[3]

For Kierkegaard the problem of God is all-important, and so it is not strange to find that the encounter of Creator and creature is central to his thought. Because Kierkegaard is an existentialist, God is a manifestation of his own personal struggles and problems and is colored by his Protestant, somewhat terrifying Christianity and by his revolt against the attempt of rationalism to depersonalize Him. Feeling that his task in life is to defend the transcendence of God and the supernatural against the natural, Kierkegaard keeps up a strong and steady opposition to Hegelian universalism.

The usual philosophic proofs for God's existence are set aside as irrelevant, since Kierkegaard, like Pascal, is not seeking the cold God of the philosophers but the vital God of Abraham and Isaac. Philosophy argues to an objective God, but God cannot be an object of knowledge, for He is always and intensely a subject. The ontological argument as well is rejected since one cannot demonstrate God's existence. One can only grasp it by faith. Consequently, all discussion moving in the direction of a proof for the existence of God is useless; the only way to approach Him is to make the "leap of faith," for God is transcendent, invisible and unprovable.[4] To commit oneself to faith in God is to lose oneself in an abyss, but risk is the way to the true self, for existence is won by choice. With the leap into the abyss, man makes his choice, believing with fear and trembling, aware that he is finite, affirming himself before God. By this means he succeeds in transcending the universal and choosing himself in the deepest sense. By it, too, he places himself in immediate relation to the supreme subject, the absolute personal God. This is the only way to assure us of the existence of God—to ignore the proof but to make the leap of belief.

Although in such an approach to God the metaphysical basis for our knowledge of God's existence is wanting, it would be wrong to imagine that reason is of no value in leading to faith. It is true that Catholic tradition holds that the act of faith has its sole and exclusive motive in that authority of God which can neither deceive nor be deceived; but this tradition stoutly maintains that reason, although unable to generate belief, does have a role in preparing for it by showing that God exists and that it is reasonable for us to grant him faith.[5]

The path to faith must somehow be accessible to reason, and reason must show that faith is possible, reasonable, virtuous; otherwise no act of faith can be elicited. For Kierkegaard, however, there is not even the possibility of a rational proof for the existence of God. Catholic theology maintains that man must *know* through reason that God exists before he arrives at faith. Kierkegaard inadequately analyzes the place of reason in laying the foundations of natural religion and in preparing the way for faith. Moreover, he confuses the rational demonstration of the truth of something which transcends reason, with the rational demonstration of the reason for belief in something which transcends reason. Although this is clearly a step in the direction of anti-intellectualism, it is not fideism per se. Kierkegaard is seeking truth—a truth that is true *for him*; not only one which he can contemplate, but one to which he can make a total commitment of self in absolute obedience to God.[6]

The nature of Kierkegaard's God is above all personal, transcendent and loving. In Him essence and existence are one. He is pure Being or eternity, a never-changing present, eternal actuality, and He is qualitatively different from man. His mode of being is neither utterly separated nor completely identified with that of finite existents, who share in being by obtaining existence from Him. Including within Himself the order of existence, He possesses a oneness of mind and object, His eternal reality appearing as a *mysterium tremendum* which evokes both fascination and fear.

Since existence, for Kierkegaard, can properly be applied only to finite being, we should not speak of God's existence in His eternal mode of being. That term is reserved for the mystery of the Incarnation, which is a matter of faith rather than demonstration. The Incarnation is the paradox par excellence, for God reveals Himself in history, in Jesus Christ and, in Him, time and eternity are freely joined. Thus the point of contact between pure being and existence, between God and finite man, is Christ.

Although certain students of Kierkegaard think that he defines God as "wholly other," this is not actually the case. In point of fact, Barth accuses him of accepting the Thomistic analogy of being. To Kierkegaard, God and man are at once alike and dissimilar. They are similar in what man derives from God; they are different, not in God's perfection, but in man's sin. This is not, however, the extreme view of the reformers, which is that there is a complete chasm between Creator and creature.[7]

In Kierkegaard's system, God is not man nor is man God. The union of the two is realized in Christianity, but this does not melt human personality into pantheism. Christianity proclaims the utter unlikeness between God and sinful man, but states that their likeness comes about through the God-man Christ. Kierkegaard's God is transcendent and infinite. He does not exist. He *is* the divine immutability itself, He is the eternal Being, this latter concept of Kierkegaard's coming close to the Thomistic notion of God as the subsistent act of existing.

Being above all else a personal God, One Who encounters man in an *I-Thou* relationship, Kierkegaard's God is the eternal essential Truth Who has freely entered into a love relationship with man. Needing nothing, it was His love which prompted Him to assume the human burden. This relationship of *I* and *Thou* is a passionate commitment whose only admittance is through faith. The personal union between Him and our individual existence is gained through free acts.

Because God is a loving God, we in turn respond with love by our trust and obedience toward Him. But we must make a free dedication of service to Him and in true Christian tradition the love of God and neighbor must be realized together. For there is solidarity and kinship with God and with each other, but only in God. The relationship to others is one of prayer, and Christian existence, union, a sharing in the divine life.

God, Who is in no sense passive in Kierkegaard's view, always takes the initiative in His dialogue with the creature. Moreover, faith is a divine gift, only to be received as a gift of God's loving kindness, impossible of attainment through human or scientific effort. Being an "imago Dei," man can never reach his complete stature without the help of God.

Rejecting the Kantian ethics of his age, according to which God became a mere sanction for the categorical moral imperative, Kierkegaard sees duty as a totally inadequate motive for eternal life; instead, he argues that man must be moved by personal love for a personal God. He condemns Kantianism for its formalism and points out the subordinate position that it allots to God. Granting that it admits the obligation to follow the moral law, it does not provide the power to perform the morally good act. The only thing that can remove the impediments to the good life is the saving grace of God. Virtue, moreover, is not an end in itself, and universal moral laws must refer back to their author. Consequently, Kierkegaard places strong emphasis on man's direct relation with God. The unique, individual vocation, such as Abraham received from God, is superior to that of the universal ethical man. If God is not at the center of the moral order, then it is not a Christian order.[8]

A different approach to the problem of God is offered by the theistic but non-Christian existentialism of Karl Jaspers. Here, the starting point is the struggling human person himself who is trying, through deliberate choice, to make of himself an authentic being. In the act of choice, I recognize myself for the first time as my own true self. Thus the Augustinian "I know, therefore I am" has become "I choose, therefore I am." Because of choice, I have become what I wanted to be, and I am the free choices which I have made. In his struggle to achieve autonomy, man encounters certain situations which limit him, making him aware of his dependent and transient nature. During such moments of time, struggle and suffering, man becomes aware of a transcendent, and once he realizes that he does not suffice for himself, that he is neither self-existing nor his own end, he begins, in his suffering and in his uncertainty, to search for it. It is then that God meets man and issues His appeal for faith. If man accepts, he moves from an experience of nothingness to faith in being itself.

Jaspers believes that the proofs for the existence of God can be refuted logically but that this does not imply the non-existence of God, since His non-existence is not subject to proof either. Yet the traditional proofs for God's existence have value insofar as they show the insufficiency of the world and its need to be oriented to God. They serve to lead man to the point where either God or nothingness is experienced. The supreme liberty of man is to accept or refuse God Whom he has met in anguish. It is only by faith, emerging out of the anguished awareness of the possibility of nothingness, that God can be grasped. In his very search for God, man presupposes that God exists.[9]

Jaspers rejects the approach to God by way of eminence and affirmation, for categories drawn from empirical being cannot be applied to transcendent being. Nor can we learn an unambiguous truth about the transcendent by our indirect awareness of existence. Instead, an act of personal freedom is necessary in order to direct our existence toward transcendence.

Thus, while affirming the possibility of transcendence, Jaspers holds that we cannot discover the nature of transcendent being. All that can be known about the impersonal transcendent is that it has being: it is "wholly other," revealed only through signs. Symbols lead us to some understanding of God, but they also lead to different interpretations. At times, Jaspers comes to the point of identifying the transcendent with God.[10]

The deity of Jaspers is neither the pantheist's immanent God nor an eternal person. Although opposing atheism, he is not strictly theistic, since he finds no positive properties or attributes in the transcendent. God is the enveloping, comprehensive being, not identifiable with, yet not apart from, the world, all of which will perish except Himself.

The analogical character of the notion of being is entirely foreign to Jaspers. Although he uses the *via negativa* to arrive at some prediction concerning the nature of God, he denies the analogy of being. God is totally other, that which cannot be thought, an empty abyss to reason, distinguishable from the world through a series of contrasts. Jaspers holds that God is undetermined being but fails to add that, in another sense, He is the most determined of beings—pure act of limitless perfection. In fact he seems to identify the indetermination of God with the character of being as encompassing all things.

To illustrate man's inability to know God, Jaspers refers to two descriptions of God. In the Old Testament, God reveals Himself as "I am Who am," while Plotinus describes "the one" as "It is what it is." The use of I and It for the same reality is indicative for Jaspers that we cannot penetrate the being of transcendence by means of philosophy or religion. As does Plotinus, he makes the One unknowable.

Although Jaspers' God is an impersonal one, his approach to the transcendental is intensely personal. Phrases such as "my transcendence" and "my God" are frequent. Since God can only be approached individually in the most personal of human acts, the unique God may reveal Himself as "my" God rather than as the God of all the world. But for Jaspers, as for Sartre, any initiative taken by a personal God is an attack upon the freedom of man.

In transcendence, as something sought for rather than as something possessed, human freedom seeks its fulfillment, its perfection, its redemption. The God of Jaspers is wholly Other, neither the tri-personal God of Christians nor Christ as the unique God-man. The latter is not divine, for no man can be God. God does not speak through man, but meets him independently of Christ in the crisis of existence, and there is no personal bond between God and man in prayer. Jaspers' doctrine of transcendence, therefore, contents itself with an attitude of transcending without ever attaining to the transcendent. Nor can it function as an open pathway to God.[11]

While he himself prefers to speak of his philosophy as the study of the mystery of being, Gabriel Marcel is usually included within the group of existential thinkers. His notion of God is directly influenced by Christian revelation. As it does with other existentialists, the human person plays a prominent role in his thought. To the question, what does it mean to be a person, he answers: to be "in a situation" is the fundamental human condition. As a human person I am essentially open to others. This concept of relationship between beings and to the Absolute Being is basic in his thought. The self-realization of man occurs in his personal relationships with others. When I am aware of the other person as a Thou rather than as an object, then I will perform only through self-transcendence, through communion with other beings and God.

"I aspire to absolute self-commitment to an absolute fidelity, I discover God as a personal transcendent and I become conscious of the orientation of my personality toward God."[12]

In self-recollection man regains self-existence by recognizing the divine source of the personal self. Thus, man is not alone but participates in Being.

Marcel's philosophy as a whole is concerned with the knowledge of God. He, too, asks the perennial question: "How can God be known?" but not out of intellectual curiosity, for theoretical knowledge of an abstract absolute seems valueless to him; his sole interest lies in personal encounter with the absolute Thou.

Marcel does not disdain the "natural light of the human reason" as this expression is understood by the First Vatican Council. But "human reason" for him is not equated with mathematical reason, the latter being only a facet of the former. Spiritual and religious reality may well be within the limits of reason, provided we do not equate it with objectivism or with "*pensée pensée*." While the existence of God can be the object of a convincing proof in metaphysics, to prove that God exists is quite a different thing from arriving at belief in His existence. One can know that He is, and at the same time deny that He is, precisely because He is who He is. In other words, knowledge of God must have the work of our liberty, in union with grace, if it is to become faith in God.

Marcel's chief interest is not in establishing the reality of God, but in showing how to approach Him Who encompasses all being. If we are able to discover ways of approaching God, it is because He has already "found" us. Consequently, the primordial question —and perhaps even from the apologetical viewpoint—is that of God's attributes: how can we be destined to seek Him Who is in us already? what are the humanly comprehensible manifestations of God? how can He be God for us?

Marcel's thought reflects many of the modern trends in theodicy. Contemporary atheism has shifted the center of gravity in our study of theodicy by forcing us to abandon the traditional question of the existence of God in favor of the question of His nature. The problem of God must now be approached through certain of His attributes. Dondeyne believes that this new state of the question is primarily due to the impact of existentialist thought.[13] Since existentialism proclaims itself a humanism, the ancient controversies about the principle of causality no longer appear to be the crucial point of encounter between theology and atheism. The vital concern today is to show how it is possible to reconcile the idea of an infinite perfect and necessary Being with man's freedom, with his acute sense of being a creator and with the historical character of his existence.

Marcel's basic effort is to avoid the rationalist dilemma, according to which faith must be either submissive to reason or unintelligible. Although at the start of his *Journal Metaphysique* he was tempted by subjectivism, Marcel never surrendered, faithfully striving to arrive at a God Who is neither an object nor a mere projection of religious experience.

In his zeal to prevent the objectification of God, Marcel is not unlike some contemporary Protestant theologians who declare that it is as atheistic to affirm the existence of God as it is to deny it, or again that every true theistic statement must be contradicted by an atheistic one (Paul Tillich). Marcel argues that we have no right to affirm that "there is" a God or that "there is no" God, both statements being absurd, since the word "existence" in itself is totally inadequate when applied to God. On the other hand, by refusing to consider Him as an object among other verifiable objects of experience, we deprive the atheistic negation of God of all its value, because Atheism tends to compare God to a "something" not found in experience. Such an "inquiry on God," says Marcel, is impossible, for to be exhaustive it should be infinite. It is also totally inadequate: God can never be the object of a search of that type. This brings us to the question of proofs in the traditional theodicy.

It is an unquestioned fact, says Marcel, that the traditional proofs for the existence of God are not always convincing, not because of lack of dialectical rigor or defect of logic, but because contemporary man to whom they are addressed is not "available" for them, not ready to receive and to experience their impact.[14] Today's world is a world without ready access to transcendence, and to the man absorbed in transforming the world into his own image, the idea of God may seem an obstacle to the realization of his potentialities. On the other hand, the pervasiveness of the scientific outlook prevents him from seeing in God anything more than an object of scientific curiosity.

Marcel's point is that the proofs of the existence of God are infinitely bound up with assent to the mystery of existence itself. So integral a part of our fundamental ontological exigency are they as to be impervious to scientific inquiry, although universally present in men. In this sense, of course, all proofs participate in the ontological proof. The latter, however, in the existential context, no longer operates with pure concepts. Its starting point is not the *idea* of God, but the presence in us of the ontological exigency. Existence in the presence of the absolute Thou implies the impossibility of doubting this Presence. Moreover, since I constitute myself as a person only in communion with the absolute Thou, to negate Him would be to negate myself.

The old objection arises: If God is the absolute Thou and all that this category involves, are we not led into pure subjectivism? We would be indeed, answers Marcel, if the truth about God were the result of my choice. But such is not the case. The act of affirming God is an assent to a Being Who envelops us, in Whose presence we are. Knowledge of such a Being is rather recognition than cognition. Similarly, the fact that the intersubjectivity (faith in the other person, the recognition of a Thou) leads us towards the supreme mystery includes the possibility of a meaningful discourse about God. There is, then, a *de jure* universality, but *de jure* only, since *de facto* this communicability is never fully achieved; it must be striven for and constantly renewed.

Existence for the existentialists is the privileged datum determining the nature of every ulterior reflection. We may say that, for Marcel, Being reveals itself in imperfect, finite ways as knowledge, love, friendship and so on. Such existential acts cannot be isolated from other authentic human acts, but participate with them in a common reality. Their ontological quality, however, is unequal, since they depend upon our efforts, and upon our participation in reality (in Being) through existential acts, which is a matter of degree. The most objectified existence is still in Being, although it is infinitely lacking in authenticity. On the other hand, existence as participation, as openness to the authentic values of life is also being—this, of course, in the fullest degree. We see now that the word "existence," for Marcel, has an ambiguous meaning, no substantial difference apparently existing between existence and Being, everything depending on the degree of our orientation, our will and capacity to expand our acts beyond the horizon of the problematic.

Existence can alternately be openness to the world, to being and to God, or closedness and refusal to participate.[15]

This ambiguity of existence is, in the final analysis, the sign of our freedom; the essence of the act of existing is freedom. And since Being reveals itself in particular acts of existence, there is a mysterious connection, an entanglement, between Being and freedom. Indeed, in so far as we are closed to all participation, the world appears to us as something strange or even hostile and we realize that we are in exile. In addition, if we become reduced to the sum of our functions, we approach the status of things.

Although the essence of the act of existing is to be free, only participation in Being renders us free in the most fundamental sense of the word. To close oneself up, to make oneself unavailable to the other "thou" and to Being, results in despair, death and the destruction of freedom. For freedom is ruined when it is not activated in participation, but is fulfilled when it chooses responsibility towards others and the world.

Marcel has come as close to the realm of religion as it is possible for a philosopher, his instrument, his method in approaching the Light, being always that of reflection. Profoundly convinced that there is and ought to be a secret convergence between philosophy and religion, he nevertheless believes that philosophy must preserve its independence. Religion is based upon faith, philosophy upon reflection. The latter, however, is no longer as radically distinct from faith as objective knowledge is. If science should one day succeed in completely explaining the natural order of things, the main philosophical problems would still remain, because they transcend us; the mystery of Being is above us and our knowledge of it. One cannot approach God like an object, a thing, because our bond with Him is beyond everything we can know in terms of an object standing over against us.

Marcel's existential ontology, which proceeds by analogy between inter-human relations and the ultimate *I-Thou* relation, gives the appearance of self-sufficiency in that it makes no direct references to Christianity. The reason for this is simple and important: Marcel refuses to speak of faith in contrast to knowledge. Although his idea of mystery is not utterly alien to philosophy, the kind of knowledge which he advocates is metaproblematic and must remain so if the gulf between reason and Being is ever to be bridged.

Clearly, in Marcel's thinking there is a close relationship between what he means by "God" and Being. But it is also evident that his God is not the same Being Whom traditional metaphysics discovers through abstraction from personal experience. Seeking the eternal in concrete relations with others and in personal experience, Marcel is able to bypass the God of philosophers as well as the Kierkegaardian God of Abraham, Isaac and Jacob. But the charge of fideism in Marcel's case does not seem to be a valid one, since he has sufficiently insisted that the experience of myself cannot be cut off from others. Self-knowledge is forever centered in the fact of intersubjectivity, and only the latter, the "We" instead of Cogito, is the starting point of metaphysics. The more my existence participates in that of others, the closer it comes to Being; the more I am egocentric, the less I exist.

Man's relation to God is never indifferent, for he can either bear witness to or repudiate the transcendent principle of Being. His vocation, then, is to make himself completely available through love, to dedicate himself to God for the sake of his fellowmen.

Marcel is interested in leading man to the encounter with God. But his attitude toward the Transcendent differs from that of Jaspers. God is knowable, the real creative source of being, and we cannot be indifferent as to whether He exists or not. The Thomistic proofs for God's existence, resting upon a previous acceptance of God, neither convince unbelievers nor are needed by one who already has experienced the presence of God. Rational proofs for the existence of God which seek only the assent of the intellect neglect the fact that the will must also be involved in the acceptance of His existence. One encounters God on the plane of the Thou, not on the plane of an It.

As the pathway to God, Marcel prefers the exploration of the experiences of persons. God is discovered by the individual in the very midst of his dynamism toward the full realization of his total selfhood.

God is Being in an eminent sense. "I am Who am" is His only adequate designation. God is not somebody, but a supremely personal God. "The problem of God gives way to the mystery of the Absolute Thou." God is essentially a Thou for whom I exist and for whom I count, not as an abstract, impersonal Him, but as essentially a knowable Thou. Each believer in God, therefore, is capable of having a unique and original relationship with God. "I am not one thing in front of another thing but a person in the presence of another person." God is an incarnate God, present in myself and in all things. There is a unique relationship between God and the individual which cannot be communicated to anyone else, and He is, moreover, the bond which seals all authentic love. Every act of charity is necessarily an approach to God, producing a concrete but mysterious relation between God and neighbor. It is precisely as fatherhood that the relationship between the living God and the faithful should be conceived. For our own essence is a gift which we receive as a result of the divine generosity.

Gilson asserts that Marcel's thought, instead of having philosophy for its object, *is* philosophy, since he has derived his way of thinking from personal experience, from original awareness of Being.[16]

Marcel is probably the only existentialist who has avoided the residual Kantianism inherent in existentialism. Karl Jaspers' transcendent, for example, is placed beyond all knowledge, whereas all that Marcel demands is that we renounce methods of investigation which are unfitted for examining questions concerning the divine Being.[17]

The chief difficulty in Marcel's thought is to be found in his attitude of scepticism towards the Thomistic proofs of God's existence. He claims that they are based upon a previous acceptance of God and that their only value consists in clarifying this original adhesion.

At the basis of Marcel's scepticism lies his mistrust of concepts and of discursive reasoning. In concert with other existentialists, he seems to be strongly tempted to identify objective knowledge with the idealistic or scientific conception of knowledge, the "concept" appearing to him as an arbitrary entity whose function is to shut us off from the concrete reality. To the medieval thinkers, however, concept was an instrument which brought us closer to the reality in all its concreteness.

Marcel's mistrust of concepts, and his simultaneous affirmation of the primacy of experience, exposes itself to the further danger of a new kind of empiricism. If experience, even in Marcel's wider sense of the word, is the only way of grasping the reality, then there seems to be no answer to the question: how, from such an experience, could we ever conclude to an affirmation of the *transcendent* God? True, Marcel speaks of a "blinded intuition," but it still remains an intuitive grasping. In fact, a consistent intuitionism offers the dilemma of either a purely natural intuition, in which God would lose His transcendence and otherness and would no longer be distinguishable from being in general, or a supernatural, that is, mystical intuition, in which, if it is to bring with it an authentic assurance of a transcendent God, there must be contained a universally valid idea of God. If this latter is not the case a supernatural experience is bound to remain on the level of interior, inexpressible feeling, possibly the privilege of the few, but without value for the universality of mankind and for philosophy.[18]

It may be questioned whether what is thus attained is God in the sense of the wholly different One. Marcel's own reflective experience does not lead him to the affirmation of a transcendent Being beyond experience. But if such an affirmation is to be possible, it must no longer belong to the order of experience, but to that of conception. From experience, from the consideration of creatures, *a posteriori,* we are able to understand that the proposition "God exists" must be affirmed; affirmed conceptually, but not really experienced: we do not understand the essence of God, we understand only that He must be affirmed as the Existent.

St. Thomas, however, found it possible to move from an existential datum to an existential conclusion.

To Marcel proofs necessarily turn God into an object. Moreover, the objective approach presumes that there is a problem of God, set over against myself, which I can impartially investigate like any other problem. But this is sacrilegious. There is no problem of God. The opposite of all attempts to deal problematically with God (to prove His existence) is the possibility of denying Him as well. Marcel, then, is in the line of the philosophers of the heart, such as Kierkegaard, Pascal, and Newman, when in his approaches to God he stresses personal responsibility and liberty, self-commitment and the sense of drama.

Marcel's work is often contrasted with that of Jean-Paul Sartre, but it is not Sartre to whom Marcel is most opposed. They share, in fact, the same existentialist concern for man in the world, for his freedom and so on. Marcel's outlook, however, is completely opposed to that of Bertrand Russell, the latter's positivistic atheism being the contradictory of Marcel's existential theism. Although Sartre and Marcel are concerned with many of the same problems, their starting points in attacking them are very diverse. Sartre thinks in terms of giving an existential answer to the challenge of an impersonal universe, whereas Marcel seeks to find an existential fulfillment of the potential of a universe created by a personal God.

The connection between Marcel and the French atheistic existentialists has an ironical aspect. Many of the entries in Marcel's journals which are concerned with what he calls the betrayal of being suggest the doctrines more recently propounded by Albert Camus and Sartre.[19] Camus' theory that suicide is the only logical attitude in an absurd world is anticipated in Marcel's work. The doctrine of radical unintelligibility and absurdity and the doctrine of escape by way of suicide are minutely outlined. In addition, Sartre's hypotheses of an absolutely creative freedom and self-deification are acknowledged beforehand by Marcel as constituting the outlook most opposed to his own, and yet possible within the context of man's interpretation of his situation. But it is wrong to consider

Sartre's acknowledgement of a theistic variety of existentialism a warrant for Marcel's philosophy. For Marcel's vigorous originality of thought is vindicated in what is his nearest approach to a "systematic" statement.

To compare Marcel and Kierkegaard is a more difficult and delicate task. Not until after his own views were established in their characteristic outlines did Marcel discover Kierkegaard's writing. Because of this, he has never been haunted by the dubious glory of achieving a latter day revival of Kierkegaard's standpoint or of transposing it into a systematic, philosophical setting. For this very reason there is more sympathy of mind between Marcel and Kierkegaard and any other existentialist. Both men offer a more realistic view of cognition, and give prominence to the free individual and his fidelity to a transcendent God. That each professes the Christian faith, and underlines its relevance for understanding existence, is reason for both agreement and disagreement. Kierkegaard regarded Christianity as a means of displacing philosophy, and his standpoint is that of Christian existence versus philosophy. On the other hand, Marcel admits not only the bare possibility of a legitimate rational discipline, but the need for a renewal of philosophy itself in an existential direction. Reluctant to call his philosophy a "Christian existentialism," he prefers to consider it a concrete philosophy centering around the mystery of being. He does admit, however, that it is compatible with Christianity and that it naturally disposes the individual toward receiving such a revelation from God.[20]

An important point of similarity between Kierkegaard and Marcel is their common regard for esthetic insight and methods. Though Marcel does not operate within the triadic framework of esthetic-ethical-religious stages, he admits the importance of the esthetic factor in human experience. Kierkegaard spoke about the need to inject new life into the old Christian and common-sense terminology. Marcel feels a similar obligation to remake the language of philosophy by recovering the immediate meanings of ordinary words. While his essays are free from the usual existentialist preoccupation with coining new terms, they uncover an unsuspected weight of significance in words and ideas that have become badly worn from superficial and careless use.[21]

Marcel's belief in God and eventual commitment to Catholicism are not discernible in his youth, for he was raised in a strict, but non-religious tradition. His history is that of one whose intelligence brought him to God, a reversal of the more fashionable process.

Nowhere in his philosophy does Marcel attempt to prove that God exists. Beginning with his personal belief in the existence of God, his first step is to warn against the usual methods of conceiving God. In the early parts of the *Journal Metaphysique,* he discusses at length the significance of such terms as "God exists" and "the existence of God," in the course of which linguistic analysis, he anticipates many aspects of the proofs that Sartre offers in *L'Etre et le néant.*[22] His main idea is that in asserting that God exists we must not try to objectify God. Since we cannot think of God, and His existence cannot be arrived at through thought, for it is only a valid starting point for thought, the only way in which we can talk of the existence of God is in terms of an experience of Him.

If the non-existence of God cannot be proven, because it is impossible for us to consider Him as an empirical object, it follows that we are unable to prove the existence of God, for the very same reason. We are without a logical passage which would enable us to bring ourselves to His level by arguing from something that is not He.

Marcel remarks that the Thomistic proofs for the existence of God are not universally convincing and ascribes it to the fact that they are valid only if one is already prepared to think theistically.

Thomistic critics have warned against idealistic tendencies in Marcel's philosophy. In point of fact, Marcel does not regard himself as a Thomist, but as a realist. In agreement with Maritain that "thought is made for being as the eye is made for light," he believes also that the judgment of existence is the most properly metaphysical judgment, and asks whether or not the intellect should in turn be studied as a mode of being.[23] Such an attitude is realistic since it seems evident that no one is ever going to "prove" the existence or the non-existence of God. Faith or non-faith is a free personal choice for each individual; though it is a choice strongly influenced by education and society. Marcel's realism comes from his honesty. With no philosophical or religious axes to grind, he is committed philosophically to no one but himself.

Marcel's belief that we must establish a personal rapport with God, the rapport of an I with a Thou, is developed very early in the *Journal Metaphysique* wherein he attempts to describe the relationship of man to God. Here, God is the Thou of the relationship, as well as the Absolute Thou.

Marcel's attention focuses, then, on the believer. For, if one believes, one must establish a rapport with God which is completely personal. God is the Thou for whom I exist and Who is therefore not necessarily for someone else what He is for me.

That which we objectify is an It. But if one defines God as an It, His existence becomes absurd, "la plus pauvre, la plus morte des fictions."[24] Although there exist certain Thous which can be considered Its, this is never true of God. He can never become an It, because He is the Absolute Thou.

The notion of freedom, so important to Sartre and Camus, also underlies much of Marcel's thought. An essential property of the relation between the believer and God is that both are free beings. For, if man is not free, then he is only an object for God, an *It* not a *Thou*. For Sartre, if God exists and is omniscient, my essence is pre-determined and I cannot be free; for Marcel, the exact opposite is true.

Actually, both positions seem plausible at first glance. If God exists and is omniscient and omnipotent, the case for absolute, antecedent predestination becomes very strong. On the other hand, if the material universe is all that exists, then man, too, is material and his actions are but the manifestations of physical principles. Marcel tries to combat the first argument by conjecturing that the divine omniscience works insofar as God considers the individual man as an *I*. Sartre uses the argument that "existence precedes essence" to deny the assertion that, without God, all is materialistic. Interestingly, the arguments against both positions are stronger than the arguments for them.

Marcel does not associate his concrete philosophy of being with a Christian existentialism. A person can accept his philosophy without being a Christian and without having any intention of becoming one, since it is based on an analysis of concrete human experiences which are not confined within confessional boundaries. On the other hand, the aim of philosophy is to elevate experience rather than to cut it off. In our historical situation, the influence of Christian ideas cannot be ignored, but makes it easier to discern the need for faith and the presence of an ontological mystery at the heart of a world arranged according to problematic requirements. The human experiences upon which Marcel's philosophy relies are deeply affected by the Christian orientation towards life. Without formally relying upon Christian revelation, Marcel's interpretation of existence accords with revealed religion and admits its existential influence. Unlike Jaspers, Marcel refuses to close off his thought from reception of the gift of revealed truth as such. For, if philosophy is not a closed system but an open participation in the mystery of being, there is no sound philosophical reason why we should place an obstacle in the way of such a gift.

Martin Buber, a theologian rather than a philosopher, is not unlike Kierkegaard in his preoccupations. Like Kierkegaard, his thinking is existentialist, and his work is closely related to that of Marcel. For Buber, the great religious traditions are different manifestations of God's revelation and, like Marcel, he is interested in investigating the personal relationship that exists between the individual and God.

Buber is, therefore, concerned with modern man's relation to God. God has become unreal for many of us. Not only has He been reduced to a moral principle, He no longer has any connection with our concrete lives. Nietzsche's saying that God is dead, that we have slain Him, dramatically sums up the end situation of the era. Since then, man has tried repeatedly to fill the empty hori-

zon. But neither Bergson nor the French existentialists who have
dedicated themselves to this task have met with conspicuous success.

Buber is attempting to discover why God is so very silent to man
today. Although He still communicates with man, as He always
will, the spirit of the age rejects this communication, for it has set
itself up in opposition to the spirit of belief and has made Faith
extremely difficult to accept. Buber sees in the evolution of modern
philosophy a process of gradual estrangement from God, beginning
with Descartes and working up to the grotesque renunciation of
Him that took place in the nineteenth century. The contemporary
crisis of philosophy is due to its "intellectual letting go of God."[25]

Philosophy, however, is not the only cause of the estrangement.
The scientific revolution, still at work today, has turned man's
mind from the personal to the empirical. But the latter is the do-
main of the *It*. "In our age the *I-It* relation, gigantically swollen,
has usurped, practically uncontested, the mastery and rule."[26] Buber
insists that God can never be treated as an *It*; unfortunately, we
have been led to think more and more in terms of the *I-It*, which
has made the *I-Thou* difficult for us to establish.

All this is not unrealistic theorizing, for the threat to the individual, the increased socialization of life and other vexing problems
of the day are closely linked to the question of human dialogue.
One does not have to travel far in contemporary America to see the
havoc wrought by the ascendance of the *I-It*, to see modern man's
palpable condition of lack of relation.

In his book *I and Thou*, Buber develops at length the idea of
relation and applies it to the case of modern man. Man exists in the
world and, as experience, the world comes under the *I-It* relationship,
for the world of the It is set in the context of space and time. But
"the primary word *I-Thou* establishes the world of relation."[27]
I-Thou relations are possible with nature, with other men and with
spiritual beings. With the latter we can establish such a relation
although we cannot perceive the *Thou*, because we can still feel
that we are addressed and that we can answer. God is the *I* to

whom it is a Thou. The *Absolute Thou* of Marcel is the *Eternal Thou* of Buber.

Man's relation with God is not the same as it is with the idols popularly conceived as substitutes for God, such as power, money and so on. For the finite goods that are idolized always remain objects of enjoyment, *Its*. It is impossible, therefore, for a man who adores idols to be led to God by a simple diverting of attention. In order to turn toward God, he must change the very nature of his movement. In the case of the religious man, the world does not come between him and God, for he does not try to profit by the world and to pray to God. Consequently, there is no tension between the world and God but only the one reality.

If man cannot find God through the finite world alone, it is necessary that God reveal Himself to man. Revelation is the phenomenon from which a man does not pass, from the moment of the supreme meeting, the same being as he entered into it. This moment of meeting is not simply an experience: a Presence is received; there is added an *I-Thou* relation that gives meaning to our life in this world. It desires its confirmation in this life and in relation with this world.

Since he is so very concerned with this world, Buber objects vigorously to a religious emphasis on other-worldliness, and in this he is close to Marcel. Both insist that it is man *in the world* who comes to know God and who is to be saved.[28] Consequently, the world we know is not to be renounced, for creation is not an obstacle on the road to God, but the road itself. God does not demand that we choose between Him and His creation or that we say Thou only to Him. It is not surprising, therefore, that Buber objects to talking of fallen creation, for that which God has made for man is good, and man does not have to apologize for being what God made him.

Since revelation is a personal phenomenon, received by a "single" man, my faith in God is different from that of my neighbor; I cannot, therefore, force upon another my personal revelation, but can only demonstrate it through my actions, and this I am obliged to do. God is there, and the key to His revelation is His saying "I am

Who am." Although He manifests His presence to me, in acquiring knowledge of Him I come no closer to solving the mystery that He is, but simply say Thou with my lips and return to the world.

The most important effect of revelation is that it gives meaning to my life. God summons me to Him and then sends me back into the world a new person, for now my world has meaning. With meaning, it receives direction and values. There is no question of inventing or creating values, for I have discerned them pre-existing in the Absolute Source and Sum of all Values.

Martin Heidegger, unlike Buber, approves of the purgation of our concept of God which was brought about by nineteenth-century atheism. However he locates his philosophy beyond the issue of atheism and theism, making it clear that he does not believe it to be the role of the philosopher to study God. The central problem for Heidegger is not existence but being. His attempt to analyze *Dasein* (human existence) is made without any reference to a transcendent being. The problem of being is not the problem of ultimate reality but of man; God for Heidegger is a being rather than a Being. The basic element of *Dasein* is being-in-the-world. The human being is thrown into a world of its own making and is left to engage itself and act under its own responsibility. Man seeks authentic existence which makes him personally responsible for his own destiny, freely choosing above all his destiny to death. Death is my personal destiny which permeates my being from the moment I am thrown into the world.[29]

One cannot study the problem of being without first examining the problem of nothingness, which produces dread and makes man ready for a new approach to reality. Heidegger, with Hegel, holds that pure being and pure nothing are actually identical. Being is purely other than anything else; it is that which is not. Being is neither God nor the cause of the world. It is broader than anything that is, but is closer to man than to any other existent.

In some of his writing Heidegger seems to imply that being is finite, and that, apart from man, there is nothing. Yet he protests against those who refer to his system as atheistic, maintaining that existential analysis of man neither affirms nor denies God. Unwilling to use the term God or to deal with problems in theology, he believes that the question of how God enters into being is not for man to decide. He has little use for the scholastic approach of defining God as first cause and highest good, for this merely sees God as the superlative among the things that are and overlooks the distinctive character of the divine. To call God supreme value is blasphemy. God is given in religious experience rather than in philosophic analysis, which is incapable of establishing the absolute as God. He is simply not to be met with on the philosophic level.[30]

Of all the existentialists, Sartre is the one most closely connected with the name, and as a result many erroneously identify his principles with the whole movement. The basic principle for Sartre is that existence precedes essence: man first exists and then he defines himself. Man is no more than what he conceives and wills himself to be and his destiny is within himself. Since there is not a God to conceive "human nature" there is no such thing as human nature. Man simply is, and is responsible for his existence. He is responsible as well for all men, since in his choices he creates an image of what man ought to be. Man is condemned to freedom and freedom is a curse, for we cannot do what we want and yet we feel responsible for what we are. Man's freedom is absolute and thus his burden of responsibility cannot be relieved by anyone. He did not create himself but, once thrown into the world, he is responsible for everything he does.

Sartre's brand of atheism is unique in many respects. Far from being totally absent, God is everywhere present in his work. "On refuse Dieu, si l'on est tenté de consentir à la présence. Dieu n'est pas rien, alors, il est 'Celui qu'on refuse'."[31]

According to Sartre, it does not follow that because there is no God one should therefore give way to licentious living or to fatalistic despair. Instead, man has the obligation to accept an appropriate moral conduct affecting himself and mankind. Believing that

the theist has created God in order to put meaning into a meaningless world, Sartre insists that man must create values, put meaning
into life, complete his own being and that of others. If it were God
and not man Who gives meaning and being, then man would have
no freedom.[32]

Unlike Pascal, Sartre is unwilling to accept a risk. Yet he is not
afraid to accept the logical consequences of his atheism. Although
he condemns the eighteenth-century French atheists who thought
God useless and a burden and yet an illusion that, for the sake of
morality and the good of society, might be maintained, he retains
the values of the theists. For the existentialist atheist, says Sartre,
there is only distress in the fact that God does not exist, because it
leaves man condemned to freedom. This is a hard thing; Sartrean
characters feel no friendly presence at their side, and there is no
strong shoulder upon which to shift their terrible burden. For God
does not exist.

Man could not be free, according to Sartre, if his nature were defined by a Creator, or if he had an end which was known and
determined by Him. In addition, a God Who is *Causa Sui* is an
absurdity. But the non-existence of God is looked upon as a postulate with no other foundation than the fact that man's freedom and
the Absolute are incompatible.

Sartre's *Being and Nothingness* reveals that a radical empirical-
ism is the real key to his existentialism. In the world of today, the
existent has been reduced to a series of appearances, Kant's distinction between the noumenal and the phenomenal having disappeared. All that is, is a totality of appearances, and this is the essence
of the real world. For Thomism, reality is a hierarchical system of
universal essences, which reflects the constant and unchanging
eternal verities conceived by God, the Source of all things. But for
Sartre, reality is manifested in the individual's subjective experiences, which are more meaningful to him than transcendent abstraction.[33]

Sartre's existentialism as philosophy depends upon the uniqueness
and immediacy of every concrete existence and the individuality of

the actions that contain it. Every existing thing is born without reason, prolongs itself out of weakness and dies by chance. Things are thrust into being and have no meaning in themselves. Being is never determined in itself, but only to the extent that it is apparent to consciousness. Essence is, then, not in the object, it is in the sensing of the object. In his *L'Imaginaire,* Phenomenology becomes an instrument of subjective analysis and this in turn leads to an existential philosophy of subjectivity.

Sartre distinguishes two notions of being; Being for itself (*pour soi*) and Being-in-itself (*en soi*). The former is human reality, the latter is everything that is not human reality. Being *pour soi* is pure consciousness but being *en soi* is "dumb, packed togetherness." The two areas of being are completely opposed: consciousness must remain active and conscious, while passive being must remain passive and dumb. With this radical bi-polarity we reach the heart of Sartre's doctrine. Being *pour soi* expends its existence in a constant struggle to become something in its own right—Being-in-itself. But this can never be, *pour soi* must seek but never find. Consequently human reality remains "no thing," and negativity is thus essential to consciousness. Precisely because consciousness is *no thing* it can become all things. Moreover, total possession of his being is, according to Sartre, the fundamental desire of man's will, out of which arises the craving to become God.[34] Thus Sartre's human struggle for meaning, for definition, for security, is a desire to be God. It may be that this identification between *pour soi* striving to attain *en soi* and man's fundamental desire to become God was made by Sartre to support the atheists' claim that God is only an ontological need, absolutized by theists in order to lend meaning to "absurdity." The *pour soi,* constantly haunted by its desire to be *en soi,* to be Absolute, knows that as long as it is in existence it can not stabilize that reality but must re-create it at every moment. And in the responsibility for this re-creation lies the anguish of the *pour soi.* As a result of this speculation, Sartre seems to be left with an insoluble dualism, precisely what he condemned in others. His philosophy seems to leave no hope because of an inherent insolvable struggle to attain to being. But if being were to be attained, consciousness would be destroyed because it must remain *no thing,* undetermined, in order to be consciousness.

As Gomez, a character in *Troubled Sleep,* leaves a New York museum which has thoroughly disgusted him with its formality and its glorification of the inconsequential, he gives in exaggerated but nonetheless vivid fashion the atheistic existentialist's reaction to life:

Outside, the octopus, a thousand suckers closed in upon him, he was dripping with moisture. . . . No matter! No matter! He was happy to have escaped the museum; the heat might be cataclysmic, but it was genuine. . . . Truth had raised high walls around him, stood blocking every vista of the horizon, there was nothing in the whole world, but this heat, these stones, nothing at all save dreams. . . eyes and grins everywhere—not to grin is a sin. . . . They are not real at all . . . and I am no more real than any of them. A make-believe Gomez took the bus and read the paper.[35]

Another equally anguished existentialist character is Roquentin, Sartre's spokesman in the novel *Nausea.* A sudden illumination seems to reveal to him the true face of reality:

Individual elements of experience are swept away as so much surface froth. Beyond the familiar relations which things sustain with us as our tool and as catering to our practical needs, the hero of the novel is brought into contact with the amorphous, blasted reality of being-in-itself. . . . He experiences a great disgust before the radical absurdity and unintelligibility that remain when the trappings of human convention are removed.
The key to Roquentin's nausea is the discovery of the complete contingency of things, the total absence of reason for trans-phenomenal being. To exist, in this sense, is simply to be there as an obtruding presence, an obscenely resistant fact. Every being that shares in the in-itself is de trop, too much of dead weight for itself and others. The in-itself surrounds and penetrates us as stifling fullness, an absolute that gives no response, no shelter, no hope.[36]

Obviously, such a view of reality could lead to a denial of God's existence. Yet this is not why Sartre does deny it. Sartre's reason for denial lies in his definition of human freedom, which is the foundation of his existential atheism and of his philosophy of being and non-being.

Is Sartre an atheist who realizes that because man is self-determining, self-creating, he is therefore free, or is he a humanist who insists on the negation of God in order to insure human liberty? Sartre and the other existentialist atheists postulate God's non-existence only in order to reinforce human freedom. In defense of his position he asks: "What is meant by saying that existence precedes essence?" It means, first of all, that man exists and only afterwards defines himself. Only then will he have made what he will be. Since there is no God to conceive it, there is no human nature and man is free to create himself.

In the gravest and perhaps the most perfect of Sartre's works to this day, *Les Mouches,* Zeus confesses to Aegisthus the secret of the gods: "Men are free and once freedom has burst into a man's soul, the gods are powerless against that man."
Orestes proudly assumed his criminal burden, for that burden is also his freedom. Tormented by the furies, he confronts his Maker with the defiance of a new Prometheus: "I shall not return under thy law; I am doomed to have no other law but mine. . . . For I am a man, and every man must discover his own path. Nature abhors man, and you too, Sovereign of the gods, you abhor men."[37]

Freedom, to be preserved, must be protected from its many assassins, the chief of whom is God. Although this is essential—this denial of God's existence—there are also other conscious beings, men who are threats and who, by their act of being conscious of us, by their very existence, challenge our freedom. In Sartre's play *No Exit* one of the characters in Hell, surprised to discover that there are no torture-chambers, is informed: "Hell is other people." Again in the *Age of Reason* we hear Sartrean freedom defended against "other people" when Daniel in reply to a bartender's query, "A double whiskey?" growls, "God damn that fellow's mania for classifying people as though they were umbrellas or sewing-machines. I am not so-and-so, one isn't ever anything."[38]

But man must also defend his freedom from himself, not allowing himself to become enslaved to any divine or human imperatives but, like Sartre's Orestes, remaining a man "freed from all servitude and beliefs, without family, a country or religion, free as a gossamer thread" (*The Flies* 1, 2). Sartre's opinion of the absurd existence of many is seen in Matthew, a character in the *Age of Reason*. Matthew can recall how as a boy he intentionally broke a valuable vase, after which he felt as light as gossamer, proud, freed from the world, without ties or kin or origins, a stubborn little excrescence that had burst the terrestrial crust. Later he cries out: "I shall achieve my salvation," and still later: "I must be free, I am self-impelled." All his life he had contemplated great things, like castles in Spain, but all his life he procrastinated. And so that life was but a vigil.

> Oppressed with countless little daily cares he had waited. . . . But through all that, his sole care had been to hold himself in readiness for an act, a free considered act that should pledge his whole life and stand at the beginning of a new existence. He had never been able to engage himself completely. . . . He felt as though he was not yet fully born.[39]

In constantly defending his humanistic attacks on God, Whom he feels to be inimical to man's freedom, Sartre gives the appearance of protesting too much. His persistent deicidal statements, in addition to his inability to prove wrong the metaphysical proofs for the existence of God based on the principle of causality, lead one to suspect that the moral problem of human freedom is the real cause of his atheism. God, to Sartre, is not a transcendent being but a directional limit of man's transcending activity, a contradiction, the object of an absurd but necessary quest.

Although absurdity is not in the nature of being, as Sartre claims, it follows logically upon a systematically developed atheism which has been integrated with an autonomous phenomenological method.

"Philosophy has nothing to say to such a position. This pining to be God, this sickness at not being God is, on the psychological side, madness. On the theological side it is satanic pride. The philosophy of Sartre is an extrapolation on man's attempt to evade the first Commandment."[40]

God cannot exist for Sartre since for Him to do so would be irreconcilable with the contingency of history and the autonomy of human freedom. Consequently, God must be denied so that human freedom may be born.

Yet this position is not without its embarrassment, for once God disappears, there disappears with Him all possibility of values. With Dostoevsky, Sartre is forced to conclude that, if God does not exist, everything is permitted. Man is thus left rootless, forlorn, alone without excuse. To escape this burden he then invents God. But the idea of God is self-contradictory, for a Being Who is infinite self-consciousness, yet at the same time perfectly self-identical without internal distinction, and Who is not involved in temporality, is impossible. To be conscious is always to be aware *of* something, to be always involved in distinction. In the case of self-consciousness, the object is the self as known. Since the idea of a divine self-consciousness is thus on all counts the idea of something inconceivable, the problem of God reduces itself to the problem of human nature.[41] For itself (*pour soi*), although always seeking completion in itself (*en soi*), does not wish to surrender its own integrity. Contradiction results, since the only stable formulation for *pour soi* is *en soi* which excludes consciousness. In trying to combine these two elements with actuality and calling it God, man is thus creating a contradictory concept, one that is both necessary and contingent.

This contradiction, however, does not lie in God or in the religious conception of God, but in Sartre's theory of the modes of being. "There is no intrinsic barrier against supposing both self-identity and self-consciousness in an Infinite Being."[42] Sartre endows the *en soi* with density of matter, thus excluding *pour soi*;

but if *en soi* is spiritual, there would be no problem; it would of necessity be an *en soi pour soi* transparent to itself and identical with itself. Actually all that Sartre does is to establish that the divine mind cannot possess the same ontological structure as man's; he does not prove that the existence of God is an ontological impossibility.

Although Sartre does not prove the non-existence of God, he accepts it as a fact. But even if God should exist it would not matter, for the real problem is not His existence but man's realization that nothing can save him from himself. Man desires to be God, the *en soi pour soi,* but knows this desire to be futile and so, for Sartre, man is a useless passion, a being who must live without God and accept the accompanying despair.

Concerning creation, Sartre theorizes that there are only two alternatives: either the world detaches itself completely from the Creator, and thus claims aseity, or the creature merges with the Creator and thus leaves no distinction between them.

But there is surely a third alternative—a world which was created, yet has relative autonomy. Sartre's alternatives ignore the theistic position, which defines a creature both by its substantial distinction from God and by its creaturely dependence upon Him. Although he denies creation he does not assert that being creates itself.

Sartre's world is one of contingent, isolated, self-enclosed beings. The neighbor is the other, an object of hate. If God existed, He would be the Absolute Other and consequently the most hated of all. "Sartre in his study of existence seems to give us a description of that nothing which is man without grace."[43]

Sartre's system is largely dependent on a personal ontological insight, the absolute distinction between being-for-itself and being-in-itself, the former being that which it is not and not being that which it is, the latter being that which is what it is.

Such a distinction is essentially a phenomenological one between the object perceived and the act of perceiving. Being-in-itself is that which is generally meant by an objective being, and being-for-itself is a person's becoming aware of a being-in-itself.

Man is continually striving to fuse the two types of being, and the limiting term of this process is called God. But if God were to exist, He would have to be, at the same time, that which He is and that which He is not, an evident absurdity. Furthermore, even if God were to exist, He could not have created the objective world, for His mode of being would have been entirely intra-subjective, and thus He would have been incapable of conceiving the phenomenal world, since He would have been incapable of detaching Himself from it before it existed.

Sartre's reasoning is both as strong and as weak as his general ontology. For, at the heart of the problem lies the doctrine of the in-itself rather than the concept of a purely actual being. But the concept of the in-itself ignores the gradual convergence of consciousness and being in the higher forms of living things.

Because he assumes that the human mode of being-for-itself is the only way in which conscious life can be realized, Sartre feels no need to discriminate between what belongs to the nature of consciousness as a perfection of being and what attaches to consciousness in virtue of special human conditions. But our human way of being-conscious always involves a real distinction between the knower and the known and our cognition is directed to an object other than itself.

Although Sartre has other arguments for the non-existence of God, they all rest on the distinction between the in-itself and the for-itself. Valuable as they are, they are not convincing, however logical and even forceful they may seem in the framework of his unique and personal ontology. His particular conception of being, nevertheless, still remains a postulatory one, which cannot be demonstrated.

Sartre accepts Nietzsche's cry, or better, shout, "God is dead" as a valid statement of fact. Granting that Sartre has accepted Nietzsche's dogma, his militant atheism becomes more alive and more understandable. For his atheism is not the result of a cold rationalistic argumentation, but of a deep and personal faith in the need to deny God. His philosophy must be atheistic, because it is the answer to the challenge of a universe which is godless.

Sartre's work is characterized by a rugged honesty. Gabriel Marcel, in his essays on existentialism, repeatedly affirms his respect for Sartre's great integrity and intelligence. In the same work, however, he labels Sartre a materialist, a charge which the latter vigorously denies. The issue is serious, because materialism necessarily leads to determinism and determinism is incompatible with Sartre's doctrine of human freedom. To Marcel, a godless universe is necessarily materialistic, but to Sartre, God and man's freedom cannot exist together.

In the Sartrean system, if God should exist, a pre-established pattern would be imposed upon human nature and man would be unable to choose his own essence. But if existence precedes essence, although the only reality man might be able to grasp is material, ontologically he has a share in shaping it, and so preserves his freedom.

Sartre's atheism is not irreligious in the sense that it denies the transcendence of God. Nevertheless, his entire doctrine is a perverted development of the proposition that the object of transcendence is a contradictory phantom, which can be neither realized nor exorcized. His whole approach to the problems that so concern the existentialist—dread, freedom, moral choice and death—is an unbroken discourse on the wisdom of disillusioned atheism.

Sartre's atheism is not merely aggressive, it sincerely tries to be constructive. In a godless world, the reasons for human existence and human values are important problems which, if we accept the existence of God, are solved for us. But to Sartre, such a solution is too simple to be valid. If God does not exist, then for what purpose is man living? Sartre's answer is: to create his own world and to invent his own values. Man is free to define good and evil, but no values exist *a priori*. Admittedly, this is a brave attempt to give value to human existence; nonetheless, it is difficult to distinguish Sartre's position from the nihilistic one.

Sartre's novel theory of human nature appears to be the consequence of certain ontological theses which he has developed and which concern man's manner of being. This relationship between ontology and philosophical anthropology is of particular importance when extending Sartre's principles into the moral field. The main reason for opposition to Sartre would appear to be the aversion many people feel toward his teaching on man.

Transcendence toward the divine is the basic striving of human nature, but it is one that by definition cannot be accomplished.

The main objection to Sartre's ideas on being and consciousness is that they are incapable of describing accurately the religious aspirations of man. Thus, he fails to distinguish between the attitude of seeking to be God and that of seeking to become like God, through participation in His holiness.

For Sartre, religious transcendence cannot be otherwise than a search after self-realization as God, since he has defined God as the hypothetical blending of human subjectivity and being-in-itself. Moreover, since he holds that a creature is either completely isolated from God or is merged with Him, he is forced to give this misinterpretation of man's religious bond with God. Hence, his position cannot stand the weight of his argumentation.

For Sartre, the denial of God is the beginning of man's self-development—if there is no God, then all things are permitted. It is because of human freedom that he places his claims concerning the liberating effort of atheism.

To prove his case, he attempts to reduce the problem of God to insignificance. Thus, he argues that it would make no difference at all to mankind if the existence of God were to be demonstrated, since, in creating man free, He has relieved him of all responsibility toward, and dependence upon, his creator.

The Sartrean self is bound by no set of prescribed rules since all rules are the products of the self and every act of the self is free. Moreover, since every act proposes an intentional project, it sets a value for itself. No laws exist for man, since there is no God to legislate for him. The only necessity which man has to admit is that of being free. In fact, his nature is such that he cannot not be free. The only idea guiding his freedom is that of making choices with full recognition of his responsibility for the ends which he proposes and the means which he takes. This is the only really free man, the one who looks at life from the perspective of an atheistic ontology.

Sartre's work is of a personal nature, his personal conception of God being essential to his ontological proofs that God does not exist. Buber and Marcel would agree that Sartre's God does not exist. For Sartre conceives of God as the absolute "other," a conception closely related to his conception of the "other" and to his idea of the value and method of love.

Many important directions of contemporary thinking come together in Sartre's work, making it an excellent indication of the spirit of the age. Psychoanalysis, Phenomenology, Marxism and Nihilism are all to be found there. To a large degree, his philosophy is a synthesis, although a very personal one, of them all. The result is a godless conception of the world, but a courageous and energetic one.

Although Sartre is the best known of the French existentialists, Merleau-Ponty is often considered their academic leader. While his atheism is close to traditional agnosticism, his system is not a humanism, for, if it denies God, it is less to affirm man than to understand him.[44] The coexistence of the sovereignty of the Creator and the liberty of the creature is unthinkable, for the existence of God would hinder man from realizing himself and would eliminate all value from existence. Were God to exist, my existence would be annihilated, since the concept of the deity sums up all reality in Himself. Moreover, my existence would lose all interest, since man is the only measure of intelligibility and value, the absolute source of his existence. Although it is proper for man to have the thought of God, this does not imply that God exists, for the basic reason for this thought is man's desire to rejoin men in another world. Clearly, existentialism for Merleau-Ponty is incompatible with Christianity.

Marcel has distinguished two types of contemporary atheism;

that of satisfaction and that of revolt. The former he finds to be a completely negative phenomenon, and a particular danger in the United States. The latter, however, arouses in him more sympathy, because it is a constructive atheism born of honest intellectual striving and attempting to give meaning to the world. To this class belongs the atheism of Albert Camus.

Camus, like Buber, is not a philosopher in the strict sense of the word but primarily a man of letters. However, he has written literary-philosophical essays, and in all his work there is a personal philosophy which he exposes with great charm and imagination. Very much an existentialist, he works in the tradition of Kierkegaard, Nietzsche and Sartre. Like Sartre, he is an atheist, but not in so rationalistic a way. Instead, his atheism is strongly emotional; according to Marcel, it is the negative source of a religious mind. Unlike Sartre, he believes that there are certain *a priori* values. Thus, for him, justice is a transcendental virtue, and he proposes charity as an answer to the evil that exists in the world.

Camus' idea of justice is essential to his atheism. Since there is great injustice on this earth and the innocent must suffer, God would be responsible for it if He existed. Therefore, Camus denies God in the name of Justice. Pledging himself to fight eternal injustice, in order to establish a human justice on this earth, his doctrine of revolt becomes a cry of protest against the unjust gods and a call to man to give meaning to the universe.

Although Camus starts with the nihilistic proposition that the universe is radically absurd, he refuses to conclude that his life is meaningless but makes a profession of faith in man, ascribing to him the ability to create transcendent values. It is in Camus more than in Sartre that we find the divinization of man proposed as the consequence of the death of God. Camus is very much influenced by Nietzsche and very much interested in the notion of the absurd. For the absurd man, if God does not exist, then he is God. For, if God does not exist, all is permitted and he is free to usurp the throne of God.[45]

Camus expounds a doctrine of metaphysical revolt in his *L'Homme revolté.* Just as the slave revolts against the master, forcing the master to recognize him as an equal, so the rebel revolts against God and blasphemes. Camus' revolt must be perpetrated against an absolute, and that absolute must be personal. Accordingly, in the West, the history of revolt follows the history of the Judaeo-Christian tradition. The first rebel, therefore, was not Prometheus but Cain. There could be no true metaphysical revolt among the Greeks, for their *moira* was a blind impersonal force. Prometheus only rebelled against Zeus, who, though personal, was far from absolute.

The figure of Christ is also important to the history of revolt, because He provided solutions to the two great problems raised by the rebel: evil and death. He endured both and preached resignation to them. Thereafter, for all who protested against them, the example of the God–Man was immediately summoned. It was not until the divinity of Christ Himself was called into question by the attack of Reason, at the dawn of the modern era, that revolt again became possible.

To modern man, revolt is counter-religious. He revolts against God, since God does not merit existence because of the injustice He has wrought against man. The rebel chooses to refuse the grace of God and to live by his own resources. In doing so, however, he must destroy the existing world and construct a new one in its place. It is here that the nihilist and the humanist rebel take separate paths. The nihilist finds himself incapable of erecting a society of justice, and so, impelled by the fury of his denial, chooses to seek annihilation by means of even greater injustice, and to say in the end that God is guilty. The humanist builds the new kingdom of justice and constructs a human community upon the ruins of the divine community.

The notion of human freedom is, of course, extremely important to Camus' philosophy. For freedom characterizes man, and God is inconsistent with it. If God exists, everything is a manifestation of His power and we can do nothing against His will. But, if God does not exist, then everything depends on us. It is ours to become gods, since to do so is simply to be free on this earth and not to serve an immortal being. But freedom is not license. If all is permitted, it does not follow for the absurd man that nothing is forbidden. Responsibility remains, although guilt does not.

Camus chooses history over eternity and chooses to struggle in time. Man's greatness consists in his ability to continue, in an absurd and mocking universe, a struggle from which he cannot hope to emerge victorious, but in which he can find himself and in which he can be happy.

Camus, considered by some an existentialist, can also be classified with Sartre as an atheist humanist. Beginning with the basic idea that man's situation is absurd, he portrays the atheistic rebel who because of the sufferings in the world feels first Godforsaken and then Godless. Such a man, having allied himself with suffering humanity, must make the non-existence of God a first principle. Camus' problem is, therefore, the eternal: how to reconcile the existence of God with the existence of evil. His suspicion is that man would be more charitable to other men if there were no God. For if God exists, all men would receive the fullness of love in the next life and consequently would have no need of charity in this one.

Curiously enough, in spite of all its ambiguities, existentialist thought has had a profound influence on professional theologians. Many of its ideas have been absorbed into theology and many of its impasses have been encountered again on the theological plane.

Paul Tillich, for example, defines God as Being Itself, the power of being everything and above everything, and like Heidegger, holds that nothingness makes one aware of the existent. There is no distinction in God between actual and potential and therefore one cannot speak of God as living in symbolic terms. God lives, not in the sense of being a person in Himself, but of being the ground of everything personal. He lives and is personal only in His relation to the creature of which He is the ground. In Himself, God appears to be naked, lifeless, impersonal being itself. Only in the *I-Thou* relationship does He become a person. To speak of God in human terms, or to define Him as the scholastics do, is blasphemy. Togetherness of being and nothing is Tillich's definition of God. It is non-being that makes God a living God and reveals Him as power and love, that is, Being Itself must encounter nothingness before it can become living and personal. God is not the living God but the ground of all created life, the highest being in which everything that we have exists in the most perfect way.[46]

Berdyaev too has borrowed insights from the existentialists, but inserts them in a much more traditional framework than Tillich does. As the Orthodox representative of the existential school in the field of religion, Berdyaev rejects any notion that sees man either as a nothing before God or as independent of God. Man's existence is a testament to the existence of the divine. It is only when man meets God in an existential encounter—that is, as personality—that there is any real understanding of Him. Purely rationalistic, objective treatment of God is merely what certain people have thought of Him, for all such conceptions are colored by anthropomorphism.

To Berdyaev the problem of the arguments for the existence of God is influenced by whatever concept one has of the divine-human elements in man. For him, the problem of God's existence is a corollary to man's existence. If man exists, God exists; but man exists. All traditional proofs for the existence of God are rapidly dismissed and he prefers to think of Him not as necessary being but as a spiritual reality always to be perceived as subject and only to be known in the *I-Thou* encounter. Our knowledge of God is thus intuitive or mystical. It is in the struggle of the human spirit that Berdyaev finds his certainty of God, not as the ruler and the Aristotelean absolute, but as one Who suffers with the world, a loving, a crucified God. In Christ, God has expressed Himself in human nature. Since it is He Who is the model of the true human personality, man to be truly human must be divine, for by vocation he is a theandric being.[47]

An intrinsic tie exists between God and man as each cooperates with the other to overcome the intolerable suffering of this world.

God is born in man, man is born in God, and thus divine life is enriched. And there is a mutual longing between God and man. Despite certain mystical phrases, Berdyaev's doctrine neither submerges man in God nor reduces God to finite humanity. Man's humanity is intercepted in Christ and in this way enters into the divine. Through Christ, man becomes a participant in the life of the Trinity.

The clearest characteristic of God is to be found in the mystery of personality. For He operates not through necessity but through freedom. Freedom exists in the encounter of God and man, grace is divine freedom, human will is human freedom. It is in the realm of the existential rather than the ontological that God belongs, for He is spirit and it is the end of man to be transfigured and assimilated to Him.

Some have considered Karl Barth also to be an existentialist, but a biblical one, whose doctrine of God is firmly based on His self-disclosure in the Bible: "God is Who He is in the act of His revelation."[48] God's Being is identical with His life, He is Actus Purus; and free act. Ultimately real, absolute and sovereign, He is above all "wholly other." This emphasis on the infinite qualitative difference does not, however, exclude the union of two totally different kinds of beings. God's being is more than perfect act, it is that of a living person, Whom we address in prayer as *Thou* and Who speaks to us as *I*. God seeks and creates fellowship between Himself and us; in this way He loves us. In fact, His being is to be defined as His loving and He cannot be placed under any category common to anything else. He is He Who exists, lives and acts and makes Himself known. Barth rejects the traditional five proofs of the existence of God, for the Bible speaks of God Who needs no proof and these proofs would terminate at an idol of reason. God proves Himself in His acts and makes Himself known in them. He reveals Himself in His Son and to this God of revelation Barth is committed.[49]

It is clear that, in spite of its defects, the Christian can obtain new insights into the problem of God through an investigation of existential thought. For such philosophizing is of value in drawing attention to the human person as a free and responsible subject, in emphasizing the importance of God and the personal relationship between Creator and creature and in pointing out new approaches to the Transcendent.

NOTES

1. J. Collins, *God in Modern Philosophy*, Chicago, Regnery, 1959, p. 370.
2. W. Herberg (ed.) *Four Existentialist Theologians*, New York, Doubleday, 1958, p. 3.
3. J. Collins, *The Existentialists*, Chicago, Regnery, 1952, p. 244.
4. J. Collins, *The Mind of Kierkegaard*, Chicago, Regnery, 1953, p. 146.
5. H. Roos, *Soren Kierkegaard and Catholicism*, Maryland, Newman, 1954, p. 3.
6. K. Reinhardt, *The Existentialist Revolt*, Milwaukee, Bruce, 1952, p. 33.
7. J. Collins, *The Mind of Kierkegaard*, p. 150.
8. *Ibid.*, p. 89.
9. Reinhardt, *op. cit.*, p. 194.
10. J. Collins, *The Existentialists*, p. 112.
11. A. C. Cochrane, *The Existentialists and God*, Philadelphia, Westminster, 1956, p. 54.
12. F. Copleston, *Contemporary Philosophy*, Maryland, Newman, p. 170.
13. A. Dondeyne, "Problem Raised by Existential Atheism," Philosophy Today, II, 1958, p. 56.
14. cf. R. Troisfontaines, *De l'Existence à l'Etre, la Philosophie de Gabriel Marcel*, Louvain, E. Nauwelaerts, 1953, Tome I, pp. 263–277.
15. G. Marcel, *Présence et Immortalité*, Paris, Flammarion, 1959, p. 241.
16. E. Gilson, "A Unique Philosopher," *Philosophy Today*, Vol. 4, 1960, p. 278.
17. J. Collins, *The Existentialists*, p. 196.
18. A. Dondeyne, *Foi Chrétienne et Pensée Contemporaine*, Louvain, Publications Universitaires, 1951, pp. 96–103.
19. G. Marcel, *Being and Having*, Boston, Beacon Press, 1951, pp. 82, 137, 148.
20. J. Collins, *The Existentialists*, p. 131.
21. G. Marcel, *Being and Having*, pp. 138, 200–201.
22. G. Marcel, *Journal Metaphysique*, Paris, Gallimard, 1927, p 32.
23. J. Maritain, *A Preface to Metaphysics*, New York, Sheed and Ward, 1939, pp. 50–53, p. 60.
24. G. Marcel, *Journal Metaphysique*, p. 137.

25. M. Buber, *Eclipse of God*, New York, Harper and Brothers, 1952, p. 31.
26. *Ibid.*, p. 159.
27. *Ibid.*, p. 6.
28. M. Buber, *Between Man and Man*, Boston, Beacon Press, 1955, p. 52.
29. Copleston, *op. cit.*, p. 177.
30. J. Collins, *The Existentialists*, p. 179.
31. H. Paissac, *Le Dieu de Sartre*, Paris, Arthaud, 1950, pp. 9–10.
32. F. Kingston, *French Existentialism, A Christian Critique*, Toronto, University of Toronto Press, 1961, p. 111.
33. J. Mihalich, *Existentialism and Thomism*, New York, Philosophical Library, 1960, p. 68.
34. R. W. Mulligan, "A Note on Negativity," *New Scholasticism*, Vol. 33, March 1959, p. 163.
35. J-P. Sartre, *Troubled Sleep*, New York, Bantam Books, 1961, p. 25.
36. J. Collins, *The Existentialists*, p. 57.
37. H. Peyre, *Existentialism—A Literature of Despair*, Yale French Studies, No. I, Middletown, Conn., Stewart Press, 1948, p. 19.
38. J-P. Sartre, *The Age of Reason*, New York, Bantam Books, 1957, p. 94.
39. *Ibid.*, pp. 52–54.
40. J. Mullaney, Review of *Being and Nothingness* in the *Thomist*, Vol. 20, 1957, p. 99.
41. F. Copleston, "Man Without God," *Month* 174, 1947, pp. 20–24.
42. J. Collins, *The Existentialists*, pp. 71–73.
43. Reinhardt, *op. cit.*, p. 168.
44. J. LaCroix, "The Meaning and Value of Atheism Today," *Cross Currents*, 5, 1955, pp. 203–219.
45. J. Collins, *God in Modern Philosophy*, p. 371.
46. Cochrane, *op. cit.*, pp. 76–83.
47. Herberg, *op. cit.*, p. 106.
48. K. Barth, *Dogmatics in Outline*, New York, Harper Brothers, 1959, p. 288.
49. Cochrane, *op. cit.*, p. 121.

The Affirmation of God:
The God of Reason

7

The God of Natural Religion

IN a very real sense, there is a kind of knowledge of God buried deep in every man, as deep as his demand for happiness. Even when making his way to the illusory heavens of false gods, he is in search of the living and saving God. Not that God is so far from us, since in Him we live, move and have our being, nor that He is so deeply hidden from the minds of men, for the world is a mirror revealing the divine nature, and everything that is, by its very existence, cries out God's name: He Who is. The book of Job says of God: "He is higher than Heaven, and what wilt thou do? He is deeper than Hell, and how wilt thou know? The measure of Him is longer than the earth and broader than the sea."[1] He is everywhere, and consequently can be approached even by natural man.

We find some of the first gropings towards a meeting between God and man in the pagan religions. Certain writers, however, consider religions as merely an idol forged by man, in which he worships himself, and which must be entirely destroyed to make room for the revelation of Jesus Christ, Who alone is God's work. For them there are no authentic values in pagan or natural religions; all are simply corrupt. More careful examination of comparative religion has shown us that what seems at first sight to be wholly corrupt, pagan superstition may actually be an authentic, although deficient, worship of the true God.[2] A superficial glance at a religion such as that of the Incas, who worshipped the sun, may suggest that they were purely idolators. It is possible, however, that

167

they were worshipping the true God under a false form just as others have worshipped idols in His name.

This idea is explored by Yves Congar, who suggests that even the atheist may be actually adoring the one God in his worship of an absolute, whether of fraternity or of community. For man, to absolutize a created value, giving it his total personal commitment and treating it as though it were God, need not be precisely idolatry, for, if the value has genuine worth, man may be reaching through it to God in Whom alone it finds absolute incarnation.

Before men began to think in terms of philosophic concepts they thought in terms of symbols or signs for realities. Continued investigation of these symbols is likely to reveal that the worshipper is not worshipping idols at all, for the symbols merely represent something which he worships and which cannot be directly expressed.

During the last hundred years Catholic teaching has maintained a more positive position towards the religions of paganism, for paganism is really the result of the idea of a human nature spoiled by sin, but not entirely perverted and hence still reaching for God. The Church indeed uncompromisingly condemns the perversions which, with exception, are to be found in all the pagan religions: idolatry, pantheism, Manichaeism, auto-redemption. But for all that, she does not deny the authentic religious values which are there, signs of that help which God has never ceased to give man, stepping-stones leading to Judaism and to Christianity.

In Old Testament literature we read of various religious characters who were authentically religious but who did not belong to Israel by race or religion and who, though they were heathen, knew and reverenced the true God. Among them are Noe, who raising an altar after the Flood and found favor in the sight of God through this offering, and Enoch, who walked with God. Melchizedek's sacrifice is presented in the liturgy of the Mass as a foreshadowing of the sacrifice of Christ. Other holy pagans are Lot, the nephew of Abraham, the Queen of Sheba and Job. The New Testament too in proclaiming to the pagans its definitive good news of God's entrance into history shows that God has never forsaken them and that it is precisely because of this that they are at fault if they have not believed in Him. Saint Paul, in the Acts of the Apostles, says to the Athenians, "God hath made of one, all mankind to dwell upon the whole face of the earth, determining appointed times, and the limits of their habitation. That they should seek God, if happily they may feel after Him, although He be not far from every one of us." God's Providence extends, therefore, to every race; and through Providence, all men are enabled to reach up to some knowledge of the true God.

One may well ask: where do these natural religions come from originally? This question was answered by the ancient Fathers of the Church with their theory of "borrowings": that is, the truths of pagan religions were regarded as loans drawn upon revelation, whether from Moses or from the Gospel. In our own time some have tried to give this theory a scientific justification basing their argument on the connections claimed to exist between the primitive character of a culture and the purity of its religion. But as a matter of fact it seems that many of the authentic values in natural religion are simply the result of the fact that God is visible in nature and can be known from the visible things of this world.

St. Paul informs us in the Acts of the Apostles that "God, Who in times past suffered all nations to walk in their own ways. Nevertheless He left not Himself without testimony, doing good from Heaven, giving rains and fruitful season, filling our hearts with good and goodness."

Belief in divinity seems to be universal among ancient people. Both in space and in time, it must have existed in all stages of civilization. Although ancient peoples differ in their conception of the nature and attributes of the Deity or in their manner of worship, all admit the existence of one or of several Supreme Beings who regulate and govern the course of life. Such unanimous universal accord is itself a proof of the existence of God, for it comes from the innermost depths of human nature and nature is not deceitful.[3] One may object that nature can be deceitful in her appearances, having deceived man for many thousands of years by leading him to believe that the earth is a fixed body and that the sun and other planets rotate around it. However, in the matter of the existence of God, the objection falls to the ground for here there is no appearance, so to speak, that could deceive us. We cannot see God as we can see the earth, the sun, and the other planets. Hence even before God's supernatural revelation, nature aided man to come to a knowledge of Him. We see this exemplified in Joel, one of the holy pagans of the Old Testament, who calls upon nature to prove the existence of God.

St. Paul, in Romans, 1, 20, says that the pagans were guilty if they did not acknowledge Him, for since the creation of the world His invisible attributes are clearly seen. Thus only a fool says in his heart that there is no God. God is visible in the sacramental cosmos for the cosmos is a theophany, a revelation of the existence of God. This is made abundantly clear in the Epistle of St. Paul to the Romans, Chapter 2, 13–14: "For it is not they who hear the Law that are just in the sight of God; but it is they who follow the Law that will be justified. When the Gentiles who have no law do by nature what the Law prescribes, these having no law are a law unto themselves." We find this again in the Acts of the Apostles, when Paul says, in his speech about the unknown God: "I see that you are most superstitious men, most religious men, and I come to speak to you about the unknown God."

God was certainly knowable to primitive man through the order of the universe. He was also knowable through conscience, as Paul indicated in Romans, 2, 13–14. Any absolute value imposed upon the conscience immediately suggests that there is an Absolute to impose such a value. It is through the absolute of the moral law that man can more easily recognize the existence and nature of Him Who alone can command absolute obedience in such a way that obedience to the moral law expresses the worship of His will.[4]

The First Vatican Council has made it clear that one can come to know the existence of God by reason, and that this knowledge is a certain knowledge. However, it does not say which approach to God is best, nor does it say, for instance, that the Five Ways of St. Thomas can prove the existence of God. It merely states that there is open to man by natural reason, unaided either by grace or by faith, the possibility of establishing with certitude that God exists. It then proceeds to suggest that the existence of God can be proved by means of causality. The possibility of the proof of God flows from the dogma of the natural knowability of God and from the fact that theologians, since the time of the Fathers, have adduced proofs of the existence of God. It would be an error in faith and in philosophy to maintain that one simply cannot prove the existence of God from reason for *in se* the proof is objectively valid. Therefore it is clear that from the process of causality in a simplified form the pagans could come to a knowledge of God.

In spite of the fact that certain true values are present in natural religions, thus representing a genuine way in which the pagan sought to reach the living God, it is to be noted also that they contain frequent ambiguities and deviations. First among them is magic, the attempt to appease, through various rites or symbols, the anger of God, to control His reaction. Belief in magic and divinization is most prevalent in the lower stages of civilization and religion; nevertheless the arts of the magician and the diviner were founded upon the same logical processes as have issued in the development of modern sciences.[5]

We also encounter, in natural religions, the deviation known as demonology, the belief in a supernatural world of spirits who can be invoked and placated. Belief in evil spirits and in magic goes back to earliest times, and was practiced among both savage and cultural races, varying from the crude to the elaborate systems of the ancient Assyrians, Chaldeans, and Persians.

The Old Testament is confronted with the question of cosmic revelation only in respect of the generations that preceded Abraham. From his time on, the Gentiles are considered as "knowing not God."[6] With the New Testament a new question arises, for the message of Christ is given to all. The call of salvation is universal. But what of the position of those pagans who had preceded

Christ? Like the Jews, had they not also received the call to salvation? If they were at fault in their idolatry, then they must have been able to know God. The Apostle Paul, confronted with this problem, affirms repeatedly the existence of a continuous revelation of God made by way of the cosmos and directed to all mankind. But this natural religion seems constantly to have been seduced from the path of reason by magic, demonology and idolatry, and in particular that form of idolatry known as polytheism, wherein the entire world is pervaded by a variety of gods. It is a basic doctrine of the Old Testament and of the New Testament Revelation that there is only one God. Dt. 6, 4 (Mk. 12.29): "Hear O Israel: The Lord our God is one Lord." St. Paul, the Apostle of the Heathens, is insistent against the heathen polytheism on the necessity of belief in the one God, i cor. 8, 4: "We know that an idol is nothing in the world and there is no God but one."

There are also theoretical errors associated with the moral life in pagan religions, such as excessive trust in the power of the human will. This error consists in saying that the good act is decisively the product of man alone. Although God has created the universe, placed man in the world, given him his human nature with its faculties, and imparted abundant graces of illumination, it is man who assents freely to God, and it is this assent which is decisive.

Another deviation frequent in natural religions is that of pantheism, the view that everything is divine, the world an emanation or part of the essence of God. In the fields of ascetics or mysticism, especially, we find the assumption that it is possible to become so one-with-God that the boundaries of personality are obliterated and one is physically identified with the living God.

It follows from all this that in discussing the natural religions we must realize that in a sense they are not at all natural. Although natural in that it was through His manifestation of Himself in "nature," in the visible world, that individuals came to know the living God, the deviations which resulted are not natural in any sense.

Historically, there was never a state of pure nature, man having been constituted from the beginning in supernatural justice from which he fell in Adam. Although God could have created us in this state of pure nature, He did not. Instead, by a special love, He elevated the rational creature above the condition of his nature, bestowed upon him, as it were, a new nature, brought him into a new universe. Having created grace poured into his soul, he is made to partake of the divine life. For created grace is a reality, a quality, a light enabling the soul to receive worthily the indwelling of the three Divine Persons. St. Thomas says of this love that it is absolute, because God wills to pour into the soul by its means the absolute eternal Good, in so far as the soul can contain it, in faith here below, in the beatific vision hereafter.

Hence, the man of natural religion was never in a purely natural state for he was already fallen man. Then, too, natural religion is not natural in the sense that it is the most primitive religion, for the religion revealed to Abraham, the Patriarchs and Moses is the earliest religion of which we know. Nor is the religion of the pagans natural in the sense that it is simply the basic religious truths which Christianity or Moses would later adorn with new truths. Instead, we find error mixed with truth, resulting always in certain deviations.[7]

The First Vatican Council has stated that in order to know the truth about God with security and with no admixture of error there is need for revelation. Without the corrective of a parallel truth every theological truth, if pushed to an extreme, will terminate in heresy. Thus when truth is pushed to an ultimate degree we must add a corrective to form a balanced point of view. (For instance, whenever we say that God is just, we must add that He is merciful.) The pagan religions, lacking that full elaboration of religious truths which revelation gives, were unable to correct one principle by another. Then too, in order to possess clear and full insight, men have always had need of healing grace which, although granted to pagans by God, was not dispensed with the same profligate profusion as in His revealed religions, Judaism and Christianity.

In paganism can be found certain things very similar to those discovered in revealed religion, but observing them and admitting the existence of authentic good in them, we must also note that similarity does not mean identity. Thus, certain symbols common to paganism and Christianity are used in natural religion to convey a particular idea, but in Christianity take on a totally different significance, for the same symbol can symbolize two totally different realities. Hence when comparisons are made, it must again be remembered that similarity is not identity.

The primary characteristic of cosmic revelation is the fact that God, as Paul told the Romans, is known in it through visible things.[8] The entire cosmos takes on a symbolic dimension: the stars and the regularity of their courses, the rock and its stillness, the dew and its blessing, visible manifestations through each of which is revealed an aspect of the invisible God. This revelation has its metaphysical basis in the analogy of being. All being is a finite participation in God's infinite reality and so bears some trace of Him. All participated goodness, power, value, truth, nobility are found in an unparticipated state in God; hence man, in finding something loveable here on earth, can realize that there is something loveable in God; if he finds power in the thunderstorm he may understand that God is powerful; if he finds graciousness in the rays of the sun, he may understand that God is benign and lifegiving like the sun. The sun, in fact, holds a prominent position amid the heavenly forms, and among the Incas as well as in Mithraism, sun-worship was extremely important. The sun also provided the final form of Roman paganism, appearing as the force that puts the darkness to flight. Thus it is an apt symbol for the divinity as the source of knowledge, and being also the lifegiving principle of the whole cosmos, it reveals God as the source of life. In contrast, the hierophany of the moon possesses a relationship with the forces of fertility.

To the pagan the existence of God was made clear by something of a metaphysical leap for, when his mind perceived the finite, he concluded through an immediate and natural illation that, if there is a finite, there has to be an infinite. This approach to the existence of God is founded on the implicit conviction that there can be no value unless there be an unconditioned value; and no beauty unless there is an absolute beauty of which this beauty is a participation.

Pagan religions make use of genuinely objective symbols. Smoke, for example, is an objective symbol of fire since it is objectively connected with it. In the study of comparative religions we discover certain symbols to be objectively connected with certain truths. The Lutherans sing: "My God is like a mighty rock." Before them, Moses said it. Christ said to Peter: "You shall be the Rock," and afterwards Paul said that the Apostles and he are founded upon the rock. Pagans also used this symbol of God. Father Daniélou comments upon Mircea Eliade's excellent analysis of the hierophany of the rock: "Nothing could be more noble and more terrifying than the majestic rock. It reveals something that transcends the precariousness of the human situation—a mode of absolute being. Its resistance, inertia, its proportions, even its strange contours, are not human; they bear witness to a presence that dazzles, frightens, attracts and threatens." The pagans used the same symbolism for God, a rock. The rock, by its enormousness and its quality of resistance to the weather, seems to intimate eternity, and God's transcendence is intimated by the might of its proportions. By the fearful contours of colors which it takes on, it appears to be numinous, causing that mixture of attraction and fear that we feel in the presence of God.

Another outstanding numinous theme in every religion is the storm, the fury and wrath of which are easily related to God. In the Old Testament the Hebrew saw Him in it. And Rudolf Otto, in *The Idea of the Holy,* says that related expressions akin to the holiness of Yahweh are His fury, His jealousy, His wrath, the consuming fire, and such. Their signification is not only the all-requiting righteousness of God, not even His susceptibility to strong and living emotions, but the fact that all this is enclosed in, and permeated with, the awfulness and majesty, the mystery and augustness of His divine nature.[9]

Water, too, is a natural symbol, for it is demoniac, a fearful and threatening thing. We recall that many of Yahweh's miracles are connected with water, and His victories over water are conspicuous. Outstanding among these victories is the classic miracle of Yahweh's Providence over Israel, the Exodus through the sea of reeds. And even before that, at the very dawn of Creation, Yahweh set a limit to the waters which they could not transgress. After the Flood, Noe and the inhabitants of the Ark having been preserved, Yahweh promised that He would never again unleash the fountains of the great deep. Thus the Flood, in effect, becomes the expression of the judgment of God on a sinful world. At that moment, Noe is man standing before the judgment seat of God, for he is sent not to a particular people but to all mankind. To a pagan world he proclaims the coming of the Judgment, bearing witness to the fact that knowledge of the Judgment comprises part of the cosmic revelation. From this we observe that God governs the world; this is His Divine Providence, that He rewards the good and punishes evil, and this is His Judgment.

If in the Old Testament God produced water from the rock, in the New Testament he continues His water miracles; we have Christ walking upon the water, Christ commanding the water and the waves "Be still," and Peter walking upon the water.

Water is also a symbol for fertility. In the pagan religions, rain is a sign of God's blessing on the parched earth, a favor always desired and always marvelled at, which gives life and joy to the earth. An association is made with the nocturnal moon which gives refreshment from the harsh rays of the sun.

Daniélou notes that in Isaias, Chapter 55:10–11, we find an excellent comparison of the lifegiving power of rain with that of God's word: "And as the rain and the snow came down from Heaven, and return no more thither, but soak the earth, and water it, and make it to spring, and give seed to the sower, and bread to the eater; so shall my word be, which shall go forth from my mouth: it shall not return to me void, but it shall do whatsoever I please, and shall prosper in the things for which I sent it."[10]

These natural signs function as symbols of spiritual blessings, the sun representing the Divinity under the aspect of understanding and knowing which we usually acquire with the aid of light. The storm is the natural symbol of Divine anger, of the intense and fearful presence of the majesty of God, the numinous quality by which we long to come nearer to Him. Thus while we are irresistibly drawn to Him, we are also frightened, because we are leaving all purely natural grounds to approach Him, and must be prepared for a crisis to arise with each new step.

Another aspect of pagan religions is myth and rite. To the pagan this relationship between God and the cosmos is revealed at the same time in the myth that explains it and in the ritual that makes it work. The myth affirms the existence, in a world of archetypes, of the patterns of all human realities. These archetypes are the immutable models in which every reality participates.

In the pagan religions the myth is played out in ritual. The meaning and purpose of the rite are that it imitates, activates and reproduces the activity of the gods before the dawn of our time. Pagan religion believed that in primordial times the gods went through all these various activities, and the purpose of the religious rite is to preserve the world in existence, in fertility, in continuity, in blessings, by imitating this activity and reactivating it in the gods. The myths, story or legend connected with each rite is what we might call primitive theology. Comparative religion can point out many similarities between Old Testament rites and pagan rites with, however, this great difference, that the Old Testament never points back to a moment in eternity and imitates this by rite, but points always to a definite single event in Israel's history. In paganism no single event has any importance, whereas in Israel it is the historical dimension that has importance. This historical dimension has two points of view—it looks to a concrete event in Israel's past, e.g. when God led the Israelites out of Egypt, and it looks to the future, to a definite moment of irreversible time when God will do something similar to what He did at the Exodus: to the day of Yahweh when He will celebrate His and Israel's victory over the world. In Israel a rite is a glance to a past historical event and an anticipation of an eschatological one at the end of time when God will come to complete all that He has done for her. To Israel, as to Christianity, it is unique Divine acts without precedent or without any need of repetition that are pointed to in rite, whereas paganism saw time as circular and the rite as referring to events that required repetition.

SCRIPTURE AND THE FATHERS

It was stated earlier that the First Vatican Council holds that one can prove the existence of God by reason, and that this is a certain proof.

For Scriptural proof we may adduce the testimony of Holy Writ that the existence of God can be known from nature. We read in Wisdom, 13, 1–9: "For by the greatness of the beauty and of the creation, the Creator of them may be seen," and in Romans 1, 20: "For the invisible things of Him from the creation of the world are clearly seen, being understood by the things that are made. His eternal power and His divinity also: so that they are inexcusable." From these two passages we discern that the knowledge of God is natural and certain.

That we can come to a knowledge of God from conscience is seen in Romans, 2, 14: "For when the Gentiles, who know not the (Mosaic) law do by nature these things that are of the law; these, having not the law, are a law to themselves. Who show the work of the law written in their hearts." The heathens (that is) know naturally, without supernatural revelation, the essential content of the Old Testament law. In their hearts a law has been written whose binding power indicates a Supreme Lawgiver.

For a proof from history we might look to Acts 14, 14–16; 17, 26–29, where St. Paul, in his discourses, shows that God reveals

Himself in beneficent works also to the heathens, and that it is easy to find Him, as He is near to each of us: "For in Him we live, and move and are."

Proof from Tradition exists in the Father's reference to the assertion of Holy Scripture, wherein are stressed the possibility and the faculty of the natural knowledge of God. We refer to Tertullian, *Apoc.* 17: "O testimony of the soul, which is by its nature Christian."

The Greek Fathers preferred the cosmological proofs of God which proceed from external experiences, while the Latin Fathers showed preference for the psychological proofs which flow from inner experience. For instance, Theophilus of Antioch writes *ad Autolycum* 1, 4-5: "God has called everything into existence from nothing, so that His greatness might be known and understood through His works. Just as the soul in man is not seen, as it is invisible, but is known through the movement of the body, so God cannot be seen with human eyes; but He is observed and known through providence and His works. Just as one at the sight of a well-equipped ship which sweeps over the sea and steers towards a harbour, becomes aware that there is a helmsman on her who directs her, so also one must be aware that God is the Director of everything, even though He is not seen with bodily eyes, as He cannot be approached by them."

Taking their stand on the authority of the Fathers, many Catholic theologians have taught that knowledge of God is not necessarily acquired by long deductive reasoning from the world of experience, but is almost innate in man. St. Justin and St. Clement of Alexandria characterized the knowledge of God as automatic . . . or as a "gift of the soul.". . .

St. John of Damascus says: "The knowledge of the existence of God is implanted (by Him) in all in their nature." But since the same Fathers teach that we must win the knowledge of God from the contemplation of nature, what is innate is not the idea of God as such, but the ability easily and to a certain extent spontaneously to know the existence of God from His works.

CONCLUSION

In conclusion, we note that one of the most characteristic contrasts between cosmic and Biblical religion is that, in the former, God manifests Himself through the regularity of seasonal cycles, while in the latter He reveals Himself in the uniqueness of historical events. Cosmic religion is bound up with permanent patterns. For it, the historical and the unique are unreal; value is given only to what is repeated. Biblical revelation, however, places us in the presence of new, decisive divine acts which modify the human situation in a specific way and are not to be repeated. Christ died and rose again once on behalf of all. The symbol of biological life, Adonis, dies every autumn and every spring is reborn again; Christ dies but once.

Israel broke through this cycle concept of time and gave us a linear concept of time with a beginning, Creation, and with an end, the day of Yahweh, thus initiating a completely different concept of time and a completely different concept of history. In paganism God reveals Himself in a cycle of recurring seasons; to the Jews He reveals Himself by unique, individual, single, irrepeatable, irreversible, historical events. The God of Israel did not reveal Himself in propositions, in ideas, in concepts, in statements, so much as in acts; and an act enters historical time, it is irrepeatable, it is single, it is not cyclic. Israel was the first one to give such importance to history, and Christianity followed her.

NOTES

1. W. Farrell and M. Healy, *My Way of Life,* Pocket Edition of St. Thomas, New York, Confraternity of the Precious Blood, 1952, p. 3.
2. J. Daniélou, *God and the Ways of Knowing,* World Publishing Company, Ohio, 1957, p. 15.
3. A. M. Mazzei, *Does God Exist?,* New York, Society of St. Paul, 1956, p. 38.
4. Daniélou, *op. cit.,* p. 21.
5. J. Hastings, *Dictionary of the Bible,* New York, Charles Scribner's Sons, 1937, p. 556.

6. Daniélou, *Holy Pagans of the Old Testament,* Maryland, Helicon Press, 1957, p. 17.

7. C. Journet, *The Meaning of Grace,* New York, P. J. Kenedy & Sons, 1960, pp. 16–19.

8. Daniélou, *op. cit.,* p. 23.

9. R. Otto, *The Idea of the Holy,* London, Oxford University Press, 1952, p. 76.

10. Daniélou, *op. cit.,* pp. 27–28.

8

Ontological Proofs for God's Existence

THERE are two traditional approaches to the problem of attaining certitude about the existence of a Supreme Being; the rational and the intuitive. In the history of Christian thought, the former has developed in the framework of the Aristotelian-Thomistic noetic and the latter in the Platonic-Augustinian tradition. It was perfectly natural for the former to gain supremacy in an analytic and logical western culture; the latter, because of its mystical and ultimately incommunicable character—incommunicable, in an Aristotelian frame of reference—has gained small acceptance and is usually referred to only by way of refutation.

The Ontological Argument for the existence of God, which is the natural culmination of the Platonic-Augustinian tradition, was first popularized by Anselm; but it cannot be adequately understood in isolation from the pre-Anselmian elements of the tradition in question. The argument takes on its fullest meaning only in the light of an Augustinian realism of essences and the other elements in Anselm's thought which are the real premises of the Argument.

The most important of these premises is a certain Realism of essences. One of the most common points of controversy in mediaeval philosophy was the objective significance of universal concepts. Did *universals* exist outside the mind, or in the intellect alone? Were they corporeal or not? Did they exist separately from, or solely in, concrete individuals? Realism conferred a certain extra-mental, objective reality upon universal concepts, in the sense that it considered the universal as the ultimate datum, as originating and preceding the particular: the individual was considered an expression of the universal and, conceived of in hierarchy of being, in a sense a lesser being than it. Beings could be said to "be" more or less, in proportion to their being more or less universal. The most universal being was considered the most "real" being. Hence we have the Ontological Argument, which claims that the concept of God is so uniquely universal as to necessitate its being actualized in extra-mental reality.

If the universal originates the particular and bestows upon it all its meaning, then everything becomes comprehensible in dependence upon the most universal, God. Hence the necessity of having contact with God in order to find Him. An obscure faith, a readiness to believe, must precede knowledge. Anselm does not suspend his belief in God in seeking to establish His existence: he only tries to give some rational, intellectual basis to the faith which he already has: his *Proslogion* is, in reality, a *fides quaerens intellectum,* a belief seeking rational support. In Anselm's eyes, to suspend belief would be to shut oneself off from the only Being which makes beings possible, from all intelligibility, and hence to make of oneself a fool.[1]

Such an approach appears illogical to one whose sole criterion in intellectual pursuits is the human intellect: it appears, in fact, to beg the question. To Anselm, however, the human mind was vain except as illuminated by the divine. God could not deceive; the human mind could. To suppose anything comprehensible without the light of the Universal was, to Anselm, incomprehensible.

Three of the more classical proofs are given in the *Monologion* for the existence of God and they all begin in the real order, quite unlike the ontological proof.

(1) All men desire the good, and so search for particular goods. But particular goods have no meaning in themselves, but only as reflections of the ultimate Good, by which we mean God. The case is the same for greatness (nobility).

(2) All which exists exists by another or by nothing, excepting

the one being which exists by Himself and by participating in Whom all others have their being. Of course, nothing is by nothing. Hence all exists (all contingent beings) by the ultimate Existence Whom we call God.

(3) There are degrees of perfection within being. "By nature, a horse is better than wood, and man is more perfect than a horse." This cannot go on to infinity. There must, therefore, exist a highest good.[2]

The proof given in the *Proslogion,* which is the Ontological Argument, was intended to be a simplification of the three given in the *Monologion.* It was meant, furthermore, to be a separate argument, dependent only on itself.[3] In fact, however, it depends upon the entire Augustinian Realism mentioned above. (The original text of the proof (*Proslogion,* Caput II) is to be found in Appendix B.)

God is defined as that, than which nothing greater can be thought (*aliquid quo nihil majus cogitari possit*). Even the "fool" evidently has this concept of God in his mind; for when the word God is used, he understands its meaning perfectly. Therefore the concept of God exists in his mind. Normally, in fact, for all *other* concepts, existence in the mind and existence in extra-mental reality are two quite different things. A painter has a mental image of what he intends to paint; but the painting does not exist in reality until he puts it on canvas. The *quo nihil,* "than which nothing greater," however, is a unique concept, in that it absolutely demands existence according to the principle of non-contradiction. If the fool should admit that he has the concept of the *quo nihil* and should further admit—and he must—that he can further conceive of the same as actually existing; then he would be saying, in fact, that *that than which no greater can be conceived is not the greatest* since mental plus actual existence is a greater concept than that of mere mental, non-actual existence. Therefore, that than which nothing greater can be thought must exist mentally *and really,* in the extra-mental order—otherwise it is a self-contradictory concept.

We should note here that if the proofs from the *Monologion* and *Proslogion* had been taken together, many of those who attacked the Ontological Argument would probably have seen no objection to the combined proof. The three arguments from the *Monologion* supply the missing factor of existing beings, from which one might argue, as did St. Thomas, to the objective existence of God. Anselm, however, intended the Ontological Argument to be taken in itself, without a consideration of existence. His argument was that, from the mere concept of God which I find in myself, I can argue to the necessary objective existence of the reality, God.

The Argument is really the explicitation of an *intuition,* as is evidenced by the prologue to the *Proslogion:* God's existence is not a deductive conclusion; it is, and must be, at least obscurely, present from the very beginning. The concept of God is co-existent with the soul, imposes its existence on the soul, and the argument simply unfolds this obscure intuition of God's presence.

The *Proslogion* was most probably written between 1070 and 1073 while Anselm was Prior of Bec. An immediate attack on it came in the form of a *Liber Pro Insipiente,* written by Guanilo, a monk of Marmoustier, near Tours. Guanilo went right to the heart of the Ontological Argument, attacking precisely those things which later authors would call into question over the centuries. Anselm's arguments added practically nothing to what had been said in the *Proslogion.* The polemic was, in reality, meaningless; for it discussed the content of an intuition in the purely formal framework of logic. Anselm had been honest in making his position clear in the preface to his *Proslogion,* but he now made the mistake of attempting to answer Guanilo in terms of the latter's logical framework. The two men found themselves incapable of understanding one another: Anselm repeated that anyone who could not see that the admission of possession of the concept of God, as given in the *Proslogion,* led necessarily to the affirmation of His reality was either dishonest or pitifully blind; Guanilo repeated that

Anselm's Argument could not possibly be logically defended. On this note of mutual misunderstanding the debate ended.

Guanilo's objections would be brought up again in the later history of the Argument, for they had not really been answered. Anselm had succeeded in silencing Guanilo only by appealing to his faith and conscience. The initial sentence of the *Liber Apologeticus* was the grain of his entire argument: Guanilo writes on behalf of the fool, but is not one himself, and is, in fact, a Catholic. He must, consequently, be answered as a Catholic.

What were Guanilo's objections?

It is claimed that I must have the concept of God in my mind, since the word has a meaning for me. Would it not be more correct to say that I have the concept in my mind because I understand the meaning of the word? If this is true, the concept has only as much objective validity as any other concept, even a false or dubious concept. It is, in fact, no more than a mere word; its objective validity must be verified by experience other than my idea.

Furthermore, this Argument could be used to prove the existence of anything to which the note of perfection is added. Thus: I have a concept of the famous Lost Island, which is the most beautiful possible. Since I can conceive it as existing, it must exist.

Furthermore, the image of the painter is a faulty one. The concept of the painting-to-be is in the mind of the painter himself: the concept of God, if we accept Anselm's concept, is distinct from His existence and does not proceed from the same subject.

Furthermore, what right has one to pass from the ideal to the real order, to argue to existence from the idea of an existent?

Anselm's answers can be summed up in his insistence on the absolutely unique character of the concept of God, the only concept which by its very nature *demands* existence. The Lost Island is a fiction of the imagination, and one would obviously not be justified in passing from the idea of such an island to its existence. It is a mere word. The concept *id quo majus,* however, is completely and utterly unique, embracing *all* perfections and hence the perfection of actual existence.

Guanilo's objection to the image of the painter completely missed the point, says Anselm. The purpose of the image was not to suggest a similarity between a passing from the concept of God to his existence in extra-mental existence.

Finally, Guanilo vitiated his argument by substituting, for a concept than which nothing greater can be *thought,* a concept than which nothing greater can *exist.* To do so is to destroy the entire Realistic character of the Ontological Argument.

The gradual rise of Aristotelianism after Anselm led naturally to the almost universal rejection of the Ontological Argument. Only a very few scholastic thinkers, for instance, St. Bonaventure and Duns Scotus, granted it any validity, and they with certain reservations. The high point of the Christian-Aristotelian system came with St. Thomas, a modified Realist who would never admit an argument such as Anselm's. He denied the very basis of the Argument, namely the inborn quality of the concept of God, and denied the validity of passing from idea to reality. The objective existence of any concept could not be affirmed without consulting the data of sense experience.

St. Thomas' *Summa Theologica,* I. quest. 2, art. I, "On whether the Existence of God is Self-evident," involves, in the second objection and reply, a direct discussion of the Ontological Argument. Things are said to be self-evident if they are known as soon as the terms are known. But as soon as God is conceived of as the *ens quo majus,* is not His existence perceived? This does not follow, says St. Thomas, because although the proposition "God is" is evident *to God,* Who knows His own essence, it is not evident to us, who do not know the divine essence. Furthermore, not everyone who hears the name of God understands it to be the *ens quo majus;* and, even if one did, only its mental existence, not real existence would follow. It must first be proved that an *ens quo majus* actually exists. Then it can certainly be argued that this existence is a necessary one.

Anselm's argument, however, despite these refutations, was to have a long life in philosophical circles. Descartes, Spinoza and many other great philosophers were to reconsider it. Just as the Anselmian treatment of the Ontological Argument had been based upon a Realistic metaphysics and upon assumptions of faith, so the Cartesian treatment was based upon one which was Rationalistic and Phenomenal. To Descartes, being was capable of being reduced to intelligible mental phenomena and all reality was to be considered, because of methodic doubt, only an appearance. The object of his metaphysics was the clear and distinct idea.

By use of the methodic doubt, by which all things were to be considered false unless they imposed themselves with necessary certainty, Descartes attained, in his Discourse on Method and Meditation, certain knowledge of the reality of the thinking self. I think, therefore, I am. But what am I? A body? That can be put in question. The one thing I can say of myself is that I am a thinking being.

From this conclusion, Descartes then argued to the existence of a Supreme Being, using three proofs, one of which was really an adaptation of the ontological argument. It can be stated as follows:

All that is clearly and distinctly seen to pertain to a being's nature or essence belongs to that being. But existence is clearly and distinctly seen to pertain to the divine nature. Therefore, God exists.

The similarity of this to the Ontological Argument of Anselm is immediately evident. It begins implicitly with a "retreat into one's own soul" or, rather, into one's own being and, without considering external reality, argues to the existence of an infinite being. Its novelty lies in its arguing from the nature of God rather than from the character of the concept of God or genesis of the concept of God, and by using as criterion of reality, that of the clear and distinct idea. The notion of a God Who does not deceive and the validity of affirmation of external reality only in dependence upon God's truthful nature are both retained. The argument remains basically fideistic. Consequently the same objection can be brought against Descartes as was brought against Anselm: Objective reality must be consulted. The argument really proves only that, if God exists, He exists *necessarily,* as a necessary being.[4]

Spinoza's philosophy has been called Cartesianism carried to its ultimate logical consequences. All reality is reduced to the object of thought in an extreme form of Phenomenalism. To every idea we have, there corresponds a sensation; and to every sensation, an idea. Between these two, there is a perfect parallelism pre-established by God. In his search for a unified system, Spinoza made all things expressions of the divine Being, Who has an infinite number of modes of existing (*Ethics,* Prop. 12), only two of which we know: thought and matter, or idea and sensation. Hence, since these are two modes of a single being, God, they must be perfectly parallel. This is his metaphysical basis for his particular development of the Ontological Argument.

Spinoza's system is basically ethical and religious. His proofs for the existence of God are fundamentally *a priori:* he defends, in fact, St. Anselm's Argument against the attacks of St. Thomas on the grounds that an *a priori* argument for the existence of God is better than an *a posteriori* one, since the latter draws conclusions from defectable, imperfect, contingent beings (*Short Treatise,* III).

Since God is perfect, He can lack no perfection, therefore He must have also the perfection of Being. Spinoza argues that God, the subject of an infinite number of attributes, could not possibly not exist. In both cases we see the Ontological Argument renewed, but now under the form of a new metaphysical conception.

A third philosopher in the Descartes-Spinoza line is Malbranche. Taking his point of departure in Occasionalism, which states that each sensation is an "occasion" for God's putting ideas into our mind, he argues that each sensation or perception also reveals to us the existence of God, since no object is known to us except by means of, and in, God. The argument is circular to one who tries to use it as a deductive demonstration; to Malbranche, the argument was the expression of a fundamental intuition and proved that the same relation of Occasionalism could be viewed from two ends; one going from God to perception; the other, from perception to

God. The argument is Ontological in that it is based upon an effort to explain the origin of ideas, and moves, by the sole means of that effort, to the necessary existence of a unifying force of ideas and perception, God.

Leibniz too was to take up the argument and once more give it a new orientation. The metaphysical basis of the Ontological Argument in his philosophy is based upon a rejection of Platonic dualism on the one hand, and of Spinoza's monism on the other, and the substitution for them of Monadic Pluralism. All of reality is conceived of in this system as composed of an infinite number of monads or dynamic unities corresponding to infinity rather than to unity. It is natural to expect a different approach to the proof of God's existence from a system proceeding from such different premises. Leibniz, in fact, considered himself the creator of an entirely new proof for the existence of the Supreme Being. For there must exist a Supreme Monad, a perfect and absolutely active unity, an ultimate explanation, in order to account for the unity and harmony within the monadic plurality. In putting this theory into logical form, Leibniz adopted the form of Anselm's Argument in the last of his own three arguments for God's existence.[5]

He did not consider Anselm's Argument a mere sophism, but simply an imperfect demonstration. Its special value seemed to him to consist in its completely *a priori* character, arriving as it does at the notion of God without consulting His creatures. One thing, however, he insisted had to be added to the Argument to guarantee its validity: the internal *possibility* of the objective existence of the concept of God. One may not always proceed to the superlative in discussing a concept; one cannot say, for example, that there exists an ultimate and consummate velocity. The non-contradiction of the concept of God must be proved, not assumed; but if we can establish that God is possible, then He certainly must exist.

If then God is possible, He exists. His possibility can be shown by an examination of the dynamic character of all possibles. All possibles tend to existence since they are to an extent active, provided that nothing prevents their becoming actual; and the most perfect possibles tend more vigorously to become actual. Now God is by definition pure perfection and pure act. Hence He, more than any other possible, contains nothing preventing His real existence, no inner contradiction. Therefore, He exists.

Something is possible, in the abstract, if the subject and predicate of its definition are not self-contradictory: it is possible in the concrete if it involves no disorder in the monadic order. In both senses, God is not only possible, but the most possible of all concepts. His existence is consequently utterly necessary, completely actual.

The Leibnizian correction only served to complicate the Argument and to taint its original Platonic character. It introduced a new aspect of the question which was not present before and which would later invite severe criticism from Kant. The question of contradiction simply did not arise in Anselm's Argument: in his idea of God, possible and real were one: His essence is to exist.[6]

Kant's attack upon the validity of the Ontological Argument represents the perfection of Guanilo's refutation of Anselm to such an extent that Hegel referred to Guanilo as the "Kant of ancient times." Kant's refutation undoubtedly marks the most serious attack made on the Argument in its history. By his argument, Kant actually destroyed the possibility not only of the Ontological Argument, but also of any *a posteriori* metaphysical argument for the existence of God. For him, all that is metaphysical, beyond sense-perception, is not susceptible of proof. But the concept of God is metaphysical, and so is the existence of God, if He does exist. Therefore we must remain agnostic, at least in the realm of pure reason, although practical reason may demand that we postulate God's existence as a sanction for the moral order, etc.

It was Kant who gave the Ontological Argument its name; for he held that the proof centered about the concept of being, that it arrived at the conclusion of an originating and Supreme Being, beyond all sense experience.

Kant's most vehement criticisms of the Ontological Argument are to be found in the *Critique of Pure Reason*.

To begin with, he states, the concept of existence includes no note of perfection and does not enrich the subject in any way at all. This was probably the most important conclusion of the work which Kant had produced in 1763, "*The Only Possible Argument for the Existence of God*." The existence of an object adds nothing to the concept of it. "To be" is a mere copula, never a predicate, and says nothing at all about the subject.

The concept of an absolutely necessary being is a purely rational one. One can attach a name to it, but it remains a mere name. From it, we can never proceed to actual existence. This evidently repeats Guanilo's objection to Anselm. One can say, for example, that a triangle without three angles in unthinkable and contradictory; but one cannot conclude that a triangle with three angles exists. If we argue that the concept of a non-existent God is impossible, we are right; if we conclude that God exists *in the real order,* we are illogical.

The most celebrated of Kant's objections is posed in the form of a dilemma. Presuming that we can consider "to be" as a predicate, "God exists" is either an analytic or a synthetic judgment. If it is analytic, nothing is added to the subject. If it is synthetic, what right does one have to form the predication without sense experience?

Kant's and Anselm's positions could never be reconciled. They started from different premises, in different frames of reference, in divergent intellectual cultures. Kant discussed in logical form an argument which was the result of an intuition, a *fides quaerens intellectum*. He denied, furthermore, the possibility of defending such an argument in the realm of pure reason; it could only be accepted in that of practical reason.

Kant's attack upon the Ontological Argument seemed, at the time of its formulation, to destroy it completely and irrevocably; but the argument showed a persistent vitality. A new defense of the Argument showed itself with the rise of Speculative Realism, advocated by Fichte, Scheller and Hegel. It was the latter who, in

addition to criticizing Kant's system, presented a positive defense
of the Ontological Argument.

Hegel's system, holding that "whatever is rational is real and
whatever is real is rational," and making reason the ultimate reality,
provided a useful framework in which to develop an Ontological
Argument. It held that a study of concepts reveals the constitution
of reality. The hierarchy of being, moving from being in itself to
being for itself, to being both in and for itself (consciousness) and,
then from subjective to objective to absolute being, naturally
culminated in the concept of God, and derived its meaning only
from this absolute spirit, who is God. Philosophy, in other words,
begins with logic (examination of concepts) and culminates in art,
pure philosophy and religion (explanation of being).[7]

Hegel attacked Kant's statement that being was not a real
predicate and added no perfection to the concept of being, that
"being" and "non-being" were mere words or abstractions. To
Kant, being did not exist in reality. Being and non-being, in fact,
could be equated in concept: since the concept of an existent sum
of a hundred thalers was no more perfect than the concept of a
non-existent sum of the same. Hegel's objection to this, as had been
Anselm's, was that the concept of God was simply not the same as
any other concept implying perfection. The Kantian analogy is in-
applicable, because, in Kantian terms, the concept of God is in the
noumenal order and that of the sum of a hundred thalers is in the
phenomenal order. There is a real difference between the concept
of a hundred thalers and the actual existence of the same. But
existence and concept, notion and being, are *identical* in God, and
it is precisely this unity of notion and being that constitutes God.
Since God is in the noumenal order, sensible experience is not
necessary for the assertion of His existence. His existence imposes
itself upon us with absolute necessity.

The argument might at that point seem to have been exhausted.
Yet soon afterwards we find a school of Italian philosophers pro-
pounding almost exactly the ontologism which Kant had attacked.
These men—notably Rosmini, Serbati, Gioberti and Carabellese—

are treated at length in Borelli's chapter on the Italian philosophers in *L'Argomento Ontologico nei Grandi Pensatori.* Their chief interest for us, perhaps, is to indicate the extraordinary survival value of this argument, and the myriad variations to which it is susceptible.

History shows us again and again the strange power of this elusive and apparently illogical argument for God's existence. It survives chiefly in the Augustinian-Platonic noetic whose basic philosophic presuppositions are quite different from those with which most Christian philosophers work. To achieve any inner understanding of the force the argument was intended to have, one must accept criteriological presuppositions foreign to Thomistic-Aristotelian metaphysics, which most people are quite unwilling to do. Despite this failure to produce conviction the argument seems to exercise a certain seduction on successive generations of thinkers. Perhaps this is because it does contain a dark intuition of a certain truth; and there is always the hope, that with a different set of criteriological assumptions (e.g., Maréchal's framework of the *a priori* dynamism of the intellect to absolute truth) it might yet be shown to be a valid proof.

NOTES

1. St. Anselm, *Proslogion . . . Guanilonis Monachi obiectio . . . Anselmi responsio,* rec. Francis S. Schmitt, Bonn, Peter Hanstein, 1931, ch. 2.
2. These arguments are outlined in the *Monologion,* chapters I to V.
3. Charles Filliatre, *La Philosophie de Saint Anselme,* Paris, Alcan, 1920, pp. 195–200. cf. J. A. Casey, *Towards an Understanding of the Ontological Argument,* Master's Thesis, Fordham University Graduate School, New York, 1949.
4. Francesco Borelli, *L'Argomento Ontologico nei Grandi Pensatori,* Naples, Conte, 1953, pp. 47–50.
5. *Ibid.,* p. 87 ff.
6. Filliatre, *op. cit.,* p. 336.
7. Borelli, *op. cit.,* p. 143.

The Affirmation of God: The God of Experience

9

Israel's Experience of God

FOR Israel there is never any problem of God's existence. Being obvious to everyone at all times, His existence does not have to be proved. Inanimate nature proclaims it (Ps. 148 9–13), the stars know God, and they sang at the foundation of the earth (Job 38.7), the trees clapped their hands at His approach (Isa. 55.12), fire, hail and snow, fruit trees and cedars, beasts and creeping things and fowl all know God (Ps. 138). The entire world is aware of Him, including the Gentiles.

> For from the rising of the sun, even to its setting,
> For my name is great among the nations (Malachi 1, 11).
> And in every place an offering is made, is presented to my name,
> And a pure offering.
> For my name is great among the nations (Malachi 1, 11).

Even the sinner knows God because the very fact of sin is a rebellion against Yahweh. The apostate himself proves that God is, because in choosing to revolt against Him, the point of reference for his sin is always Yahweh, God.

The nearest approach to an indictment of atheism is the crticism of the fool who has said in his heart that there is no God (Ps. 53.1). But this is the practical atheism of the sinner who questions the works of God, not His existence. What he is denying is that God involves Himself in human affairs and human events, that He will act as Judge and Savior. Never denying the fact that God is, the

199

fool denies that God acts in the concrete, individual providential situation to control, to save and to judge. Because he refuses to recognize God, to relate himself to Him, to submit to His judgment, he is always also a corrupt man in the Old Testament. Nor could he be otherwise, with the light of his intelligence darkened by his evil moral attitudes.

The biblical problem of God is that of the "Living God," as He is called in Scripture. The question is always discussed in terms of the biblical "knowledge" of God, that is, entering into a total and vital relation with Him. For the classic virtue of the Israelite is fidelity to this knowledge: accepting His word, adhering to it, obeying and submitting to it. Israel is never interested in conceptualized or theoretic knowledge; her God is not the God of the philosophers and scholars, but that of Abraham, Isaac, and Jacob, and the knowledge proper to Him is essentially concrete, intuitive, synthetic. Such knowledge cannot be confined to the intellect alone but always involves a personal encounter and an inward conversion.[1]

The word, *yada* to know (God), signifies a knowledge acquired through interior experience rather than through discursive reasoning. "Know the Lord" implies recognition of His true nature and acceptance of His moral will. But this involves experiencing the Divine reality, acknowledging His supremacy, and therefore submitting to Him.[2]

In addition, the term "knowledge of God" has an intensely personal connotation in the Old Testament, indicating an intimate and spiritual relationship that induces conduct in agreement with the will of God. Thus, in the book of Osee, the prophet announces that when Israel is betrothed to God she "shall know the Lord" (2:20). He asserts that there is no fidelity or "knowledge of God" in the land (4:1) and for want of knowledge the people are destroyed (46). The nation, in seeking the divine favor, exclaims:

> Come, let us return unto the Lord:
> For he has torn, but he will heal us;
> He smote, but he will bind us up; (6:1)

> Let us know, let us press on to know the Lord;
> As soon as we seek him we shall find him;
> He will come to us like the winter rain,
> Like the spring rain that waters the land   (6:3)

God announces His delight:

> For I delight in piety, not sacrifice;
> And in the knowledge of God, rather than burnt-offerings   (6:6)

The Old Testament affirmation is clear stated: God is our God, the God Who knew us and Who in knowing us gave us to know Him. But to be known by Him implies that He has chosen us; that He cares for us, exercises what we call Providence, will one day judge and save. To know God in the Old Testament means to believe and to adopt a total practical attitude toward life as a consequence of that belief. There is mention too of the search for God, a search which is also a finding, an idea repeated by St. Augustine. Thus the problem of God is posed and answered in terms of the assertion of His presence and remoteness, His closeness and inaccessibility. Man's answer is contained in the whole-hearted acceptance which the Bible calls the "knowledge of God."[3]

REVELATION

It was little by little and in different ways that God spoke in old times to our forefathers the prophets, but in these latter days he has spoken to us through his Son.   (Heb. 1. 1)

Although it nowhere argues the case for the existence of God, the Old Testament is greatly concerned with what He has revealed of Himself. This revelation is manifested through encountering the divine, achieving God through personal experience. Apart from this revelation, no other knowledge of the living God is possible to man. As a creature, he can never know the limitless God in the fullness of His Divinity, for even when revealed, He necessarily remains a hidden God (Isa. 45:15). Because man cannot comprehend the hiddenness or the transcendence of God, it is necessary that he be freely granted this personal knowledge.[4]

The testimony which God gives of Himself is expressed by the Word, and his Word, a guarantee of divine perfection, makes known something of the mystery of His inner existence which then becomes the object of faith. The activity of God is synonymous with this Word by means of which He manifested His creative activity. When He spoke, things began to exist (Gen. 1:3; Ps. 33.6, 9). In the Exodus He revealed Himself to Moses, establishing the Sinai Covenant and bringing man into a fellowship with Himself (Osee 2:22; Jer. 31:33f). God's purpose in thus revealing Himself was "to cause men to see" (Amos. 7:1 4, 7) (Jer. 38:21), His will being "to make known His Will" (Gen. 41:39) and to "instruct" or teach men His intentions (Isa. 2:3; 28:26). But it was especially to "speak His Word" (Jer. 1:4ff) that God made Himself known.

This revelational knowledge of God depends wholly upon the divine initiative manifesting His love in certain great acts which bring to man the fullness of life.[5] Through his own efforts man can never know God in a personal way, but revelation transcends the experience of the individual. In order to make them mediators of that revelation, God manifests His nature to Abraham and His Name to Moses. Awareness of this divine nature is communicated by the Old Testament concept of revelation, whose purpose is to redeem man and to bring him into communion with God.

That God might also enter into a Covenant relation with Israel, individual patriarchs were chosen to serve as mediators of the divine revelation (Lev. 26:12), and the prophets too became the heralds of God's message: "Surely, he will do nothing, the Lord God, Except he reveal his purpose to his servants the prophets (Amos. 3:7)."

Recalling the fact that the knowledge of God and His will, founded on the divine authority, was transmitted to men, the prophet says:

"As for me, this is my covenant with you," says the Lord: "My spirit which is upon you, and my words which I have put in your mouth, shall not depart from your mouth, nor from the mouth of your offspring, nor from the mouth of your offspring's offspring," says the Lord, "from henceforth, even forever" (Isa. 59:21).

Having made use of words to reveal Himself and His spiritual truths, God selected the prophets of Israel to convey His word to others, and the faithful Israelites must listen.[6] The prophets are charismatic figures, with the right to judge history and events, including those institutional figures of power, the priest and the king. The fact that the prophets have the courage to testify to their convictions even to the point of martyrdom makes it evident that they are not simply the deluded victims of some psychic experience.

The revelation of God as a manifestation of grace made the Hebrews a unique people, one set apart from their pagan neighbors (Deut. 18:9ff). Throughout their history those to whom the Word of the Lord had come were not outstanding for their learning, wisdom or power. What they did, however, was to speak in the name of the Lord, proposing the divine Will as the rule of every activity of human life here and now. Other religions saw their divine communications as pertaining only to the future, their adherents being less concerned about the will of the gods concerning the affairs of this world.

The manner in which the Hebrew prophets spoke was also different from that of the religious leaders of the ancient world, for their messages often ran counter to existing practices and conventions, with no thought of pleasing their listeners. The "peculiar religious genius" of the Hebrews can only be attributed to the word of the Lord to which the prophets testified, fully aware of the divine reality present in themselves, in the world, and in the course of human events. Indeed, the most striking feature of Hebrew belief was this keen perception of the living, divine personality, a knowledge which directed the process of human life toward God Himself.

It was the mission of the prophets to maintain and deepen among the people this precious knowledge of the one true God.

REVELATION OF THE LIVING GOD

But the Lord God is the true God; He is the living God, the everlasting King; At his wrath the earth quakes, and his fury no nation can bear (Jer. 10, 10).

The concept of God as a living God is the characteristic concept of the Old Testament and is basic to an understanding of its doctrine of the revelation of God. The meaning of the term "living" as applied to God is clearly shown in the passage from Jeremias.

Because Yahweh is the living God, divine revelation, the activity of God in History, and His creative activity in nature are all seen as necessary realities. Life is His essential characteristic, and He is continually active as the Creator and Sustainer of all, the One Who gives life to all. This is why every creature, by its very existence, sings the praises of God, as is seen in Dan. 3:57–82.

All ye works of the Lord, bless the Lord . . . O ye heavens . . . O ye sun and moon . . . O ye stars of heaven . . . fire and heat . . . frost and cold . . . nights and days . . . lightnings and clouds . . . mountains and hills . . . fountains . . . seas and rivers . . . fowls of the air . . . beasts and cattle . . . O ye sons of men, bless the Lord; praise and exalt Him above all forever.

All the creatures of the world rejoice in God as the source of life, their dependence upon Him revealing some of the glory of His life.[7]

God's creative power and His communication of natural life are evident throughout the Bible, all creation being dependent upon its Author and directed toward Him. He alone, the essential cause, supports and sustains life, His providence maintaining all creatures in existence. Moreover, His supernal life distinguishes Him from other gods. Idols represent the gods which have no life, but the living God has power to save. Israel's faith contrasts the weakness and inadequacy of the foreign gods with the might of Yahweh, the living God (Jer. 19:10).

As the Fountain of Life and the Source of Light (Ps. 36:9) and of all that constitutes life (Ps. 34:12), only the living God could create living things. To describe this creative power, the Old Testament uses verbs rather than abstract concepts: He is the God Who delivers Israel from the bondage of Egypt, Who entered into Covenant with Israel (Deut. 5:26). Always, even from the beginning of her Covenant relations with Yahweh, it is Israel's belief that Yahweh is guiding her continually (Ps. 107:4ff).

Yahweh is the active God Who delivers His people. Present in universal history, He disposes of empires, using even the Gentiles as His servants. The Israelites swear their most solemn oaths by the living God (1 Sam. 14:39) and the psalmist, depressed and concerned about the problems of life, is cheered by the thought that His God is a living God, One Who is always able to be personally encountered, "My whole being thirsts for God, for the living God: How long till I come and see the face of God?" (Ps. 42:2). As David faces Goliath his strength is renewed in the same thought (1 Sam. 17:26, 36).

Since God is a living God, He operates in and through the historical process, demonstrating active *power* such as no other god had ever shown. As a result of this practical consideration that God is supremely, uniquely alive, genuine monotheism arose, the idea of God as the One God of Israel.[8]

The concept of the living God attained its most vivid expression in the anthropomorphic language which Israel adopted for its educational value, speaking of Him as it knew Him, in action, as though He were a man. Because He is known to the Israelites through immediate experience, their God is no abstract idea or principle but an active powerful being about Whom they speak with a convincing realism. To them He is a living personality Who talks, walks, even whistles (Isa. 7:18). He has eyes (Ps. 34:15); ears (Isa. 59:1); face (Jer. 44:11); head (Isa. 50:2) and a mouth (Isa. 40:5). He walks, listens, answers, is angry.

The divine nature of God is continually revealed as subject to human emotions: rejoicing over His people (Isa. 65:19); moved to pity (Joel 2:13); provoked to anger (Deut. 32:16). Such human terms give the God of the Old Testament His vivid personal traits and, bringing Him close to man as a living person, preserve and strengthen religious life.

The absence of artistic images of the Lord among the Israelites proves that they were aware that these human terms cannot adequately describe the divine reality, that nothing in fact in the universe can be likened to the Lord, for He is beyond human experience and knowledge. It proves too that they were conscious of the divine reality and of the danger of reducing it to the level of the created. Although mythological language was criticized by the Greek philosophers as a form of idolatry, they found they were unable to preserve the character of the living God within their philosophic language. Instead, their cult was directed to "a diffuse deity" rather than to the living God. But the metaphorical language of the Bible served to safeguard the most absolute teaching about the divine reality in the old alliance: belief in the one living God.[9]

THE CREATOR—GOD

As Israel came to know her God through personal encounter with Him in history she also came to know this Sovereign Lord of all things as Creator, an idea which is not the earliest aspect of His nature to be stressed in the Old Testament. Originally, it would seem that the Israelites saw in Yahweh their king and protector; only gradually, through personal experience of His help and protection, did they become aware that He was the only true God, the Creator of heaven and earth.

In the Old Testament, the God of revelation, the Lord of all creation, reveals Himself through natural phenomena (Ps. 19:1–6) (102:25). To the Israelite these were the expression of a personality above and outside nature, of a God Who is never identified with the universe He has made but is wholly and utterly distinct from it, supremely transcendent and independent.

Only the power of God as Creator could control the natural order, achieving His preconceived goal by simple decree: "God said, 'Let there be light!' And there was light!" (Gen. 1:3–4). The supreme power of God, seen in His acts of Creation, is announced by Isaias (Isa. 40:21–22; 40:26). That He is infinitely superior to all other so-called deities appears in His relation to the natural order, for nature is inexplicable except on the assumption that God exists. From Him, man and the universe derive their existence and consequently are neither self-contained nor self-sufficient.

God reveals His activity in nature, natural phenomena being evidence that God's creative and sustaining Word still operates in the world (Ps. 147:15–18). Thus Isaiah came to a clearer conception of the God of revelation through the wonder of the stars (40:25f). God is made manifest in the thunder and lightning (Ps. 18:5ff. Ex. 19), in the control of stars (Judg. 5), in the sun and the moon (Isa. 38:7ff).

Creation, as seen by Israel, is a free and sovereign act, the purpose of which is expressed in terms of God's providence. Thus in the universe all nature coheres and is unified, a visible form of His presence and a revelation of His power.

In the Old Testament, Yahweh is conceived as the sole, genuine, universal Creator, Who freely made Israel the people of His predilection and drew the entire universe from nothing by a free act of His will. Nor is there any evidence that the origin of the world was ever attributed by the Hebrews to a cause other than Yahweh. While the term "causality" was unknown to them, they did have a strong belief in causation and in the idea that the only conceivable cause was a personal agent Whom they saw as the Master of all the natural world of earth and sea and sky as well as the supreme arbiter of the fate of nations and men.[10] Thus their faith in God as Creator enabled them to have a coherent view of the cosmos and to draw upon it for light and spiritual energy at critical periods in their history. For Israel, Yahweh was all-sufficient and would achieve His purposes.

God is supremely free and independent, with all things subject to Him in a relationship of dependency and contingency. Lord of all that existed and of everything that happened in both the physical and moral order, Yahweh exerted profound influence on the world, on history and on the life of the individual. It is because He was the author of the entire universe that the Old Testament saw all things as dependent upon Him.

NEIGHBORING RELIGIONS

Israel's idea of God, utterly unique among the concepts of the deity in the world of the ancient Near-East, reveals itself as most distinctive when seen against this background.

According to historians of religion, Israel's religious genius is unique, with a concept of God that could never have been derived from surrounding cultures. This fact alone is remarkable because everything else in Israel's culture was absorbed from that of neighbors. But at the very heart of her culture, her religion was not only not identified with those of her neighbors but was opposed to them in every way. No intelligible explanation for this is possible aside from the fact of God's revelation.

The Canaanites, the Mesopotamians, the Assyrians who surrounded Israel were larger and more powerful nations, yet her God is in no way like theirs. They were first of all, idolaters, although not necessarily in the most primitive sense. At the heart of their religions is the worship of natural forces: fertility, power, money, war, the state, the race. The gods of these peoples were all too human, fighting, stealing, being cruel, committing adultery and suffering the same moral conflicts as fallen mankind. But all this is as remote as possible from the traits of Israel's God: total sinlessness and ineffable holiness.

Moreover, these were gods who could be placated by magic, particularly the many lesser gods among them. Demons could be controlled by magic, thus preventing harmful things passing from them to men. The enormous amount of magical literature in countries such as Mesopotamia proves how relatively pure was Israel in this regard. Although she practiced magic, it never became part of her official religion.

Sacrifices made to the gods of Israel's neighbors were human sacrifices. The word *Gehenna,* hell, is taken from the name of the valley in which they were offered to the god Moloch, to the unspeakable horror of the religious Jew whose God did not permit such abominations.

At the center of the religious culture in the Semitic countries surrounding Israel there is a drama which was enacted by the high priest or the king as a representative or incarnation of the people. The meaning of the ritual symbolizing the fertility cycle was that the world was re-created each year through the efforts of the king and the people re-enacting the cultic drama. The sun, the rain, the cycles of the seasons are due to the will of the gods, who refuse to produce them with regularity and to preserve the order of the cosmos unless men symbolically act out the activity of the gods themselves. Creation itself is viewed as a cosmic struggle with chaos. After the main god had conquered, he then had union with his consort, the fruit of which was fertility upon the earth. Obviously, the role of woman in such a religion is simply that of a chattel, owned and possessed as an instrument of pleasure. Society and law are created to protect those who have the good things of this world and to make the "good life" possible to all. The basic philosophy is irreligious secularism in which material wants, natural forces and sexuality are all deified.

A further development was the deification of the state. While in Semitic religions the king personifies God, in Israel, God is King and the latter never comes to be considered as God. Yahweh is the supreme God, from Whom the king receives His authority. In the neighboring cultures the king personifies God and he is also the state, with the consequent loss to the individual of personal worth, personal dignity and liberty, eventuating in his complete submission to the king and the state. This destructive theory is common to all forms of statism, including the same emphasis on material satisfactions. Modern variations simply add that the historical process, as it inevitably develops, will produce statism automatically, whereas the ancient Semites looked to the cultic drama as the cause.

In such a theory the state is God, Whose purpose is to wage war and to provide slaves and captives. Such deification glorified and rendered sacred war, pillage, rape and all the aggressive instincts of man. The gods of this society, having no inner consistency, were unprincipled and unpredictable, capable even of betraying their worshippers. Worship of such gods, pushed to its ultimate term, could only dehumanize and de-divinize human beings.

The Israelite concept of God is infinitely superior to this and it is one that cannot be explained by the process of comparative religion. For Israel, the most vital question in life is: What is the will of Yahweh for me and how shall I obey it? Such a faith is a radical and unique departure from that to be found in the other religions of her time. The problem of life is not analyzed with respect to nature, which played only a subordinate role, but with respect to the will and purpose of the transcendent Lord.[11] The election of Israel is part of the universal redemptive purpose of God (Gen. 12:3). By acts of grace and love and the covenant He binds His elect to Himself and expresses His will. The reality of this election, confirmed in the deliverance from Egyptian bondage and in the gift of inheritance, shows that He is not a power immanent to nature but One Who reveals Himself in historical acts, transcending nature and history and destroying the basis of all pagan religion.

Israel's God is wholly different in many ways, and first of all from man. Man is defective, fragile, weak, sinful; God is the utter breath of holy and transcendent Power manifested in the elements, in history and in His miracles. Because He is so completely different from man, He fills him with awe and terror. Whereas man is weak, God is strong; whereas man's span of life is short, God is always living.

God is wholly different also from the gods of the nations. Moral, with an absolute will that must be obeyed with interior submission, He can neither be controlled by magic nor manipulated by sacrifice. Pagan worship centers on the efficacy of an individual's magic or sacrifice (food for the deity's need) or the mystical experience, but in Israel worship begins with the proper inner attitude toward

God, with holy reverence, faith, and love. Sacrificial rites have lost their pagan setting in which the physical needs of the gods for food and drink are ministered to. Instead sacrifice provides the means of worshipping God, atoning for sins, and re-establishing communion with Him. Not human sacrifices are wanted but the expresion of utter dependence upon Him. Moreover, He does not merely promise natural benefits to man; on the contrary He frequently threatens him with punishment and extinction. And His promised reward is not that of the gods of the nations.

Israel's God has no cultic goddess-consort. Yahweh is distinct from the world, not its prolongation but the One Who has created it through His sovereignly independent choice. No element in it ever resisted Him because every part is His sovereign, effortless creation. All men in comparison with Him are defective and because of their creatureliness and wickedness are separated from Him.

Yahweh is, then, completely different from the gods of the nations and from mankind in His purpose and intentions. Had the Israelites had their way with Yahweh they would have wanted the identical things that the other Semites asked of their gods. But Yahweh would not permit them to distort the revelation which He granted them. The means by which He arrived at these intentions were peculiar, frequently involving suffering on the part of His people who could not understand why Yahweh, Who was so sovereignly powerful, could not use other means to carry out His plans. Jeremias, for one, complained against such peculiar approaches to reality. God therefore is not remote from Israel but governs every detail of life, His will being the supreme law of life which He insists the Israelite must live by. In fact, the meaningfulness of human life results only from adhesion to that moral will. There is no question in Israel that He is the Lord of universal history, that His power stretches from end to end, disposing of all things mightily and graciously. Consequently, to the Israelite there is no such thing as secular existence; every object, person, place or deed has a religious significance.

Israel's faith is plainly rooted in history, the plan of God, His revelation and Will, unfolding through the pattern of actual events. Having accepted the intervention of God in human affairs, the Israelites had so strong a sense of reality that they saw His creative power operative even in secondary causes, and were fully aware of His guiding and divine Providence.

In contrast to the cosmic pantheism of Babylon and Canaan and its deification of the forces of nature, Israel's God is the personal, transcendent Creator in Whom all reality "lives, moves and has its being." His activity, while permeating the world, remains distinct from it. "Yahweh is a living God" Who guides His chosen people by His Providence and miraculous intervention, binding Himself to historical events and through them manifesting His purpose. The Biblical revelation of God is the knowledge of the ways of the living God through His acts in the history of salvation. Thus He raised up leaders to declare His will, who, while remaining entirely dependent upon Him, would act as intermediaries between Him and His people. The only nation of the ancient world to have a genuine theocratic sense of history, Israel saw that the unity in all human experience was due to the Lord of history Who initiates, wills, and directs it all (Isa. 7:18, 8:7–10, 10:4ff.).

This conviction of the active work of God in redeeming and directing universal history is one of Israel's chief contributions to man's religious knowledge. In Biblical revelation God is made known through His manifestations; these are not the regular seasonal cycles or the motion of the stars, but Divine interventions in the history of salvation.[12] Since history has a goal and the Lord of history has called Israel to co-operate with Him in the realization of it, God reveals Himself through precise historical experiences, and these are the starting point of faith. Present also were prophets who interpreted the events in their relation to the living God and the Covenant. Revelation presupposes a divine intervention in the spirit of certain men chosen by God to reveal His divine will. In the case of the prophets, God gave them signs which led Israel to consider the revelation of God as authentic.

Israel's history as God's people goes back to the Exodus and it is a history which, inspiring and directing faith, becomes a dialogue with God. For all its events revealed God to man as the saving and redeeming Lord.

THE EXODUS

When Israel was a child, I came to love him, And from Egypt I called him (Osee 11:1).

The primary notion of Israel's history is God's self-revelation, and His greatest revelatory act, the focal point in Israelite history and faith, was the Exodus (Ex. 67). This is the luminous center toward which successive generations would always turn. The Exodus is the classic, pri-mordial, archetypal deed of Yahweh: His rescue of an impoverished people from the great powers of this world and His leading them to salvation.

Israel, an oppressed minority in Egypt, was miraculously delivered, led through the wilderness and given a land in which to dwell. As a result, Israel came to think of God as the One Who, having control of the forces of nature, liberated her from bondage, as a sign of power and a manifestation of Himself.[13] Before this historical event, Israel did not really "know" her God. With the Exodus, His action in the redemption of His people was seen, and it was at this moment too that God revealed His inner essence as that of saving power and purpose. For one of His main purposes was to make Himself known to men.

A close relationship between God and Israel was established in the Exodus event. In the Book of Exodus we read the whole mystery of the creation of the people of God, their liberation, their training and their purification. The deliverance from Egypt, seen as the fulfillment of God's promises to the Patriarchs, is especially clear in Genesis and Exodus, wherein the framework is precisely that of promise and fulfillment. Yahweh calls Abraham, makes the election promise to him, and repeats the promise to each of the

Patriarchs. The Exodus and the conquest then follow as a witness to Yahweh's faithfulness to His word.

Israel was to keep alive her sacred traditions in the temple liturgy. Having permeated the religious history of Israel, the Exodus transformed her liturgy into a commemoration of the escape from Egypt, recalling her supernatural birth and her creation as the people of God. In renewing the deed of the Exodus, the prophets made it a permanent act of God, so that it became each year the supreme moment when Israel renews her communion with its God.[14] This trust in the protection and nearness of God is at the center of her most personal piety.[15]

Israelite faith looked also to a future salvation and a still greater manifestation of Yahweh's glory and redeeming love. In the second part of Isaiah there is evidence pointing to the future in terms of the past.

ELECTION

For you are a people consecrated to the Lord your God, the Lord your God having chosen you out of all the peoples that are on the face of the earth to be a people of his very own (Deut. 7:6).

The explanation of the Exodus was the doctrine of the chosen people. How else could Israel explain the deed except by the idea of election? The Old Testament, however, does not teach that Israel was chosen because she was better than other nations, but because, in a miracle of Divine grace and in spite of her weakness and worthlessness, God willed to lavish His love upon her. It was through His love that Israel came into existence.

It was not because you were the greatest of all peoples that the Lord set his heart on you and chose you (for you were the smallest of all peoples), but it was because the Lord loved you, and would keep the oath that he swore to your fathers, that the Lord brought you out by a strong hand, and rescued you from a state of slavery, from the power of Pharaoh, king of Egypt (Deut. 7:7–8).

Yahweh did not impose His choice but out of His grace He offered it. The primary motive for that choice was love, unconditioned by anything in Israel that was good, wholly unmerited. There was nothing about the Israelites that entitled them to God's special claim; they are described as a stiff-necked race, little inclined to virtue (Deut. 9:4–6).

Having demanded that the people respond, Yahweh summoned them to a task within the divine purpose. Israel freely accepted the Covenant, solemnly placing herself under obligation to obey the Ruler and the Law which He gave as the constitution of society.

God's action in history is primarily to use the historic people of Israel for His end—

And they kept calling to one another, and saying, "Holy, holy, holy, is the Lord of hosts; The whole earth is full of his glory" (Isa. 6:3).

The Old Testament reveals the story of how God educated men to render them capable of receiving the divine gifts destined for them. Before the Incarnation and the working out of the mystery of the salvation of the Nations, the Word of God began by preparing His way in history. That Israel was chosen to be the covenanted people, and through them all men, is evidence of divine love permeating history.

Thus between God and His people there exists a relation of tenderest love, providential care and exclusive proprietorship: they are God's possession, a holy people. Here the word "holy" has a negative and a positive aspect. Negatively, it implies separation from all other peoples, and since holiness demands purity all alien elements must be removed from the Covenant community. The positive aspect is one of admission or introduction into communion with God. Having been separated for a special service, "You shall be to me a kingdom of priests, a holy nation" (Ex. 19:6); vocation to this worship of the true God is the main idea in the priestly character of the covenant people.

In His love, God demanded of His people that they would belong wholly to Him and would have no other gods as was set forth in the decalogue (Ex. 20:1ff). No matter that other nations might worship gods who personified their desires. Israel's personal God was the powerful, holy One on Whom depended the whole course of history.

To Israel God continually made Himself known in concrete affairs and relationships, thus revealing the divine dimension of meaning. Since election was for service, it was not election to a privilege but election to responsibility, the basis for which is not obedience to a code of law but an inward personal response to Yahweh's deeds of love and kindness. Having manifested His love through His just works, God demanded of Israel that she imitate His manner of dealing with the weak and oppressed, reminding her that her people had once been slaves in Egypt.

Israel's election was not merely to reflect the will of God and so to delight His heart; she was chosen for service to the world and therefore has a mission to the nations. Because of her intimate share in the Lord's strength and purity, to see this people as a mediator among the nations is to learn something about the true God. Jeremias and Isaias, with their forward view, look for a new covenant in which all people will worship the one true god, Yahweh, according to the way He wills to be worshipped.

THE COVENANT

I will set my dwelling in your midst, and will not hold you in contempt, but will move among you . . . (Lev. 26,11).

The doctrine of election found its most concrete expression in the Old Testament language of Covenant. The entire Old Testament was an attempt to acquire a loving understanding of the themes fundamental to the religion of God's people. Yahweh, the transcendent and personal God, had brought His chosen people into the intimacy of His Presence; the Covenant introduced the creature into a living relation with the Holy One and the Creator for the purpose of man's salvation.

The meaning of Covenant is that God binds Himself to a people and that the people are therefore bound to Him. Thus Israel is the Covenanted community, a relationship between God and Israel founded upon history. Although the Israelite enjoyed a consciousness of salvation and an assurance of being in Covenant relationship with the living God, the sovereign will of God is the ultimate basis of the Covenant. It is He Who bestows this grace on Israel, summoning her into His holy presence. Throughout the Old Testament it is implied that Israel's Covenant is an unconditioned one, God having chosen Israel because He willed to choose her.

For you are a people consecrated to the Lord your God, the Lord your God having chosen you out of all the peoples that are on the face of the earth to be a people of his very own (Deut. 7:6).

The characteristics of the Covenant are that it is a free gift, God having willed to separate this people unto Himself and give them a special task, that Israel is now established in a supernatural communion with God, and that obedience must be rendered to the terms of the Covenant. Israel will receive the beneficent goods of God and His providential protection provided that she lives up to the terms. But if she fails to live up to them, God will punish her. Yet the prophets, and especially Isaias, with his notion of the remnant, insist that despite Israel's infidelity, God will exercise His *chesed,* His fidelity towards her. With God, fidelity is nothing less than the very life of divine love. It was because God insisted on maintaining His part of the Covenant, even when Israel had failed to keep hers, that there was any continuance of it, and any hope even for a remnant. Israel's continued existence has always depended upon God doing more than was required. Here is where God's love is distinctive, showing itself in that determined persistence which is the characteristic significance of the word *chesed.* This continual increase of His love is precisely what makes His *chesed* so firm and steadfast. It is a love evinced in the Covenant-keeping character of God; by faithfully keeping the promises made in the Covenant bond, God manifests His love and kindness.

> Though the mountains should be removed,
> And the hills should waver,
> My kindness shall not depart from you,
> And my covenant of peace shall not waver,
> Says the Lord, who has pity upon you (Isa. 54:10).

This firmly established relationship of love implies solidarity, the involvement of man with God Himself. Such reciprocal fidelity is fundamental to all Old Testament religion. From his own personal experience, the Psalmist interprets the history of Israel: "The Lord is faithful in all His words and holy in all works" (Ps. 144:13).

> I will call for help by day, O Lord, my God;
> I cry before thee at night;
> Let my prayer come before thee;
> Incline thine ear unto my call.

> For I am surfeited with troubles,
> And my life verges on Sheol . . . (Ps. 88:1–3).

Fidelity, a feature of divine holiness, expressed God's loving, constant effort to enlighten and sanctify man, and to allow man to explore His mysterious depths.

The establishment of a Covenant can be traced to Creation itself, Genesis being its story (Ch. 1–11) and the beginning of the history of the chosen people (Ch. 12–50). The organization of the world and its creation is for the Covenant, in a plan of love. From the beginning all things are oriented towards man and particularly toward Israel, the future instrument of God's design for the universe.

This Covenant with mankind becomes a special Covenant with Abraham by which God makes the patriarch part of His plans, an event essential to the history of the world. God freely chose a people, and first of all a man, Abraham, in such a way as to enter into the closest and most familiar relations with him. The origins of the people and the origins of the Covenant are interwoven because the Hebrew people, on their own testimony, do not exist apart from it. The Covenant made with Abraham is one of promise and it looks forward to its fulfillment.

The Covenant with the Patriarchs is then elevated by solemn ceremonial into the Covenant of Sinai between God and His people. Considering the Scriptural passages dealing with the events of Sinai, we conclude that God had previously dealt with the Israelites by means of a Covenant. At the burning bush Yahweh identified Himself as "The God of thy father, the God of Abraham, the God of Isaac, and the God of Jacob" (Ex. 3:6). Having recognized that the One Who spoke to him from the burning bush was the One Who had made the promises to the Patriarchs, Moses has simply to tell the Israelites that the "God of your fathers" (Ex. 3:18) had sent him unto them. His role then was that of a mediator. The God of their fathers had made known His purpose, His demand and His promise.

Because it is at this point that God yields and makes the Israelite people His own, through Moses, His messenger, the Covenant of Sinai, with its Ten Commandments, is at the heart of the Old Testament. The Israelites, having been reminded of what God has done for them, are now chosen as His own and bound to Himself. In doing His will, something of His powerful presence in them would enable them to transform the world. The covenant as a mutual presence and communion of love is also a field of action. "If you hear my voice and keep My Covenant, I shall keep you for Myself...."

By means of gracious leading, unmerited love, and severe chastisement God accomplished His purpose through Israel. The election and the Covenant being linked together, loyalty to the Covenant required obedience to the Will of God. But there is also a place for individual Covenants, extensions and renewals of the prime Covenants of Abraham, Sinai, Exodus. Such, for example, is the Davidic Covenant of 2 Sam. 23:15, which incarnates the people again when God Covenants Himself to the Davidic dynasty. He is thus renewing His Covenant which He will build in the eschatological times through the agency of a descendant of David. The relationship with Yahweh and the messianic king of the future is also presented as a Covenant (Isa. 49:6). One of the great achievements of the Davidic era is this very conceiving of kingship in Israel as a Covenant between Yahweh and David. The Messiah to come would be a king of David's line in Whose Person the promises made to David would be fulfilled.

The Covenant relationship, binding the people together in brotherly solidarity, brought a sense of God's concern for each person. Yet in the Biblical view, man is created by God for community and stands in relationship to God and his fellowmen. When he lives in isolation from the community he suffers the greatest loneliness and misery. Even Jeremiah, who is often called the prophet of individualism, did not advocate an individualism apart from the Covenanted community. Men have access to God, to salvation, but only within the community.

It is interesting to note the variation of imagery used in the Old Testament to picture the relationship between God and His people. Thus the vine is frequently employed as a figure for Israel, it being regarded in ancient times as a symbol of vitality which is able to produce an immense number of shoots. Osee 10:1 employs the symbol when he refers to Israel's failure to bring forth fruit as a healthy vine ought to do. The vineyard is Israel, the hope of Yahweh, and from her should spring the fruit of obedience, love and utter devotion to the will of Yahweh.

The Covenant at Sinai seems to have been more clearly presented to the Hebrew mind under the figure of a Covenant of marriage than under any other form. Through all the troubles that broke the marriage bond between God and Israel, His love for her never changed. Although the Hebrew *chesed* includes the warmth of Israel's marriage love, and her first glad obedience to God's demands in respect of conduct, these are secondary to the main idea of faithfulness to the marriage bond. Israel may have rejected God, but He will lure her back to the wilderness and will speak to her heart again, for His steadfast love for Israel is a love which nothing, not all her waywardness and apostasy, can destroy.

Another expression for Israel's special relationship to God is the title of "son." God has called this peculiar people and adopted them as His son, for no other reason than that He loves this son (Deut. 4:37). As a consequence of the pact or Covenant made with the patriarchs and to be renewed with their descendants, Yahweh regarded Israel as His son: "Israel is my son, my first-born" (Ex. 4:22). This relationship was conceived to exist primarily not with the individual, but with the people as a whole.

Thus the Covenant constitutes the heart of God's self-revelation in the Old Testament. Each feature of salvation derives its value for Old Testament theology from the prominence of the Covenant between God and man as the basis for a continuing, redemptive relationship, and no other aspect of Israel's faith is as conspicuous as this. Within its scope may be found all that is relevant to her basic religious beliefs. It is clear that God's way of salvation is present in the Covenant itself, as it dramatically and historically reveals what God has done in creating man, in endowing him with His own image, in showing mercy when man repents of his evil and in faithfully rewarding the righteous by His gifts of material blessings and of His Spiritual Presence.

ISRAELITE THEMES CONCERNING GOD

"I the Lord your God am holy" (Lev. 19:2). The Hebrew word *qodesh,* or "holy," indicates all that is set apart, reserved for the worship of God. Sanctity implies the idea of separation and belongs properly only to God. In the Old Testament, "holiness" stands for the divine Being itself, ineffable in its transcendence and perfection. Isaias discovered this quality in the Triple Sanctus which comes to us from the heavenly liturgy (Isa. 6:1-5).

Divine holiness expresses the sovereign reality of God, for which no similar analogy in human life can provide a basis of comparison. God has revealed it to the Israelite as the sum of His nature and being and man's experience of it is expressed in these words: "No man can see God and live."

As a distinctive and fundamental attribute of God, holiness cannot be ascribed to anything created, "Who is like Thee among the gods O Lord? Who is there like thee, so glorious in holiness, so awe-inspiring in renown, such a wonder worker?" (Ex. 51:11). Moreover, God is recognized by His distinctive characteristic, His own sign and seal, manifesting His holiness in the midst of the theophanies and miracles.

> Incline thine ear, O Lord, answer me,
> For I am afflicted and needy.
> Preserve me, for I am a godly man;
> O thou, my God, deliver thy servant who trusts in thee . . .
>
> (Ps. 86:11–2).

Holiness receives its particular orientation from its relationship with the God of the Covenant. God has engaged Himself to be faithful to the people of His Covenant, and because it is a Covenant holiness, it is ordered to redemption. It is a holiness which God wishes to communicate to His faithful people and which manifests itself in all the acts of deliverance for Israel's sake.

Holiness also signifies God's great transcendence, His majesty, His fearsome and awesome difference from humanity. This is the awful otherness of God, which nonetheless makes possible the nearness of His redemption.

The Hebrew people tried to express the mystery of the divine holiness in their prayer of adoration, experiencing a reverential fear of God in the presence of this divine sanctity which separated God from creatures. Their consciousness of the transcendence of the divine holiness included awareness of the fact that all things consecrated to Him are set apart.

You may not serve the Lord and foreign gods as well; for being a holy God and a jealous God, he will not forgive your transgression nor your sins . . . (Jos. 24:19).

The thrice holy God desires to bestow upon His creaturs His unique sanctity. He said to His people: "I am the Lord that will sanctify you" (Lev. 20:8).

It is in God's dealings with Moses that the qualities of divine holiness are especially evident: for instance, in the scene on Mount Horeb, when the impact of God's transcendence and mercy is made known. The creature sees the mystery of God's holiness in His transcendence and mercy which persists in seeking the sanctification of His creatures. Moreover, God reveals Himself to the Patriarchs as one Who blesses and corrects; He is the bestower of all blessing, life and fruitfulness (Gen. 48:15–16) (49:24–26); under the guidance of Moses the people learn something of the holiness of God.

So a central communication in the Old Testament is the revelation of God's holiness, which combines all the divine perfections and allows man to become aware of it only to the extent that it is communicated to him. This intimate and profound communication exceeds our capacity for knowledge, and through it we learn that the divine holiness exists in apparently contradictory attributes: transcendence and mercy, justice and kindness, power and gentleness, distinction and unity.

The Holy God is a living God, a personal Being. The word "holy" is repeated throughout the Old Testament as an expression of the sovereign perfection of the God Who is infinite and changeless, the God of Israel Who loves (*agape*) and wishes to be loved in return.

TRANSCENDENT AND PERSONAL GOD

The transcendence of the God of the Bible is suggested in His revelation of Himself as the All-Powerful and the All-Loving. Human understanding cannot comprehend His unsearchable decrees and thoughts.

> A stupid man cannot know,
> A senseless cannot understand this . . . (Ps. 92:6).

> "For my thoughts are not your thoughts,
> Nor are your ways my ways," is the oracle of the Lord
> "But as the heavens are higher than the earth
> So are my ways higher than your ways,
> And my thoughts than your thoughts" . . . (Is. 55:8–9;
> Pss. 40:6; 71:19).

Though living, present and ever ready to intervene in the historical process, God remains always ineffable, unspeakable, undefinable, transcendent and incomprehensible. He is different, "wholly other," not in the sense of being distant, apart, inactive or without the breath of vitality, but in the sense of being unimaginably different, free and independent, infinitely above all creatures.

The God of Israel is different from the gods of her neighbors in His purpose and intentions. Man's desires are in conflict with the intentions of God, and the means He chooses to accomplish these are not the ways of His creatures nor can His ways be comprehended by the human mind. In fact, those who dare to approach too near to that which is sacred to the Divinity deserve the most severe punishments (Ex. 19:12). But gradually Israel's idea of God's unlimited power and universal control become more explicit (Isa. 45:5–13). Because He was the only God, therefore He was transcendent. Whereas each of the several deities of the polytheists possessed certain limited power, for Israel Yahweh alone is God and all power belongs to Him alone.

Yahweh sustains the natural order, yet intervenes as a climax of His power by a sign we call a miracle. This is not an infraction of the natural order but a concentration of the glory of God by which He shows that He is the Lord of Creation, nature and history. A miracle always points to the future time when the world will show forth its complete submission to God, reflecting Him from all sides and in every aspect.

The divine power has animated the forces of nature: "O mortal man, stand upon your feet, that I may speak with you" (Ezechiel 2:1).

The elements were transfigured and yet they remained but a weak analogy of the ineffable transcendence, "I will heap on the wood, and kindle the fire; I will cook the flesh and brew the broth, till the bones are burned" (Ezech. 24:10). Ezechiel emphasizes this transcendence in an attempt to translate his vision: "This was the vision of likeness of the glory of the Lord" (Ezech. 2:1).

The elements reflect the glory of God Who deigned to reveal His divinity, but the God revealed by these manifestations is necessarily a hidden God. "Verily thou art a hidden God" (Isa. 45:15).

A holy and transcendent God makes Himself near and present in order that man may penetrate His intimacy. Knowledge of the true God as personal implies a personal encounter which makes it possible to enter into communion with Him. An inward conversion is brought about through the revelation of the God of Abraham who "speaks," "governs" and "loves" His people, thus making it possible for man to be able to speak to Him and to love Him. The whole meaning of the history of Israel is the discovery of the personal God Whose will has a personal impact upon men. Thus the divine personality becomes the very basis of religion.

The Old Testament emphasizes the personal nature of God by revealing and communicating the personal will of God. It is the personal God Who speaks to the prophets and psalmists in the Old Testament, the personal Creator Who watches over His creatures (2 Sam. 14:11; Ps. 18:46), and delivers the people of His Covenant.

In the creation of Israel, the living God reveals Himself to a people formed by a common history. Giving them His Face and His Name, God wholly fashioned them into a living unity which developed slowly in the course of time. The Hebrews saw the reality of God in His Name and in the imageless worship paid Him, and their knowledge and worship of this one God, so real and pervasive, made them a people.

THE ONE TRUE GOD

> Know now that I, I am he,
> And that there is no god beside me;
> It is I who slay, and bring to life;
> When I have inflicted wounds, it is I who heal them,
> With none to give deliverance from my power (Deut. 32:39).

The idea of divinity held by Israel's contemporaries was that of a superhuman force which was to be kept favorable and to be used by man. The idea of Divinity in the Old Testament is a notion of one Supreme, Loving God Who had made Israel His people. The Hebrew belief in God was not, however, the philosophical idea of monotheism, since it was never looked at from a speculative point of view, but always from that of practical religious experience. Israel's dependence upon Yahweh for material blessing in the form of strength in battle, prosperity, and long life, led to the exclusive worship of the God Yahweh. But He was a jealous God Who would not have strange gods before Him and the First Commandment expressed this claim to exclusive worship, a unique feature in a Semitic world completely surrounded by the worship of various divinities.

Adam, Noe, Abraham and Moses were witnesses to the true God in the midst of various forms of idolatry. Adam, living in the brightness of the divine radiance, knew the reality of the living and true God, and even the Divine voice was familiar to him. "I heard the sound of thee in the garden," he replied, "and I was naked; so I hid myself" (Gen. 3:10). Noe, living at a time of universal corruption, was saved from destruction and offered worship to the true God. God spoke to him and protected him. "But Noe found grace before the Lord . . . He walked with God" (Gen. 6:8-9). The one true God was to be glorified in the posterity of Abraham who was to become the father of the Covenant. With Moses the chosen people received God's word on Sinai, that Israel was to preserve the divine inheritance and to defend it against the pagan nations. Israel's vocation was to safeguard the belief in the one true God.

With Moses we have definitely arrived at monotheism. Yahweh is a jealous God and the Israelites are forbidden to worship other gods (Num. 25:11). Such gods are "no gods"; they are "abominations" (Deut. 32:21; Jer. 10:15). During the Exile this thought gradually becomes more explicit, Yahweh insisting that He alone is God. The Israelites ridicule the strange gods because they are unable to do anything for their clients; they are inefficacious because they are dead. Implicit in the religion which Moses taught his people is the notion that there is only one God. This is not elaborated theoretically or speculatively, it is not even said explicitly. What is said to Israel is that Yahweh is living, the other gods are dead. Yahweh has no rival among them; He is superior to all the gods. Utterly and absolutely exclusive, He is unlike all others, beyond comparison. Therefore, there is no common note between Him and the other gods. Jeremiah hails the God of Israel:

> There is none like thee, O Lord!
> Thou are great, and thy name is great in might.
> Who would not reverence thee, O King of the nations?
> For this is thy due, and there is none like thee
> Among all the wise ones of the nations, and among all their royalties
> (10:6–7).

Second Isaias tells us explicitly that there is only one God:

> For thus says the Lord who created the heavens—
> He is the God Who formed the earth and made it—
> He established it—He did not create it a chaos,
> He formed it for a dwelling-place: I am the Lord,
> and there is no other (Isa. 45:18).

> Let them take counsel together, then let them show
> us, and bring forward proof of it!

> Who announced this of old, foretold it long ago?
> Was it not I the Lord—no other God than I—
> A righteous and saving God—none apart from me?
> Turn to me, and be saved, all ends of the earth!
> For I am God, and there is no other—by myself have I sworn
> (45:21-22).

In the condemnation of idols, God's jealousy appears as a continuation of the nuptial image of *chesed* between Yahweh and Israel which will not tolerate the unfaithfulness of His people. No creature is to receive the absolute homage of love which is due Him alone. God's jealousy here is a concrete sign of monotheism.

Yahweh, the great and mighty God, with all the power of His grace and fidelity, is the God of Israel, one and transcendent, living and personal, omnipotent and infinitely holy. It is God Himself Who speaks to man, mysteriously revealing Himself. In accepting the revelation made by the living God, each individual can repeat with all the Old Testament:

"O Lord, . . . Thou art my God!" (Ps. 15:1-2).

NOTES

1. J. Daniélou, *God and the Ways of Knowing,* New York, The World Publishing Company, 1957, p. 54.
2. J. L. McKenzie, S.J., *The Two-Edged Sword,* Milwaukee, Bruce, 1956, p. 198.
3. J. C. Murray, S.J., "On the Structure of the Problem of God," *Theological Studies,* XXIII, 1962, p. 4.
4. J. G. S. S. Thomson, *The Old Testament View of Revelation,* Michigan, Eerdmans, 1960, p. 10.
5. G. A. F. Knight, *A Christian Theology of the Old Testament,* London, SCM Press, 1959, p. 89.
6. Paul Marie of the Cross, O.C.D., *Spirituality of the Old Testament,* St. Louis, B. Herder, 1961, Vol. 1, pp. 15-16.
7. A. Davidson, *Theology of the Old Testament,* New York, Scribners, 1955, Vol. II, p. 198.
8. O. J. Baab, *The Theology of the Old Testament,* New York, Abingdon Press, 1949, pp. 26-27.

9. J. Giblet, et al., *The God of Israel, The God of Christians,* The Great Themes of Scripture, New York, Desclée, p. 235.

10. E. Jacob, *Theology of the Old Testament,* New York, Harper and Brothers, 1955, p. 51.

11. G. F. Wright, *God Who Acts,* London, SCM Press, 1952, pp. 21–22.

12. Dom C. Chartier, *The Christian Approach to the Bible,* Maryland, Newman, 1958, pp. 112–115.

13. C. Tresmontant, *Toward the Knowledge of God,* Baltimore, Helicon Press, 1961, pp. 77, 89.

14. J. Guillet, *Themes of the Bible,* Notre Dame, Indiana, Fides, 1954, pp. 2–3.

15. Giblet, *op. cit.,* p. 46.

10

The Way of the Heart to God

MARITAIN has said that there are as many ways of man to God as
there are paths on earth or avenues to the heart of man himself,
a remark confirmed both by the history of theology and that of the
apostolate.[1]

Pascal and Newman illustrate the apostolic concern to bring men
to God. Each in his own field was a genius, Pascal in science, Newman in literature. Each was also to a marked degree a religious
genius. While neither was a philosopher in the technical sense, both
contributed major philosophical insights to the problem of the
existence of God. Both were concerned with a knowledge of God
which would be not only an assent to fact but also a personal commitment to a Personal God. Theirs is the testimony of converging
witness.[2]

Products of different countries and centuries, deeply marked by
the conditions and intellectual climate of their times, these men
reacted in accordance with their convictions, and succeeded in ex-
erting an influence that continues today. Their approach to God,
commonly known as the way of the heart, manifests striking
similarities and striking differences.

Both stem from the Platonic-Augustinian tradition, an approach
to knowledge markedly different from the widespread Aristotelian–
Thomistic tradition in Catholic thought. For Augustine, knowledge
of truth is a means to an end: beatitude. Realizing his own insufficiency, man reaches out to an object both greater than himself and
capable of bringing happiness; knowledge of this object is a condi-

231

tion for its attainment. Augustine himself had been spurred on in his search for truth by a strongly-felt need. Having found it in the full sense, he knew peace and happiness and from then on equated the search for Christ and Christian wisdom with the attraction of that divine beauty, ever ancient, ever new, the Christ. The psychological process in which he analyzed his experiences has enriched our understanding of the soul's dynamisms, but Augustine was not interested in formulating a theory of knowledge for its own sake. Assuming that man could have certitude, he gave his attention to the question this assumption posed: "How then attain it?"[3] This was also to be the attitude of Pascal and of Newman, particularly the latter.

Perhaps because of the influence of Augustine on their theory of knowledge, neither Pascal nor Newman showed much interest in the Thomistic Five Ways of proving the existence of God. Both in fact depreciate the argument from design in the world when it is used in its most naive sense, and fail to see much value for their particular purpose in the approaches from causality. Concerned more with particular, concrete individuals, with ordinary men who, lacking philosophical training, are beset by difficulties in regard to the existence of God, they seek to lead them to accept it as a fact and to go beyond it to faith that affects one personally, that leads to inward conversion. Their purpose is to engender in man a personal encounter with God.

While neither thinks that the metaphysical proofs for the existence of God are of great value for this goal, their attitudes towards the proofs are radically different. Pascal sees the effort of reason to arrive at knowledge of God as a danger, the outcome of which is more likely to be idolatry, i.e. worship of the intellect, and he terms the effort blasphemy. Such an effort leads not to the true God, but to an idol. Newman's position is somewhat more balanced, for, assuming that the Five Ways are valid, he sees worth both in the efforts to prove and in the truth at which they arrive, but is not interested in the Ways themselves precisely because they do not make a personal approach to the man with difficulties. In his thought, acceptance of the existence of the Unmoved Mover is likely to leave the searcher unmoved, whereas what Newman seeks is an intellectual conviction re-enforced by affectivity: in other words, a real assent.[4]

In evaluating the effectiveness of the Five Ways for their particular purpose, the two men may well be correct for, while the Five Ways prove, they do not necessarily persuade. The proofs which Pascal and Newman offer for the existence of God are, in the Augustinian tradition, a knowledge which involves a vital commitment to this truth.

The attitudes and convictions of Pascal and Newman stem from their ideas of man. Both have a high sense of individual differences and characteristics and of their effect on the difficulties which each man experiences in his approach to God. Both are gifted with sympathetic understanding, an ability to enter into the problems of the individual, to understand the reasons for these problems, to see the difficulty—and perhaps, in some instances, the impossibility—of arriving at a solution. This insight is a key factor in their approach and in their success. Of all the philosophers and theologians of times past, they are best able to maintain dialogue with modern man. Neither Pascal nor Newman suspected the unconvinced individual of insincerity.

Both Pascal and Newman show a characteristic originality in taking the interior of man as the starting-point for their argument. The classic approach had been to use external nature as the beginning of one's argument, to prove God as the First Cause, or the Cosmic Orderer. But the God at which one arrived by these proofs seemed to these teachers the God of the philosophers, not the God man must meet in the historic world of sin and grace. They disliked the approach to God by way of the clear and distinct idea, an approach which insists that formal logic is always valid in proving His existence, and while granting that syllogistic or mathematical reasoning is valid in itself as a way to prove that existence, they believed that under certain circumstances its very inappropriateness either to reach the person or to produce the results would make it illogical.

Like all Augustinians, Pascal and Newman insist that there are different types of knowledge and that these types depend upon the object to be known and are regulated by it. These types of knowledge are not necessarily scaled from the highest to the lowest, for they are all valid, though different, and the difference depends on the object to be known. Since logic will not enable one man to know another, there must be a fitting of the approach to the precise object we seek to know.

To a degree Pascal and Newman look at man from the same point of view, as a complex, incomprehensible, thinking reed placed between two infinities, the abyss of nothingness and the abyss of greatness. In their concern to establish proofs by touching the human freedom of man and soliciting it, the living God of history, the God of the Bible, the "God of Abraham, Isaac and Jacob" as Pascal calls Him, is their end. A personal God, One Who exercises providence over the work of His hands, Who is good in His relationship to man and to the world, should be the conclusion of their proof. The problem of evil then becomes much more than a difficulty to be explained after it has been demonstrated that God is and must be infinitely good. It becomes a neuralgic pain to both Pascal and Newman, which is not only present to them from the very outset of their proof, but which even dictates to them the curves of that proof.

For the acceptance of a value, both intelligence and will must be prepared. Pascal and Newman emphasize that when we approach a value, such as God, truth, love, the human person, we must prepare and dispose our will as well as our intelligence if we are to know the object validly. The individual should labor to grasp the metaphysical principles involved in the problem of truth and to cultivate a veritable passion for truth, a personal commitment to it. Only in this way can he understand certain problems connected with truth or with any other value. The will is here performing the indirect but essential task of excluding prejudice, keeping the mind active in seeking truth, overcoming such moral obstacles as fear of the consequences of truth or the hesitancy induced by laziness, and, finally, urging the mind toward a love of the value in question, for there must be initial love, if a value is to be grasped intellectually.

Again, in the Augustinian tradition, Pascal and Newman are inclined to distrust any knowledge which fails to end in a real assent, to inspire action. They admit the usefulness of the rational, but the full knowledge they seek when dealing with a value must result in affectivity, the commitment of the heart. What they want is that the free center of liberty, the whole person, be committed to the object at stake.

Neither Newman nor Pascal indulge in the usual dichotomy of faith and reason so popular in sixteenth and seventeenth century rationalism, though both have been accused of depreciating reason. Newman had discussed the question when writing of the necessity of recognizing the limitations of reason as a manifestation of the will of God.[5] But this is not to devalue reason, and neither Pascal nor Newman ever did so, although some of their statements are open to such an interpretation. Their position is genuinely Catholic, namely, that unaided reason can arrive at the knowledge of certain religious truths (both accepted the Five Ways as valid proofs from reason), that this is difficult to achieve, as is evident from various false religions and philosophical aberrations, and that reason without the aid of faith cannot attain to the full knowledge needed to live the Christian life. As to the difficulty of the achievement, Pascal and Newman place the cause precisely where it belongs: in the wound which human nature received in the Fall, Newman accepting reason in the reality of this condition and its resultant effects, Pascal rather exaggerating both.

The approach of each man to the existence of God is in a sense a reasoned approach, the key to which lies in what Pascal understands by the word "heart" and what Newman understands by the term "illative sense."

Pascal's exact meaning is disputed. Some think that with Pascal

heart and intuition are synonymous; heart being the faculty "which
perceives both principles and order," which grasps and loves, in
which knowledge and feeling cooperate.[6] It is certainly not opposed
to the intellect, except in the sense of the intellect as discursive reasoning. Pascal himself says that we need both heart and reason to
know the truth, and since truth is the intellect's object, Pascal apparently considers "heart" and "reason" as modes of operation of
the intellect.[7]

Newman defines the illative sense as the mind's power of reasoning, judging and concluding, in its most perfect state, and explains
"sense" in this context as parallel to our use of the word in "common sense," a "sense of beauty," and so on. In addition, it is the
instrument by means of which convergent probabilities effect complete certitude, a process of argumentation in which we employ informal and natural inference. The former reaches conclusions by a
mental comprehension of the entire situation, a discernment of its
gist, and a resultant summing up of the whole; the latter governs
"the unconscious, implicit transition from one known thing to another." It is not precisely scientific reasoning; but when possessed
in a sufficiently high degree, it is genius.[8]

For Pascal and Newman, then, "heart" and the "illative sense"
do not prescind from reason but are a kind of intuitive reasoning
somewhat opposed to formal logic. Both, and perhaps Newman
especially, sought an intuitive awareness of God; not that of simple
knowledge without affectivity, but that higher knowledge of a
person, which, when conditioned by a free decision, leads to trust
in God and therefore acceptance of Him and of all that He reveals.[9]

Such an approach to a proof of the existence of God was a break
with traditional patterns and one which showed a higher sense of
existential reality than that manifested by many nurtured in
scholastic modes of thought.

Blaise Pascal, a layman of seventeenth century France, learned
his religion in the first instance from his father, whose curious
dictum that what is an object of faith cannot be an object of reason

should be understood as putting faith above reason rather than as denying reason any part in faith.[10] Pascal himself seems to have arrived at the conclusion that, although reason cannot produce faith, faith is reasonable. Deeply religious as he matured, and experiencing two "conversions," he was influenced by Jansenism to an extent impossible to determine. The milieu in which he lived was intellectual; his friends, classed as libertines, were trained thinkers more interested in problems of mathematics, science and theology than would be common today. Theology, in fact, was widely discussed in all the salons of Paris at the time, with a keenness of interest that, as Newman said later of the efforts of unaided reason, could flare up in the fierce flame of passion, and the "all-dissolving" scepticism of the intellect.[11] Although the libertines went by the name of Catholic, they neither accepted the authority of the Church nor practiced the faith. Highly interested in Pascal's work, many of them were also attracted by Jansenism, and concerned for the reform of the Church which the Jansenists were urging.

Pascal became embroiled in the theological disputes of which the Jansenists were the focus, through being urged by the Port Royalists to come to their assistance, particularly in the question of grace. He began with what may have been reluctance, but having once tasted the elation of battle, threw himself into the writing of the Provincial Letters. Eighteen in number, written in the literary style that has caused Pascal to be read through the centuries, they brought the theological controversies alive and caught the popular fancy. He was not a theologian, and apparently realizing that he was going beyond his depth in the Letters, he shifted his point of attack from the order of dogmatic theology to that of moral theology. Although he won a victory at the time, the verdict has since gone to the system he attacked.

Since the one great aim of his life came to be the conversion of his libertine friends, Pascal conceived the idea of writing an Apology in which he would present Christianity in ways calculated to win their assent and to lead them to conviction.

It is not easy to interpret Pascal's argumentation, for the projected Apology was never finished. His *Pensées,* or little thoughts, on various aspects of the Apology were written on separate slips of paper in no particular order and with unfortunate results. In writing the *Pensées,* Pascal experimented with various literary forms including dialogue, in which the sceptics he addresses express their scepticism. These remarks have been interpreted as indicating that he himself was a sceptic. Yet a careful reading of the *Pensées* does not bear this out.

Pascal is without doubt a great religious genius. He is also an enigma. But is he a Catholic? The question remains open. A number of authorities hold that he is a Catholic, and that, although possibly tainted with Jansenism during part of his life, he was not sufficiently versed in the subtle distinctions of theology to be aware of it. This would seem to be borne out by his insistence, in certain theological disputes, that it was a question of fact, not of faith; that if the Holy Father were fully informed the decision would be different. It is also true that on his deathbed he asked for and received the last Rites of the Church. Since he was under suspicion of Jansenism, the priest, the Abbé Beurrier, asked the necessary questions and received the answers that entitled Pascal to receive these Rites, a fact that the Abbé himself made known, although he later wavered in his statement. But his memoirs, published in 1908, finally settled the question in favor of Pascal. There is perhaps confirmatory evidence in Pascal's statement in the *Pensées,* that if the Roman Pontiff was to declare all his works wrong he would submit without the slightest hesitation, that he wished to think only according to the mind of the Church. Although, like the Abbé Beurrier, Pascal sometimes reverses himself, his last words on the matter, as recorded in the memoirs, are those of submission to the Vicar of Christ, the Sovereign Pontiff.[12] For the rest, Pascal remains a mysterious character of perennial interest. Although his philosophy and theology can not be put into ordered systems, since he neither did this himself nor left the means that would enable others to do it, it is possible to see and examine his point of view.

Pascal attacks both the Cartesian and the current Scholastic proofs of the existence of God. They were not very dissimilar, for in Pascal's day Scholasticism in the seminaries was strongly influenced by Cartesianism. Consequently, in attacking Scholasticism Pascal attacked a Cartesian variety, with its heavy emphasis on clarity and distinctness as a norm of truth, as well as a certain dualism between body and soul and between the soul and the world.

Pascal strongly attacks the argument from design in the universe, maintaining, as do many modern critics, that it does not prove, but merely confirms a previously established proof of, the existence of a wise intelligence, which has established this order but whose relationship to man might be completely impersonal and who, therefore, could not be God.

Pascal makes little use of the proof from causality for the same reason: although establishing the existence of an Uncaused Cause, it will not arrive at the living God of Revelation. Certainly no personal relationship will be established if the search goes no further and, since the possible outcome is an obstacle, it does not seem probable that it would come to such a state. But he uses to some extent another Platonic approach, that of divine ideas, the idea of the immutable truth in God, holding that from the existence of immutable essences which impose themselves upon our mind we should be able to argue to their one Immutable, Eternal Source. For example, if a man who had never encountered the idea of justice in the real order of his human experience were in a dream to meet the ideal order, to encounter a situation in which he would see "justice" shining before him, on awakening he would realize that justice was and had to be; that it had an inner consistency which imposed itself upon his mind once it had been grasped; that it had to exist in the real order also. The same would be equally true of any of the Divine ideas or eternal verities. Even though encountered only in an ideal existence, these truths would impose themselves with necessity and consistency upon the human mind, forcing it to recognize that they exist. If there is truth, there must be an absolute truth, and an absolute, wholly consistent source and support for truth; if there is love, there must be an absolute love.

And yet, although inclining toward this proof, Pascal does not develop it to any extent, perhaps because of his dislike of Descartes who was preoccupied with the eternal verities.

Pascal's objection to the metaphysical arguments is that they are useless from the point of view of apologetics since they are alien to the normal modern man's way of thinking and therefore unacceptable to him. Again, even if they are accepted they lose their force the moment the demonstration has been finished. So complex, so metaphysical, so far removed from human concern are they that any assent to them must of necessity be fleeting. Unable to serve as a force in human life, that is, unable to produce conviction, they fluctuate in value and are inoperative. Consequently, Pascal is led to examine the human condition, to show man his greatness and his smallness, and to make it clear that without God he too is incomprehensible. This is his introduction to his proof for the existence of God.

Man's nature, says Pascal, reflects both greatness and misery. His misery rises out of the deep inconstancy of his nature, for, while he has within himself the desire to attain to lofty goals, he finds himself incapable of fulfilling his aspirations. Continually, he is forced back upon himself to realize the inconstancy of his will. Wanting to be great, he finds himself petty in his pursuits. Longing to be sincere, he finds himself to be deceitful, seeking honor even where he would abase himself. Even in writings against vanity, writers still seek their own glory. Regarding truth as praiseworthy, to be highly esteemed, to be possessed, man has many times embraced falsehood, his escape from reality. Though recognizing it as worthy of a man to act with courage according to convictions in spite of ridicule and difficulties, human nature, in the face of this situation, resorts to the cowardly device of pleasing man.[13] Man seeks happiness and finds himself miserable; experiences dependence in regard to everything and yet cries out for independence. The cravings within him are never really satisfied; to achieve one ambition is to beget another. This constant striving keeps him in a state of anxiety and restlessness, and restlessness makes him seek diversion; even if he found the rest he yearns for, it would not last, for he would be continually thinking of the difficulties already experienced or apprehensive about future misfortunes. Ever in a state of unrest he is hemmed in on all sides by the forces of his own being.[14]

His knowledge too is limited. He seeks to know more than he can understand and, since he is a composite of a material body and a spiritual soul, the problem is even more complex. Unable to understand his body, much less his mind, how can he be expected to comprehend the unity of both? Truly, he is a mystery even to himself.[15]

Man has the gift of reason, yet often reasons falsely, swayed in his judgments by feeling or passion, by false appearances, by custom. Instead of deciding and acting as he knows he should, he permits custom to make the choice. He permits his imagination to substitute its fantasies for the reality of things, and his efforts to gain knowledge are confronted by conflicts from without and from within. Reason and the senses deceive each other in turn, the senses misleading reason by having things appear other than they are, reason having her revenge by applying the same "trickery" to the senses.[16]

Even in the proper sphere of its activity reason has its limitations. Certain truths are beyond the scope of human comprehension, man coming to know them only through "intuitive insight"; they are felt rather than understood.

Yet man, in spite of his misery and weakness, is also great, for he can think. The fact that he can know his misery indicates his greatness, marking him off from the rest of creation. Even if the universe were to destroy him, it would only prove his greatness, for man would be conscious of being destroyed. The fact that he recognizes his weaknesses, and suffers from them, is an indication of the truth that he was created in a higher nature from which he has fallen.

Such is Pascal's view of man: supreme greatness and utter misery, neither godlike nor brutal but something between the two, not infinite, but finite, although not everything, still not nothing. Man is a mystery that cannot be solved by scepticism or rational dogmatism, for while the one may explain his greatness and the other his misery, neither can explain both. The philosophers cannot solve the enigma of man's greatness and wretchedness, for while one makes him God's equal, another would liken him to the brute. The sceptics release man from pride and vanity only to plunge him into sloth, despair, or sensual appetites which are the heritage of the brute. The rationalists avoid this extreme, but only to lead him into pride.

How is man to escape from his dual nature, of which reason cannot render an account? How is one to explain this man of complexities and contradictions, manifested through the conflict of his cognitive faculties? For Pascal the only explanation is to be found in Christianity, for in Jesus Christ one finds both the greatness of God and the misery of man. Only in Christianity are the inner conflicts of man given an understandable order and man invited to the society of the redeemed.

Hence the need arises for man to hear God, once he has become aware of his weakness and greatness. Reason must be humbled and nature must be silenced, that man can learn from God the nature of His true condition. Since this is a call to religious conversion, man must respond with a personal commitment, based on principles that are known intuitively, not founded on reason but disclosed by the heart—"God felt by the heart." For those to whom God has granted such a knowledge, the truths of religion are believed and accepted with conviction; but for those who do not have it, one can only prepare the way by reasoning. Reason, in the narrow sense of argument, can lead the unbeliever toward the kingdom of heaven, and can help man recognize his desperate need for God. But only God gives insight into the truths that clarify man's meaning.[17]

The expression "felt by the heart" does not imply feeling alone, but an act of the intelligence and will—both moved by the action of God's grace. With the intellect grasping the truth and the will being drawn to accept it, the movement is made, not through deductive principles but through intuitive ones.

While reason cannot give perfect assurance of God's existence, it can help, if aided by history, tradition and religion, to gain immediate experience of God.

Pascal attributed to man three ways of knowing, namely, through the heart, the senses and reason. The heart is capable of intuitive knowledge, which Pascal considered the highest order of knowledge, but to attain it the heart must be regenerated by grace. The senses, concerned with the physical world of observation and science, have authority in those spheres. Discursive reason is, in a sense, the least of the cognitive faculties, for its function is to aid the other two, to help the senses know the material world and the heart to understand the order of charity. Although responsible for interpreting and classifying the data of the other two faculties, it is not entirely sufficient in itself.

For while reason cannot convincingly demonstrate the existence of God and the other dogmas of religion, it can show that the mind should submit to these proofs. Human reason can lead one to *approach* God but it cannot lead one to *understand* Him Who is beyond our powers of comprehending and conceiving.

The inability of reason to achieve truth is owing to the impeding "parasitic powers"—imagination, memory, sickness, custom, self-interest and that escapism which hinders the intellect from functioning impartially. Among these, the chief offender is the capricious imagination which misrepresents rather than lies.

Reason of itself can never lead one to a persuasive and full knowledge of God, for such knowledge is supra-rational, above the sphere of human reasoning. Since the sphere of God is the supernatural, He can best be known through direct revelation, through faith, and to be known He must first manifest Himself to man.

Pascal disliked the metaphysical proofs of God, for they do not lead one to the personal knowledge that will prompt an act of faith. Once the fact that God exists has been established, then we may use the metaphysical proofs to confirm it. It is this God, personal and loving, that Pascal is concerned with and not the "cold God of the philosophers."

Nevertheless, the metaphysical might well be accepted by the *believer,* as a reasonable foundation for his faith. Already enlightened by the gift of faith, the believer has no difficulty in seeing that the work of creation is attributable to none other than his Creator. But these proofs are not really necessary for the believer, nor convincing to the unbeliever. In fact, to a cold, scientific mind they are inconclusive. To inform the searcher after truth that he has only to regard the things around him to see God displayed is to convince him that the proofs of our religion are weak. To the unbeliever seeking the light of faith, these proofs bring only obscurity and darkness. It is the heart that makes one say "credo" and not "scio." God is experienced by the heart and faith is to Pascal "God felt," not by the reason but by the heart. Reason may lead the unbeliever to the threshold of faith but it cannot induce him to cross it.

In order to see the validity of the metaphysical proofs, the "heart," that is the intimate depths of one's being, must be infused with good dispositions. But these can only be given by God, since they refer to the point at which God's grace penetrates human nature. Grace is therefore a precious necessity if the human reason is to be capable of understanding the evidence for the truth of religion.

Humanly speaking, one must know a thing in order to love it, but in matters divine, one must love them to know them; one enters into truth only by way of charity.

Pascal's idea of man obviously belongs in an atmosphere of a Calvinist theology which depreciates nature and its capacities. Human nature has been wounded by original sin and man's nature, that which makes a man what a man is, has been altered and changed in its intrinsic constitution as a consequence. Not only has it suffered the loss of all its preternatural and supernatural gifts but it has been intrinsically diminished, darkened, almost corrupted.

With that Calvinistic framework for his thought, it is natural for Pascal to distrust the intellect, as it is easy to see why he thinks that philosophic knowledge of the existence of God by the Five Ways is always an obstacle to man's faith. For such knowledge generates pride in intellectual achievement and terminates in a God Who is a stranger to the God of Revelation. Pascal is afraid that the end product will be deism, admission of God's existence without personal commitment to Him, without belief in a particular providence over the individual man or warm, loving, concern for his soul. The fact that this type of deism is associated with affective morality does not diminish Pascal's strong aversion to it. To him, it is almost as bad as atheism.

Newman, on the contrary, sees validity in the metaphysical proofs but regards them as incomplete. In this Newman and not Pascal is in accord with St. Paul who said that we can arrive at some knowledge of God from visible creation and that man is to be condemned if he does not act upon this knowledge (Rom. 1:19-20). Moreover, Pascal's distrust of the intellect differed both in kind and in degree from that of Newman, for the two men are products of different theologies, Pascal's being tinged with Calvinism and Newman's being wholly Catholic.

Both Newman and Pascal believe that there is in man and in the world an irrationality, a principle of destruction, a cleavage between what should be and what is. Fully aware that all men are sinners not only because of personal failings but also because of a "mysterious solidarity in evil" which we know as original sin and its consequences, both Pascal and Newman concluded that it is only within the order of redemption, grace and revelation that man is fully intelligible to himself. For Pascal, to really know God as a Savior we must know Him in relationship to the breach which we see in ourselves: the double law in our members—the law of life and the law of concupiscence, the law seeking virtue and the law seeking death. To know God man must know sin.

But since the God man seeks is a Hidden God, both Pascal and Newman insist on the limits of human knowledge, and repeat

Augustine's statement that when man thinks he comprehends God, he does not, for God is incomprehensible. God is not so hidden, however, as to make atheism the normal conclusion. Although hidden in such a way that He cannot be easily arrived at by rationalistic expositions of facile philosophical argumentation, He is not so hidden that man terminates his search in agnosticism or fideism. God has left traces of Himself in His world that man may "grope after Him and find Him for He is not far from any one of us" (Acts 17:27).

Pascal's approach to the existence of God, then, is to look upon the mystery that is man and to see its solution in the admission of the existence of a personal God involved with man, a redeeming God Whose grace inclines our intelligence to truth and our will to the freedom of the children of God.

Because he was exaggerated in his idea of man as a creature in whom both nature and intelligence have been corrupted, Pascal's search for proof for the existence of God results in false alternatives: utter scepticism, practical atheism (which he sees as proof of the existence of a God but not of the saving God of history), or faith in the Christ of history. The Catholic position is that man can have valid but incomplete knowledge of God, perfectly correct in its realm but calling for completion by faith.

Pascal also falsifies genuine difficulties in proving the existence of God, for he insists on placing them all within a moral and religious perspective. But not all such difficulties are moral or religious; there are genuine philosophic difficulties to proving the existence of God, even though the proofs are valid in themselves. A further flaw in Pascal's approach is that in spite of his rejection of causality as a proof of the existence of God, his Wager Argument is in a sense based on causality since it begins with the assumption: I exist because I am a caused being.

Pascal's argumentation is characterized by an appeal to the heart, an informal inferential sense which engages will, affectivity and intelligence.

In the effort to establish this relationship Pascal seeks to make his friends receptive to argument for the existence of God by showing them man's greatness and smallness and his utter incomprehensibility without the saving God. He then offers the religious proof, the history of God's interventions in the world, the miraculous interventions for Israel, the theologian's proof from history and from the moral sancitity of Christ. Finally, he advances a rational proof on the basis of the wager. The situation being what it is, he suggests to the free-thinkers that it would be to their advantage to wager that God exists and then to proceed to act as though He did exist. There is little to lose; if they win the gains are infinite.

In Pascal's view there are three kinds of persons—those who having found God serve Him; those who are occupied with seeking Him; and those who live without seeking Him. The first group he considers "reasonable and happy" because they are already enjoying the advantage of faith. The third group is "foolish and unhappy." Although filled with uncertainty they will not inquire into the doubts which confront them, preferring to remain uncertain until death or the destiny that awaits them.[18]

For Pascal, such an attitude induces anger more than pity. The fact of death itself which threatens us all at every moment will place one in the absolute necessity of being forever either annihilated or unhappy. Reflection on this should lead one to the conclusion that there is no good in the present life except in the hope of another. But to refuse to concern one's self with this important question is to act in a manner that cannot be conceived as reasonable.

The second group Pascal considers "reasonable and unhappy." They are reasonable because they are seeking their ultimate end, and unhappy because they have not yet been able to attain the faith they desire. For them he has only compassion since they spare no pains in making this inquiry their principal and most serious occupation. It is to this class of people that Pascal addresses himself in the form of a wager.[19]

Pascal begins by stating that man is capable of knowing the finite with regard both to existence and nature, since man is himself finite and has extension. He is also capable of having knowledge of the infinite with regard to its existence, but not with regard to its nature, since the infinite has extension like man but is without any limits. Being finite, man cannot comprehend what God is, because His nature is beyond the scope of man's understanding.

Pascal goes on to argue that, if according to natural light there is a God, He is infinitely incomprehensible, having neither parts nor limits and consequently being without affinity to man. Since man is incapable of experiencing God, he cannot know either what He is or if He is. Yet who will undertake to decide the question?

Christians admit that they can offer no necessitating proofs and that Christianity is full of obscurities. But this very lack of proofs shows the consistency of what they are saying.

Still the one who is confronting this situation finds it difficult to accept the fact that those who believe in Christianity do so without necessitating proofs.

Now with regard to the question of whether God exists or not, there are equal odds for and against the Christian religion. Religion is unable to offer, in such a manner as to constrain all minds, a necessitating proof that God exists; but neither is it possible to discover a proof which will convince all minds that God does *not* exist. In view of these facts must one give up all further investigation? Not at all; since one who is in life must of necessity make a choice, one must "bet" for or against the existence of God. If reason is to make a choice, it must be made in the form of a wager. What does one's own interest suggest? One has two things which one is capable of losing, the true and the good; there are two things in the balance, reason and will, knowledge and happiness; and nature has two things to avoid, error and misery. Now reason is not shocked by choosing one rather than another, since of necessity it must take a choice. Therefore, one point is settled. But what about one's happiness? Here it is necessary to weigh well the gain and the loss involved.

If one wagers for God—and God is—the gain is infinite, heavenly goods infinite in duration and extent; if God is not—there is no loss; one has simply lost finite earthy goods. Since there is a chance of gaining the infinite and losing the finite, the possible gain is infinitely superior to the possible loss. For in the presence of the infinite, the finite is mere nothingness. Consequently, it is reasonable to "bet" on God's existence.

But if one wagers that God is not—and God is—he has infinite loss; if God is not, he has neither loss or gain. Yet in this position his risk of loss is greater—for he stands a chance of losing everything in the event that God is and he has wagered against Him. In the first case where he wagers for God, the loss involved is not as great, since he risks only the finite to gain the infinite, whereas here he risks all to gain nothing. In such a position, one would be wise to make the wager, which insures his winning all or at worst losing nothing, that is to say, to "bet" on God's existence.

Even in the face of this argument the free-thinker may still hold out, saying "for all that, I cannot succeed in believing." Pascal does not then suggest further proofs but the abating of one's passions, since it is they which prevent one from seeing one's own true interest. The free thinker should "stupefy himself," that is to say, he should live as though he believed. By acting as though he did believe, by making the gestures of belief, he will come to believe.

To act in such a manner is to lose nothing, for such a man will gain in this life by virtuous living and will eventually arrive at faith.

It is certainly true that Pascal's reasoning can convince without persuading to action, for it is necessary to pass from the "idea of God to God." Reason prepares the way for the disposition to accept, but for the actual ascent to God in a personal commitment of oneself, grace is necessary. Yet the argument of the wager could help much to prepare a sincere seeker to receive the gift of faith when it is offered.[20]

In stating the argument of the wager, Pascal knew for certain out of his own experience that there was valid ground for it. If a man of good will manifests in practice the deeds and gestures which ordinarily proceed from religious experience, there is offered a channel through which he may receive grace, a bridge which will link intellectual assent and the actual experience of God, and thus supply a continuity otherwise missing. Pascal was ever conscious of divine grace and it became clear to him that, if sincerity is present, such elementary moral conduct as is here in question might provide God with the opportunity of election.

Pascal defends as reasonable the action of a man who, though uncertain, acts as though he believed, for many things in the natural order are uncertain, and if a man were to act only on certainty he would do nothing. Consequently, to act on the principle of chance, as demonstrated in the wager, is to act in a reasonable way.

Even chance dictates that man should put himself out to search for truth, since the fact that he will not remain forever in this present life should lead him to speculate upon the possibility of another. And he cannot be indifferent since he is already in life. Even in the case of a doubt about the existence of God, it is safer to act as though there is a God, for if there is and a man dies without seeking Him, he is certainly lost. To the objection of those who contend that if God wanted man to worship Him He would have left signs for man to recognize it, Pascal affirms that God has done so, but that man must seek them sincerely.

The argument of the wager was not intended by Pascal to give one faith, but to dispose the unbeliever to be willing to accept the faith. For faith is a gift of God and only God can bestow it. Yet reason can aid man in his search for God and a reasonable argument may well prepare the heart for the reception of faith. Revealing to man what the senses do not tell, faith is not contrary to what he sees, but is above all sense-knowledge.

The accusation of blasphemy has been brought against Pascal by some outraged at his daring to speak of man's ultimate concern in terms of a wager. But this is a superficial charge. Pascal is by no means blasphemous or irreverent; he is trying to induce the sceptic to "leap" from unbelief to belief. For this reason he wishes to clarify the conditions under which a man might approach, not knowledge of God, but faith in Him. He is convinced of the pre-eminence of faith over knowledge, for through faith there results man's personal commitment to God based upon God's self-revelation. It might even be said that there is a Scriptural precedent for the argument since Christ himself had asked, "For what does it profit a man, if he gain the whole world but suffer the loss of his own soul?" (Matt. 16:26), using the terms of a commercial transaction as the basis of a religious proposition.

Nor was the wager argument new, having been used by apologists since the early days of Christianity to prove the immortality of the soul and even by apologists contemporaneous with Pascal. In the history of apologetics, we find Silhon using the argument to prove the existence of God, but only as a preliminary to proving the immortality of the soul. Raymond de Sebonde, one of Pascal's predecessors, used it to prove the existence of God but confined it to the moral plane. The statement is made that Pascal is the only one who "dared apply" the wager argument directly to the existence of God. Certainly he is the only one who used mathematics in his approach, transposing it to the plane of the spiritual. Perhaps it would be better to say that Pascal is the only one who had sufficient originality to use the wager argument with this emphasis and in this particular way.

As to the objection that it is a brutalization of human freedom to suggest that man should live in accord with what he does not believe, one should remember that Pascal is merely utilizing the psychological principle that in man, being a composite of body and soul, not only does the soul act upon the body but the body also acts upon the soul. When, in the *Pensées* Pascal speaks of "proofs by the machine" he is not suggesting that the free thinker should abandon reason and act like a brute: he has in mind the interaction of body and soul and the fact that such efforts will help the individual to understand the physical basis for his reluctance to commit himself, and to work for concurrence, not opposition, through development of a new set of bodily habits and feelings.[21]

In the last analysis, the libertines themselves are the reason why Pascal used the wager argument, for, fascinated as they were with mathematical mensurations, they had asked Pascal to employ his mathematical genius to discover the calculus of probabilities. Completely devoted to chance, they had the spirit of daring that goes with this attitude. So Pascal was on solid ground from the psychological point of view. The mathematics of probability, he told them, are in their favor.

Pascal wishes to shake, even to shock, the free-thinker out of his neutrality, his casual agnosticism, his assumption that it is all a peripheral problem of no great concern to him. That might be true, Pascal says, if you were not in this life. But you are in it, adds Pascal, implicitly appealing to faith in his argument that life without God is anguish, nonsense, absurdity. Although the sceptic may reply that, such being the case, he will live it as best he can, Pascal shows the absurdity of this agnostic approach. Since you are already in life it is to your advantage to find out if there is not some meaning to your existence. Without God you are incomprehensible, for only grace and original sin explain the mystery of man.

Like Pascal, Newman was concerned with the practical life. His own search for the truth, his friendship with others in the same situation, his correspondence over the years with sincere people unable to assent to the existence of God, and who suffered accordingly, gave him ample experience. His keen sensitivity, his remarkable gift of insight and understanding, his unfailing personal interest, all prepared him to enter into their problems and to work toward a solution.

Newman's life is a graphic illustration of God's providence over the individual and over the work He intends him to do. Like Pascal, Newman experienced two conversions. The first occurred when, as a boy of sixteen, he turned from a merely moral life to a life that was both moral and religious. Through this conversion he received a strong impression of the immutability of dogmatic truth and became wholly aware of something he had sensed only dimly before—conscience, to which he gave full assent by complete submission. These two elements of his initial conversion stand out all his life.[22]

Przywara, the German Philosopher, associates St. Augustine and St. Thomas with Newman as typical representatives of their respective epochs—the ancient, the medieval, and the modern. Newman is indeed modern, and unlike many of his contemporaries, he has become more significant in our time than in his own, for his mind had accepted positions not yet reached in his era. Bouyer writes that "nothing in Newman seems more remarkable than the reality, or as we should say nowadays, the deeply 'existential' character of his spirituality. No unreal 'words' but the fact of God entering in our most personal history not as a motion but as the most real and commanding of all beings."[23] In Newman we see an anxious man of integrity dealing with the perennial problems that vex humanity: above all others, the relationship of the finite being to a Personal God.

It must be remembered that Newman was above all an apologist writing primarily for English non-Catholics. The deistic spirit of his day which considered God aloof from the intimate life and interests of men impelled him to turn for conclusive proofs of God's existence to the moral rather than to the intellectual side of man. Seriously doubting the effectiveness of the scientific apologetics of his day in the individual believer's approach to God, he declared: "Logic makes but a sorry rhetoric with the multitudes. . . . Tell men to gain notions of a Creator from His works, and if they were to set about it (which nobody does) they would be jaded and wearied by the labyrinth they are tracing. . . . After all man is *not* a reasoning animal; he is a seeing, feeling, contemplating, acting animal."[24] At Oxford, Newman had seen individuals arrive at opposite conclusions from the same external evidence; he had seen men convinced on very little evidence, while others remained sceptical after full proof. He found an explanation for this in the existence of some hidden evidence, of some previous considerations influencing the mind and either depriving the positive proofs of their force or supplying their defects. In his search for this hidden evidence, Newman looks to his own inner experiences and consciousness and reaches the following conclusion, "Were it not for this voice speaking so clearly in my conscience and my heart, I should be an atheist, or a pantheist, or a polytheist when I looked into the world."[25]

He does not provide us with the popular scientific proofs of God's existence in the *Grammar of Assent* because his intent is to give only such a proof as influences himself. The book is the autobiography of his mind to a great extent, and in it he uses the argument from conscience because it alone appeals to his practical sense.

Newman distinguishes two modes in the act of conscience. The moral sense is an original judgment connatural with the human mind which distinguishes right from wrong and which is evidently natural to human beings since it exists in all classes of men from the moment of reason. The second mode, the sense of duty, is a magisterial dictate to do or to avoid a particular act, whose commands are as clear as an internal voice, so real and personal that they lead man spontaneously to refer them to a Being outside himself, the Supreme Judge. Thus the sense of duty is the creative principle of religion, as the moral sense is the creative principle of ethics.[26]

Just as the inner voice leads to the knowledge that God exists, so its quality leads to the knowledge of His attributes. The God Who so insistently demands truth, purity, justice, kindness, must Himself possess these attributes in their highest degree. But if all that He demands is good, then He must be the all-Good. To obey one's conscience at all times helps to form a clearer image of God together with a clearer awareness of His voice. However much it may suggest about God, its most prominent teaching is that He is our Judge: The one who is angry with us and threatens us.

In the chapters of the *Grammar of Assent* which deal with natural and revealed religions, Newman enumerates the truths attainable by human nature without the aid of supernatural revelation but through the teaching of conscience. The chief doctrines are: the existence and attributes of God; man's dependence on

Him; his responsibility to Him; his prospect of future reward or punishment; his need of reconciliation with God by expiation; the utility of a priesthood to effect this; the use of rites of atonement; the notion of a possible revelation from God; an expectation of it as probable.

When God at length gives the long looked-for sign, a man on the alert needs little evidence; certainly miracles are not necessary. That a revelation conveying a message of reconciliation with God and free from positive error claims to be divine suffices for most men. The decisive reason for accepting it as divine is, according to Newman, not so much the external evidence, as the harmony between chief doctrines of the new message and the inner, intimate teachings of conscience. "It was this instinctive apprehension as we may conjecture which carried on Dionyius and Demaris at Athens to a belief in Christianity though St. Paul did no miracle there, and only asserted the doctrines of the Divine Unity, the Resurrection, and the universal Judgment."[27]

Such in general is Newman's description of the moral state of a good man, which moral state is, without the special intervention of God, an indispensable condition of saving faith. His general term for this moral character is love, by which he does not mean the theological virtue of charity which must follow faith, but rather that initial, spontaneous going out to the supreme good, that longing and yearning for happiness, for God, which exists in all men. Whatever way towards God that the intellect may indicate, the moral sense may approve as good, and the sense of duty may urge to be followed—that way will such a will eagerly embrace.[28]

The principal external evidences which Newman finds in favor of the divinity of Christianity are not miracles strictly so-called, but a cumulation of converging probabilities which by inference lead to certitude. In point of fact, the *Grammar of Assent* is a defence of that moral certitude, arising from a convergence of many probabilities, on which our belief in everyday facts depends and on which our proof of the claims of Christianity is based. The illative sense, the sense which discerns the unity and meaning in an apparently disordered mass of detail or evidence and grasps the point of an argument, or a moral problem, or a religiou issue, is the faculty by which we know when these probabilities converge and are sufficient to allow us to be certain.[29]

This process generates a genuine certitude and not merely a probability. Although Newman calls it moral certitude, he does not mean by it the moral certitude defined by the scholastics as a high degree of probability, but a type of certitude one is expected to have in this situation. While it is as convincing as mathematical certitude for mathematics or logical certitude for logic, it is not demonstrable.

Everyone spontaneously embraces the doctrine of the existence of God as a first principle and a necessary assumption. It is not so much proved to him as borne in upon his mind irresistibly as a truth which it does not occur to him, nor is it possible for him, to doubt, so various and so abundant is the witness for it contained in the experience and the conscience of everyone. He cannot unravel the process or put his finger upon the independent arguments which conspire together to create in him the certainty he feels, but certain of it he is and he has neither the temptation nor the wish to doubt it, and he could, should the need arise, at least point to the books and the persons from whom he could obtain the various formal proofs on which the Being of God rests and irrefutable demonstration thence resulting against the free thinker and the sceptic. At the same time he certainly would find that unbelievers had the advantage of him so far as this—that there were a number of objections to the doctrine which he could not satisfy; questions which he could not solve; mysteries which he could neither conceive or explain; he would perceive that the body of Truth itself might be more perfect and complete than it is. He would not indeed find anything to invalidate that proof, but many things which might embarrass him in discussion, or afford a plausible, though not a real excuse for doubting it.[30]

It was statements such as these that caused Walgrave to say that Newman never worked out his proof for the existence of God. "He has left an outline of such a proof but its achievement did not come easily to him. He testifies that he had not succeeded in stating a proof that satisfied his reason."[31]

Newman himself points out the advantage of this form of proof. It is at once true and peculiarly fitted to contemporary needs. It is within the reach of the learned and simple, pagans and Christians, and all men from infancy bear in their inmost experiences its essential elements. A thing of real consequence, closely bound up with actual life, it is no purely theoretical conclusion of abstract reason, but it goes to the very source of religious life and doctrine. Finally, it arrives at an authoritative Personality Who imposes obligations on a man, Who appeals for a response from the full center of personal liberty.

In itself such an argument is weak "insofar as it implies a confusion of thought—existence and extramental-existence, and has idealistic implications." However, in evaluating it several points must be kept in mind: Newman is less concerned with proving God's existence than with explaining how one can gain an image of Him which in turn can elicit a real assent to the proposition that He exists.[32]

Can I attain to any more vivid assent to the Being of God than that which is given merely to notions of the intellect? Can I enter with a personal knowledge into the circle of Truths which make up that great thought? . . . Can I believe as if I saw? At first sight it would seem as if the answer were in the negative, for how can I assent as if I saw, unless I have seen? But no one in this life has seen God. Yet I conceive a real assent is possible and I proceed to show how.[33]

Newman does not overlook the fact that the very nature of conscience is subjective. In *Difficulties of Anglicans* he writes: "But the sense of right and wrong which is the first element in religion is so delicate, so fitful, so easily puzzled, obscured, perverted, so subtle in its argumentative methods, so impressible by education, so biased by pride and passion, so unsteady in its course that in the struggle for existence amid the various exercises and triumphs of the human intellect this sense is at once the highest of all teachers, yet the least luminous." Yet, this subjectivity may be perfected through correct objective values. "Our conscience too may be said to strike the hours and will strike them wrongly unless it is duly regulated for the performance of the proper functions."[34]

To what extent this initial knowledge comes from without or within, how much is natural and how much implies supernatural aid cannot be determined. What Newman wants to show is that men can gain an image of God above mere notions. Whether the elements of this knowledge, latent in the mind, could ever be elicited without extensive help is doubtful. Yet it is certain that it can become brighter or darker depending on each one's individuality and circumstances. Transgression, neglect of duty, succumbing to temptation, lead to a gradual loss of the sentiment of fear and shame which are the witnesses of the Unseen Judge, and thus reduce the apprehension of God to that of a mere notion. On the other hand, if this image is cherished it will expand and a real commitment to the Personal God will be made.

In Newman's mind, England of the nineteenth century presented a twofold danger to faith: secularism, for theology was being crowded out of the schools as irrelevant to the purpose of education, and the growing liberalism of the divines that was breaking down the barrier to rationalism. This liberalism was not so much a direct attack on religion as the proposition that theology was hypothetical and inconclusive. Newman traced it back to seventeenth-century deism and saw far better than his contemporaries the bitter fruit that would come of it: loss of religious truth, and false worship as men filled the vacuum by making a religion of business, or came to worship the race, the nation, class.

As a priest Newman was particularly concerned with the practical import of proof for the existence of God in terms of concrete, personal assent, not merely that assent of the faculty of abstraction which of its nature is only notional, but the real assent which means personal commitment of the whole man to the truth accepted. The age of Newman favored the argument from order in the universe and outstanding Anglican divines based their entire proof for the existence of God upon it, propounding it with mathematical clarity, in their belief that only such an argument was demonstrative and cogent. Newman, however, was unique among the nineteenth century divines in perceiving the growing tendency toward an ambivalent interpretation of nature. He believed that in view of the scientific studies of evolution then current, of which Darwin was a foremost exponent, and of scientific investigations as well, the scientist was in the position to find the universe a completely consistent system without God, or to find God from the order in the universe. Still, if he found God in this order it would be by virtue of philosophic principles extrinsic to his scientific investigations of order and design; if he denied the existence of God he denied it on the basis of philosophic presuppositions extrinsic to his perceptions in the scientific order. In other words, Newman had a highly modern approach to the value of science, of evolution, and of the proof from order, and drew from this, and from his knowledge of man as he is, the conclusion that, while mathematical proofs are valid when we wish to arrive at a conclusion which is a principle, they are valueless when we want to reach as the term of our conclusion an existent, a person, or a fact such as the existence of God.

His approach to the value of logic and his understanding of personal difficulties was far in advance of that of his contemporaries. Denying that any demonstration can force the assent of the mind, even though it be valid and perceived as such, he asserted that there is always a hiatus between the conclusion and the moment when we see that this conclusion has reference to us, when we see that it is, in fact, not only of concern to us, but clearly for us. This hiatus, he argued, cannot be closed by mathematical considerations; a person must be led to accept the conclusion. It is false therefore to say on the one hand that legitimate assent can only be given to mathematical, logical propositions, and it is also false to say that mathematical logic can force an assent, although it is true to say that it may force a conclusion. In point of fact, assent can never be forced, since it always involves a commitment by a person which of its very nature is a free act. Newman was clearly in opposition to the trend of his century in maintaining that there is no coercive proof for the existence of God, as witness many of his friends, men of sincere good will who yet lived their lives in harrowing uncertainty.

Newman agrees with Pascal that personal insight is always required for conviction and that, for the truth to become operative through commitment, the individual must see in it a value for himself. His accord with Pascal here is on three points: speculative assent to the existence of God is valueless—although here a difference appears: Pascal thinks that such proof may be harmful, Newman holds that it is valid but incomplete, supplementing it with his proof from conscience. He agrees with Pascal that God is hidden, is incomprehensible (a statement made centuries ago by Justin and drawn from Isaias 45:15) but he does not depress the value of human reason as much as did Pascal. Further, he agrees with Pascal that there is a real drift of natural reason to atheism for he saw his own age rife with it.

Newman maintains that the three most self-evident and luminous truths in the world are one's own existence, through which the existence of God appears, which in turn makes clear that of the external world. In considering his own existence he observes the phenomenon of conscience, from which he concludes that since it is evident that he is not binding himself in moral matters, he must be bound by Another, and this Other must be authoritative, personal, supreme.

The argument from conscience arrives, not at a Cosmic Orderer or an impersonal God, but at an authoritative living God Who personally imposes obligations and command upon me, One to Whom, therefore, I must respond from the center of my personal liberty. Newman believes that the argument from conscience is in a certain sense presupposed in the argument from causality, since the latter ordinarily proceeds by virtue of accepting the realism that the external world exists, has reality, is not a projection of one's mind, an illusion. But the only way to establish the existence of the outside world is from conscience. He argues as follows: conscience establishes the fact that it is bound by Another, therefore God exists. But if the outside external world were merely an illusion God would be deceiving us. Given the nature of God this is impossible. This somewhat circuitious way of arriving at the existence of the world leads Newman to conclude that the argument from conscience lies at the very basis of the argument from causality.

Objections have been made to Newman's argument from conscience on the score that it arrives only at a probable conclusion; Newman himself is said to have admitted this. The difficulty here seems to be semantic, for Newman does not say that the arguments from conscience will force assent any more than other arguments, but that even those who are not convinced by it have had presented to them a line of thought on which to reflect and through which they may obtain conviction.

For those who accept the argument, a genuine certitude results, as strict in its order as mathematical certitude for mathematics, or logical certitude for logic. But it is a different type of certitude, one better suited to the matter under investigation. For Newman, the "probable" is a technical term indicating opposition to abstract demonstration. Now his purpose in the matter under consideration is to end, not with a principle in physics, mathematics, or philosophy, but with an existent, concrete person, which since it is not abstract he calls probable. Further, the argument from conscience is based upon experience and is therefore an inductive argument drawn from it. Finally, it is concerned with one, concrete, individual existent fact, and again, for this reason he calls it probable. Yet Newman, although a master of words, acknowledges that even for him, as convinced of the existence of God as he is of his own existence, to attempt to explain his reasons is to discover that words are poor vehicles for what his mind holds and his heart believes.[35]

According to Newman, the argument from conscience leads to a conviction and to a conclusion. The conclusion is acceptance of the fact that there is no logical flaw in the premises, major and minor, and that they are therefore true. The conclusion is: God exists. But the argument also leads to an assent, by which Newman means a conviction firm enough to withstand opposing arguments and difficulties. We remember his dictum: A thousand difficulties do not make a doubt.

Newman's assent is both notional and real, notional in the sense that it accepts the argument as valid, intellectually firm, logical and capable of being proven; real in that it engages the whole person in a commitment to the truth and to its consequences in one's personal moral life. This real assent has been called the key to his entire grammar of faith and knowledge. Newman himself called it the absolute, unconditional acceptance of a proposition, and certainly it is of prime importance if the assent is to be unconditional, concrete, a stimulus to action. But assent does not stop at the notional and the real; it must include simple and reflex assent, the former because it should have the power, spontaneity, and personal quality of a pre-philosophical immediate assent to an obvious truth; the latter because it should lend itself to being explored, discussed, reconsidered, drawn out in a reflexive manner. So Newman is looking for an assent to the existence of God which is natural, real, simple and reflex.

But the argument for the existence of God is not the first step in winning assent. Newman insists that no one should ever assent unless he has been prepared to do so. His understanding of the difficulties involved is partly owing to his own experience and partly to the fact that he looked at the individual as a person shaped by a particular environment, whose philosophic and cultural background must be taken into consideration, and who must be trained to *see* certain facts and to accept certain principles which he may already be holding implicitly.

Newman touches on this when he says that the syllogism as such will never compel assent in those who see its validity, and that not all who consider it are able to see that validity. Yet the assent is not conditioned on the argument being seen. Nor is acceptance of the validity of the argument sufficient, for no argument has value or is effective unless the individual seizes it, makes a synthesis of it, and contributes something of himself in the process.

The fourth point of Newman's approach to God is basic: when discussing with a person anything that touches moral or religious problems there are four factors to be considered. The first is the cultural. Our thinking is sociological, tending to accept the principles and the images which our culture gives us even when we are unconscious of them. Consequently, if we wish to win a person to acceptance of a new truth and new values, we must take this element into consideration. Here is a first principle in all missionary endeavor whether to an individual, a nation, a race. The second factor, Newman reminds us, is that of the problem of semantics. We must understand the language of the person we seek to convince, just as he must understand the language we use in conversing with him. Thirdly, we must remember that any value commitment always demands a personal synthesis of the argument and a personal grasp of its probative value. Fourthly, an instructor must be aware of the climate of opinion in which the person moves. It is not at all necessary that an inquirer should be asked to abandon this climate in order to accept the truths presented, if he can accept them as well within it.

After the person has drawn the conclusion that the argument is valid, Newman distinguishes four possible attitudes to take: remain completely passive and uninterested; acknowledge that the argument is true but claim that one cannot see where it has any personal relationship to oneself; admit the conclusion and give no assent, refusing to seize it personally; or, give assent but with the qualification that the proof is too complicated, that one cannot see and answer objections against it. This need not be an irrational procedure. The person concerned has considered the proof but in the end he withholds assent, not precisely because of the proof itself but because of some other element connected with it of which he is perhaps not fully conscious. In other words, an informal inference has been joined to the formal inference.

The validity of these inferences is passed on by the illative sense which is personal in each individual and which each uses in his own way to judge the truth of the concrete. Newman calls it the power of judging and concluding, when the mind exercises this power in its perfection, and is convinced that independent probabilities can lead to a certain proof when they all point to the same conclusion.

Newman has a marvelous sense of the way in which God reveals and at the same time conceals Himself. God never reveals Himself with startling, unambiguous behavior; He allows traces of Himself to be seen, but the signs are always equivocal, able to be read in two directions. His presence in the world is something like the miracles Christ performed before the Pharisees who saw them but were not convinced. A person must have a certain attitude of mind beforehand to prepare and dispose him to be able to see that a miracle exists. The same thing is true of finding God's presence in the world. It is there, but to find it a person must first have a susceptibility to religious truth; then a willingness to believe if sufficient grounds are given to show that it is reasonable and credible to do so; and finally a moral preparation of humility and openness to truth, allowing one's self to be dictated to by being, instead of having one's self dictate how being should be. God is concealed and revealed in the cosmic order and in human history, sufficiently hidden always to allow man to turn away from Him and to opt for atheism; sufficiently revealed to allow one who searches for Him in humility and truth to find Him. Pascal gives us a clue here in his statement that to know divine things one must first love them.

Newman sought for the Lord of the human heart and wanted those he influenced to see that the universe is truly sacramental, not in the sense that everything is an immediate image and symbol of God as the nineteenth-century divines thought, but in the sense that it veils God and unveils Him at the same time. For always God remains the Hidden God.

Both Pascal and Newman have a value for the modern world. They are able to continue the dialogue with today's atheists and free-thinkers because of their preoccupation with the personal, concrete conditions of assent and their preference for existential reasoning rather than metaphysical argumentation. Pascal is more pessimistic than Newman, believing that a conclusion that is sterile is invalid, and that human reason needs to be chastened and humiliated. Newman holds neither of these views but maintains that reason should see its own limits and accept them as the will of God. He does not believe that grace destroys nature or abrogates its ability to reach God, whereas Pascal seems to want man to give up philosophic knowledge and to leap into the great world of faith.

NOTES

1. J. Maritain, *Approaches to God,* New York, Harper & Brothers, 1954, p. xv.
2. J. Collins, *God in Modern Philosophy,* Chicago, Regnery, 1959, p. 325.
3. F. Copleston, *A History of Philosophy,* Vol. II. Westminster, Newman, 1950, p. 50.
4. Collins, *op. cit.,* p. 330.
5. C. F. Harrold, *John Henry Newman,* An Expository and Critical Study of His Mind, Thought and Art, London, Longmans Green & Co., 1945, pp. 156–157.
6. J. Chevalier, *Pascal,* Paris, Plon, 1922, pp. 270, 272.
7. Hubert, Sister Marie Louise, *Pascal's Unfinished Apology,* A Study of His Plan, New Haven, Yale University Press, 1952, p. 135.
8. Harrold, *op. cit.,* pp. 152–155.
9. G. McCool, "The Primacy of Intuition," *Thought,* XXXVII, 144, p. 57.
10. Hubert, *op. cit.,* p. 56.
11. H. MacDougall, *The Acton-Newman Relations,* Cambridge, November, 1959, p. 170.
12. E. Mortimer, *Blaise Pascal,* The Life and Works of a Realist, New York, Harper & Brothers, 1959, pp. 178–179.
13. J. Howie, "Pascal's Doctrine of Man," *Philosophical Forum,* XVII, 1959–1960. p. 65.
14. J. Mesnard, *Pascal: His Life and Works,* New York, Philosophical Library, 1952, p. 151.
15. F. Mauriac, *Pascal,* New York, Longmans Green and Co., 1940, p. 78.
16. J. Howie, *art, cit.,* p. 63.
17. F. T. H. Fletcher, *Pascal and Mystical Tradition,* New York, Philosophical Library, 1954, p. 82.

18. C. W. Eliot (ed.) *Blaise Pascal,* New York, P. F. Collier & Son Co., 1910, p. 94.
19. W. Clark, *Pascal and the Port Royalists,* New York, Scribners, 1902, p. 195.
20. E. Cailliet, *Pascal, The Emergence of Genius,* New York, Harper and Brothers, 1961, p. 331.
21. Collins, *op. cit.,* p. 338.
22. J. H. Walgrave, *Newman the Theologian,* The Nature of Belief and Doctrine as Exemplified in His Life and Works, New York, Sheed and Ward, 1960, pp. 29–30.
23. L. Bouyer, "Newman's Influence in France," *The Dublin Review,* vols. 214–217, Oct. 1945, pp. 140–158.
24. John Henry Newman, *The Gammar of Assent,* Image Books, New York, Doubleday, 1958, p. 90.
25. John Henry Newman, *Apologia Pro Vita Sua,* Image Books, New York, Doubleday, 1956, p. 319.
26. Brother J. F. Kaiser, F.S.C., *The Concept of Conscience According to John Henry Newman,* Washington, Catholic University of America Press, 1958, p. 90.
27. Grammar of Assent, *ed. cit.,* p. 329.
28. S. P. Juergens, S.H., *Newman on the Psychology of Faith in the Individual,* New York, Macmillan, 1928, p. 174.
29. M. C. D'Arcy, S.J., *The Nature of Belief,* St. Louis, B. Herder, 1948, p. 101.
30. E. Przywara, S.J., (ed.) *A Newman Synthesis,* New York, Sheed and Ward, 1945, p. 2.
31. J. H. Walgrave, *op. cit.,* p. 358.
32. Kaiser, *op. cit.,* p. 97.
33. *Grammar of Assent,* p. 96.
34. *Grammar of Assent,* p. 106.
35. A. J. Boekraad, *The Argument from Conscience to the Existence of God, according to J. II. Newman,* Louvain, Nauwelaerts, 1961, pp. 70–75.

11

New Approaches
to God's Existence

"Abyssus abyssum invocat," cried the psalmist, pondering on his soul's quest for the God Who made him. From the moment of reason, man seems plunged in total darkness when faced with the impenetrable abyss of Light to which his gaze inevitably directs itself. God is distant, incomprehensible, and yet man, although he cannot comprehend Him, can know that He is, and know it with an unshakable certitude. The fact is that men do know Him, and therefore this knowledge is possible and actual, not only among the learned but also among uneducated people. How do they attain this knowledge of God, especially if they do not seem to have the gift of faith? What is the source of their awareness of God among those who have never had a rational demonstration of His existence? How is it that some reflect a knowledge of God, of the absolute, without apparently adverting to Him directly?

Several new approaches to the existence of God will be discussed in this chapter in the hope that they may suggest answers to these questions. The approaches themselves are called "pre-philosophic," that is, they are ways of knowing God's existence through a process of thought which does not involve explicit philosophical reasoning.

One might question the validity of proceeding without the use of explicit philosophic reason since it seems so alien to traditional notions of knowledge and proof. Yet we are aware of the apparent inadequacy of the classic proofs for the existence of God, for convincing others that God is. So many objections are raised against the philosophical demonstrations of this fundamental truth that perhaps a pre-philosophic approach may be more successful. Again, a living knowledge of God, certainly more desirable than a purely speculative knowledge, may perhaps be more easily arrived at through these pre-philosophic approaches to God's existence.[1]

That God exists can be known by man with certainty through the use of his reasoning powers. The Vatican Council, in defense of man's natural ability to attain this truth with certainty, defined that God can be known by reason from the things that have been made.

> The same holy Mother Church holds and teaches that God . . . can be known with certainty by the natural light of human reason from the things that He created. . . .[2]

The Council did not say that this truth could be demonstrated, nor that any particular proof was valid or to be preferred to others. It did say that such knowledge could be arrived at and that such knowledge is certain. Since several points in the definition were controverted, the Oath Against Modernism clarified them by stating that the existence of God can be demonstrated, a clarification aimed at those who maintained that God could be known by internal experience only. The way of causality is also clearly stated in this second document (". . . as a cause from its effects").[3]

The problem, or perhaps the mystery, arises when we begin to speculate about the "how" of knowledge concerning God, for, when we do, we experience a sense of uneasiness, realizing that God is beyond comprehension and that He is never the direct object of our senses which are the starting point of all knowledge. In stating that God can be known by reason, both the First Vatican Council and the Oath Against Modernism refer to St. Paul's Epistle to the Romans, where Paul chides them for not knowing what they should have known concerning God—not only that He exists, but also His invisible attributes (Rom. 1, 18–21). Paul meant that the pagans should have had a knowledge of God which was unique and personal, involving conscience and the obligation to prayer and adoration. His point is that man can know God's existence and that those who do not honor Him are inexcusable. God would be unjust if He did not make it possible for man to know Him. It seems too that Paul suggests that this knowledge is arrived at by a proof from causality.

St. Paul also points out still another way in which the pagans knew God: through conscience (Rom. 2, 12-15)—for they kept the precepts of the natural law, which they knew without any revelation, and one of these precepts is concerned with the worship of God.

The early Fathers of the Church repeated St. Paul's arguments about this natural knowledge of God, St. Ireneus, Clement of Alexandria, Tertullian, Origen, St. Jerome, St. Basil and St. John Chrysostom all mentioning it in their writings.[4] St. Athanasius in *Oratio Contra Gentes* indicates that it is certainly possible to draw the knowledge of God from visible things.[5] Jerome, commenting on Psalm 95, states that the whole human race naturally knows God, and that there are no people (*gentes*) who do not naturally know Him.[6] It might very well be that this "natural" knowledge is actually the pre-philosophic knowledge of God with which we are concerned in this chapter. St. Augustine, in his commentary on the Gospel of St. John (Tr. 106), also notes that God is *naturally* known to all men as the author of the world.[7]

How do most people arrive at this knowledge without having followed an explicit rational demonstration of a proof for God's existence? Do they, in a simple, implicit fashion undergo a process of thought that is actually a proof from causality? Such a way would be a pre-philosophic or natural approach to God's existence and would seem to be what St. Thomas had in mind when he wrote: "To know that God exists in a general and confused way is implanted in us by nature inasmuch as God is man's beatitude."[8]

Maritain in his *Approaches to God* describes several of these pre-philosophical or natural approaches to God's existence. The word "approach" is used deliberately since these ways are not proofs in the strict sense. A proof is a demonstration of a truth and is ordinarily expressed in syllogisms. Syllogisms in turn have the substructure of concepts, and are the caused sequence of knowledge which is based upon the caused sequence of being. The foundation of proof being reality which exists outside the mind but is known by the mind, proof consists in perceiving, in the reality of the created world which we can see, the grounds for asserting that there is another reality, an absolute existent. Proof, then, reproduces in knowledge what is so in existence. This particular type of proof is called *a posteriori,* since it proceeds to discern a truth *after* knowing existing things. In an *a priori* demonstration on the other hand, one would argue from what is prior absolutely.[9] St. Anselm's proof is just such an attempt. The Five Ways of St. Thomas, however, are *a posteriori* proofs elaborated in abstract, conceptual terms. To many, these proofs are quite convincing; yet to others, they are not. Many people, besides, have never followed nor imagined such elaborate proofs for the existence of God and yet have firm certitude about that truth. How do they arrive at it?

THE PRIMORDIAL, NATURAL APPROACH

It is possible that many come to be convinced of the existence of God simply and directly, at the same moment that they become aware of the very fact of existence.[10] At some time they become aware of the existence of things around them—objects, others, the world. These things exist, each with its own act of existing, and yet they have nothing at all to do with our own existence. Existing outside ourselves, they are and were and will continue to be without our help. Our own individual existence is very real too, but it is apparently a more fragile type of existence than that of the sky, the mountains or the sea, for it is a threatened existence; there was a time when we did not exist and there will be a moment of death. This reality of death can be a sharp goad pressing us on to think further . . . to the point where we realize that there must be, somewhere, somehow, a type of existence that is not threatened, but is absolute, not marred by the possibility of fading. This trend of thought follows a simple pattern: a person grasping the reality of God in this existential way is not a metaphysician; his conclusion might be: here I *am*, living. What explanation is there for my being here? There must be someone Who is, which is the reason why the things which I see *are*, and is the reason why I am, and that is God.

This is the fundamental way, according to Maritain, by which most men who are not philosophers come to affirm the existence of God. Realizing that he is a being-with-nothingness, one who exists but need not have existed, since there was a time when he did not exist; realizing too that the world of which he is a part, and upon which he depends, is also being-with-nothingness, a man concludes that the universe itself cannot be the explanation for his existence. The mind grasps then that there must be a Being-without-nothingness, the explanation of all existing things. According to Maritain, this process of thought is almost an instantaneous progression, a natural way of arriving at the truth that God exists.[11] Moreover it is precisely this existential grasp of the Absolute Being of God that is at the root of the Thomistic proofs, and the Five Ways of St. Thomas rest upon it. If we are to be successful in convincing others of God's existence, through any of those Five Ways, this pre-philosophical knowledge of God is a prerequisite. Not that the Thomistic proofs for the existence of God are to be discarded—the mind needs such proofs as well; but the mind could not work out these elaborate, highly conceptualized proofs unless it had previously encountered God in some obscure fashion.

Romano Guardini may be describing this primordial approach when he speaks of knowledge of God through realization of His Presence. This is the most precious mode of awareness of God: the simple knowledge that He is present. But it is a presence not easy to talk about because there is really nothing to be said about it. "The all-important thing is that He is present and that He is He."[12]

If "nothing really could be said about it," how is it that we can elaborate such a lengthy analysis in terms of concepts? The answer is that existence is affirmed before any abstract idea of it is formed by the mind. Existence is *apprehended* first, even before the mind abstracts any notion of the essence of a created object. Only after abstracting the essence of a thing, does the mind go further to form the *concept* of existence, which it realizes each specific essence must possess or it simply would not be.[13]

Maritain's existential approach to the existence of God seems to be a good reply to the objections of some theologians against the Thomistic proofs. Karl Barth, for example, rejects any philosophic approach to the existence of God on the grounds that such knowledge leads to an idol.[14] The only valid knowledge we can have of God's existence is arrived at through faith. A God Who could be known otherwise than through Himself, through revelation, would have already betrayed that He was not the one and only one, and so was not God. Since God cannot be put into a genus, nor be made evident to us, any attempt of philosophy to subject God to human reasoning is futile and misleading. Even the Scholastics admit this, when they affirm that an idea of God has to be corrected through the process of affirmation, negation and super-eminence. *We* do not enclose God in our arguments; it is He Himself who envelopes our thought all the way.[15]

Maritain points out that our arguments do not actually give evidence of the Divine existence itself, of the act of existing which is in God and which *is* God Himself. This would be to have evidence of His essence, for existence and essence are one in God. Our arguments only give us evidence of the fact: the Divine existence must be *affirmed;* consequently, it is correct to attribute the predicate to the subject in the assertion, "God exists."

The explanation of man's natural, primordial way of arriving at this truth answers the objection that philosophic knowledge of God results in an idol, for in the existential approach abstract concepts are relied on less heavily, the reality of God being grasped in an almost instinctive way.

The thinking involved in this existential approach is the activity of the speculative intellect, and the knowledge of God arrived at through it is a conscious knowledge. One knows that God exists and is aware that one possesses that knowledge. But there is another way in which God is known, the way of the practical intellect which refers its activity to some action to be done. Here the knowledge of God that is attained is a pre-conscious or implicit knowledge. One such way of knowing God is involved in the activity of a person's first free choice for good.

MORAL OPTION

When a person first chooses to do a good action simply because he realizes that it is good, he is making an implicit reference to some indefinable but absolute norm and in that moment of decision affirming implicitly the fact of the existence of God. This moment of decision marks a turning-point of his life, and therefore seems to involve a total commitment of himself to good. (The possibility, however, of reversing that commitment remains.) In such a decision or choice for good, God is known in a natural or pre-philosophic way.

In order to choose to do something good, it is clear that a person must know the distinction between good and evil, and that he is acting from a formal desire to do the good because it is good. This implies that there is some ideal or perfect or higher order in which our actions agree with our essence, a "law of human acts," that is above material, visible facts. This law indicates or reflects the further fact that there must be an order of reality that transcends the whole empirical order, which is Goodness itself. Clearly, the law governing human acts subsists in this Goodness for it depends upon this higher reality. When a person makes such a choice for good, he is actually choosing or ordaining his life to this Ultimate Good as well, even though he may not explicitly know God with any kind of conscious, reflex knowledge. In such an act he knows God in a preconscious way, and although will is a "blind" faculty, such a person would know God because: "by virtue of the internal dynamism of his choice of the good for the sake of the good, he wills and loves the Separate Good as ultimate end of his existence."[16]

Quite possibly such a person might even be an atheist, not an absolute atheist, but a pseudo-atheist, one who claims to have rejected God but is actually rejecting a false idea of God. We occasionally find this tendency in those who are approaching adulthood. Doubts arise in them concerning the existence of God because they see flaws in some of the ideas which they have been taught about God. If at a certain decisive moment they choose a good simply because it is good, and in that decision commit their lives to the Good, this action reflects the fact that they have accepted God in fact, in reality, though not consciously. Because of the vital dynamism of this choice, it is possible that it may lead to a conscious knowledge of God. If they do not arrive at a conscious knowledge of God, they are in an abnormal condition and their personalities may experience the anguish of a subconscious contradiction.

It will be patently easier for those thus committed to good to *recognize* the God, Who is Goodness Itself, Whom they have implicitly known all along.

POETRY AND ART

This is still another pre-philosophical way of knowing God implicitly—the way of poetic or artistic experience. While the ordinary process of knowing reality terminates in *ideas,* and the entire intellectual process depends upon outside things, as a cause of our knowledge, poetic or artistic knowledge terminates in an expressed or uttered word. Such knowledge, called "knowledge" only by analogy, would be more accurately termed "experience," since it is a creative activity. As such it presupposes a preliminary pre-conscious knowledge, prior to the artistic activity, but actually extrinsic to it. It is "not formed by a thing in order to know, but forms a thing in order to place it into being."[17]

Maritain describes this poetic experience as knowledge of the mirrors of God. Unable to know God directly in this life, man's knowledge of God is an indirect, reflected knowledge seen in the mirror of creation. The knowledge of poetic awareness is the result of glimpses of Him, seen and experienced by the poet in created beauty, and expressed by him in the work he produces. In the artistic experience, the poet tends toward God, and gains an implicit knowledge of Him. He cannot do otherwise, for beauty is a transcendental spiritual thing whose source is Infinite Beauty. The beauty of poetry is a reflection of the Spirit from which it proceeds. This creative act is a spiritual "tropism" in the direction of God, an obscure, silent movement, a vulnerable but genuine beginning, not of mystical experience, but of knowledge of God, even where the poet has rejected Him or has no explicit awareness of Him.

But if the poet knows God, explicitly, through faith or through reason, one can at times sense in his work the joy of the discovery of God, and can more easily detect the Beauty that he has experienced. This is the case with much of the poetry of the Israelites, many of the Psalms being touched by this sense of beauty and of the wonder experienced by the human author:

> Bless the Lord, O my soul:
>> O Lord, my God, Thou art very great.
> Thou art clothed with majesty and beauty,
>> Robed in light as a mantle. (Ps. 103)

> The heavens tell the glory of God. . . .
>> Day unto day pours forth this word,
> Night to night sends out this knowledge. (Ps. 18)

Here the inspired poet seems to be proclaiming the knowability of God through the beauty of visible creation, as St. Ambrose points out in his *Hexaemeron*.[18] Although the poetic experience of the sacred author resembles in this instance the contemplative's mystical knowledge of God, mystical knowledge of God differs from poetic experience of Him. The contemplative is overcome with wonder and awed into silence at the awareness of God's beauty in creation, while the poet is moved to utter what he has come to know. In the poetry of some of the psalms, both types of knowledge are found, God being known implicitly in the poetic experience and explicitly through faith.

Poetic knowledge is vulnerable in as much as it seems to stem from an emotional experience and so to lack the support of reason. But, as Henri de Lubac points out, it is God Himself who leads us to the knowledge of Himself. On whatever plane we may be, that of the natural or the supernatural, God precedes any activity by which we come to know Him. The perception of beauty and the expression of the beautiful in a work of art or poetry is a *natural* "witness" to the truth that God exists.

The dynamic activity of mind is still another way in which God is known implicitly. The mind seeks truth, and in seeking it, finds God. In the words of St. Thomas, "all cognitive beings know God implicitly in any object of knowledge."[19]

Here again it is a question, not of conceptualized but of lived or implicit knowledge. As such it needs study and analysis in order to be clearly understood.

J. Maréchal, in the fifth volume of *Le Point de Départ de la Metaphysique,* while demonstrating the validity of ontological knowledge, establishes also the existence of God, the ultimate foundation of all thought.[20] In a sense, he may be said to provide a philosophic underpinning for a pre-philosophic intuition concerning the nature of thought.

The point of departure of Maréchal's reasoning is that judgment is a real operation, a real thing. Since all our human knowledge is of existents, that is, of things that exist, our judgment is a *real* activity, depending on experience, on sensible things outside ourselves.

Now when the mind seeks to know things, such activity manifests a dynamic finality. This finality constantly draws the mind to seek more and more knowledge, both in the shape of new things, and about the things it already knows. What the mind is seeking in all this activity is really God, Infinite Truth.

At this point we may review how the mind of man gains its knowledge.

Man has no innate ideas, his knowledge being derived from the senses, the starting point of the whole intellectual process. From the senses, a phantasm or sensible representation is produced in the imagination which the intellect then works on in order to make it intelligible to itself. In the formation of an idea, the intellect manifests an active and a passive aspect, the work of the possible intellect. The agent intellect, having abstracted the idea from the phantasm, joins with the latter to produce an abstract "impression" based on the phantasm. This impression, called a *species impressa* or "impressed species," is then stamped by the agent intellect on the possible intellect and this in turn forms the *species expressa* or "expression," which is the idea or the concept.

The *species impressa* is not a mere intellectual representation of the sensible phantasm. If this were so, all the knowledge that comes to us through the activity of the agent intellect would be a mere addition of facts, *ad infinitum,* a "boxed" or static thing. As Maréchal states, the impressed species or, better, the intelligible species, is a dynamic relation to a phantasm.[21] All the things that we know are referred implicitly to something else. In the dynamic relation of which he speaks two terms are implied, the second of which is quite simply, God. The object of intelligence is being which the intellect seeks to know in order to be perfected. The mind is dependent upon the senses in gaining its knowledge, but there are many things with many characteristics that come into contact with the senses. This multiplicity of things reaching our senses is referred to the Unity of Being by the dynamic relation effected through the intelligible species. In fact, the countless objects impinging on our senses only "make sense" by this reference to the Unity of Being.

Now, since the beings that we perceive are always quantitative things, it might seem as if the speculative unity of Being is merely a unity of quantitative being. But this is not so since there are things which are not material quiddities at all—for instance, abstract, universal ideas or the fact of contingency—all of which we can know in spite of the fact that they cannot be represented by the mind. Although the mind can only form representations of essences of material things, *we know* that we have the power to know things that are not representable. That there must be a principle within us making this possible is evident. St. Thomas offers a satisfying solution with his explanation that in our concepts of objects the mind can have a twofold kind of knowledge. Our concepts can represent material things, while at the same time signifying or "meaning" immaterial things which are not representable at all.[22] Yet in doing so, some form of representation is present which we know *means* something more. For example, when we think of the soul, we represent to ourselves a kind of fluid, hazy substance permeating the body. Obviously this is not correct, since the soul is an immaterial substance. Yet what we really mean or intend to signify is something else, the soul.

This manner of knowing applies also to our knowledge of God, which sems at first to be a "lived" fact or reality discernible only by the process of analogy. Unable to know God directly, we know Him through His effects, between which and Himself there is a relation. (Creation, in fact, is termed the "constitutive *relation of dependence* of created beings to God.) Our concepts about created things and about God cannot be univocal, that is, they cannot mean the same thing, for they are not the same thing. Yet neither are these concepts equivocal, that is, totally different. There is something that is truc of both. Therefore we say that our concepts of God and of creatures are analogous, that is, they apply to God and creatures partly in the same way and partly in a different way. Therefore, when we form a "concept" of God, we really form a representation which is based on material things. Yet because of some kind of instinctive "knowledge" mysteriously present to us we know that representation signifies much more, for God is not a material being and He is incomprehensible to us, that is, our finite minds cannot comprehend God. Moreover, we cannot make a representation of God through an objective concept because in God essence and existence are identical. In creatures they are distinct, that is, every creature is an essence and an existence. Because every objective concept delimits an essence, it is clear that we cannot form an adequate or true representation of God, Whose essence we cannot comprehend. Yet we do "make up" one, so to speak, and then we correct the representation thus made. We say in effect: God is a being. Yet He is not any kind of a created being which we know, but is something much more. He is a Super-Being.

But how can the mind make this correction? If our knowledge, which is effected through the intelligible species were merely a static thing, it would be impossible. According to Maréchal, we must postulate in our objective knowledge something other than an inert gathering and abstractive analysis of ideas. We must postulate a *movement* of thought which constantly moves us above that which is representable through concepts, a kind of "metempirical *anticipation*." Maréchal calls it the "dynamic finality of our spirit."[23]

Every act of knowledge is a *movement,* a passing from potency to act. A movement, however, indicates an end. But what is the end of all our intellectual activity? Certainly not the knowledge of created, finite objects, for these do not satisfy the craving of the mind, precisely because they are finite or limited. Yet how could the mind realize that they were limited unless it had a principle within itself able to go beyond the limit? How can the mind grasp the fact that creatures are limited, relative or contingent, unless it has already implicitly referred them to an Absolute? As Maréchal points out, if we suppose that there is a definite relation between the creature and God, and that this relation, such as it is, manifests itself to us in the creature, as *relative,* this would give us some notion of the higher term. If we see an arrow being shot from a bow, we can know, from the direction in which we see the arrow launched, the position of the target. That is, in effect, what happens to us: "we know creatures as relative to an Absolute Principle and by that—by that alone—we know God."

Thus by studying the way in which the mind forms its concepts, we discover how God is known implicitly in the activity of knowing. The same thing applies also to the way in which first principles operate in us. Actually we exercise these principles in everything we know; thus, each time we come to know something, we affirm that it *is;* we also affirm "Whatever is, is." But we could not affirm that about any created thing because only God *is,* absolutely speaking. Anything else *is,* only because God *is.* For example, we see a thrush and our mind thinks, "That is a thrush." But in the same thought is the implicit affirmation that the thrush *is* as well, that is, that it exists. But it could only exist because God is, and we can only know that the thrush is, because we implicitly affirm that God is.

Maréchal analyzes the dynamic finality of the mind in relation not only to the concept but also to the judgment, for judgment is actually the foundation of the intellectual life. In proving the fact of the dynamic finality of the mind, he indirectly proves the existence of God. His study of the mind's activity in gaining knowledge reveals that the implicit affirmation of the Infinite is a constitutive *condition* of *all* our particular apperceptions of objects. But in positing the dynamic finality of the mind, Maréchal points out the only way to avoid the errors of ontologism, which would hold that we have innate ideas, and agnosticism, which would doubt that we could have any metaphysical knowledge. We are aware of the fact that we can know transcendent Being, but not through any innate knowledge or direct intuition. We realize that we do not seem to have in our knowledge the form of transcendent Being, for we cannot represent it to ourselves adequately. But because of some principle within us, we find that we can know It, can correct our notions about It. This principle is not a direct intuition, but the activity of our judgment which is called affirmation. "Affirmation is the dynamic substitute of intellectual intuition."[24]

To explain this more clearly, it may help if we recall that when the mind forms a concept it always does so in judgment. As has been said, it is really the judgment that is the foundation of our intellectual life. Concepts alone could not suffice, for they cannot adequately explain or give us knowledge of immaterial realities, which we realize we do *know,* in spite of the fact that we cannot form any representation of them. Our judgment or power of affirmation is the activity within us that produces this knowledge. It occurs at the moment when the possible intellect *expresses* that which the agent intellect has impressed on it, namely, the intelligible species. Only at that moment is the mind conscious of the object which it knows, while simultaneously conscious of its own activity of knowing, in a way that is almost "intuitive." If we could know things intuitively, if we did not need our senses to gain knowledge, and if we did not have to reason discursively, we would know immediately the fact of our implicit affirmation of God in every act of knowledge. We would know directly that existing things would not be intelligible to us except by our referring them implicitly to God.

But as things are, to perceive this implicit link we are forced to use all kinds of reflective analyses and dialectical effort. We have to study the activity of affirmation and to see how it reflects a constant movement, never satisfied with affirming finite things; seeking always to know more and more. Since this tendency could not be oriented toward an impossible end, one that would never be attained, man cannot be moving toward non-being, or to a mere abstraction. Actually, his mind betrays an activity that will never allow it to rest until it rests in the Absolute, and therefore such an Absolute must exist. As Maréchal says, "The possibility of the subjective end (of intelligence) presupposes the *reality* of the objective end. In order that the assimilation to the Absolute Being be possible, it must first be necessary that this Absolute Being exists."[25]

This reasoning seems to resemble somewhat Leibniz's ontological argument for the existence of God: If God is possible, He must necessarily exist. But Leibniz meant that if we *imagine* or *think* of a Being such as God, and this *thought* involves no contradiction, then it is possible, and must exist. This may be true in the realm of thought but it does not necessarily follow that it is also true in the realm of reality. Maréchal, however, does not mean this. He is speaking of the fact of the activity of the intellect manifesting a

natural desire for an end that is Unlimited. Moreover, when we
place any intellectual act whatever, what we do is to will this end
implicitly or explicitly, and thus the avowal of a subjective end
necessarily *willed* carries with it the affirmation of an objective last
end necessarily *existing*. Finality and causality are really analytically
linked terms, and to know God as universal End is to know Him
as Universal Cause, for these are two sides of the same relation.

Maréchal's approach, we think, represents an excellent solution to
the Kantian objections concerning the proofs for God's existence.

It has often been argued that the existence of God can be proved
by examining the natural end of the human will, which can be
nothing other than the Infinite. If there is order in the Universe,
natural ends must be attainable. Therefore, God exists. What
Maréchal claims to do, however, is to apply to the theoretical intellect an argument parallel to this argument from the natural end of
the will. Arguing from its natural end, he attempts to show that
God can be known by the unaided theoretical intellect, or, in other
words, by the light of natural human reason.

The first thing to be established in arguing from the natural end
of human intelligence is that the intelligence is a real thing, that the
process of "intellection" really takes place. Now philosophy makes a
distinction between actions perceived as external to us and actions
perceived as internal, for instance, intellection. Materialists have
argued that only external actions are "real," thus dismissing acts of
the pure intellect. There is no such thing as real intellection, they
contend, and indeed the very statement of it is subject to distortion.
But the statement either represents a real intellection or it is pure
fiction. In either case, intellection rests secure. Also, to ask whether
intellection is as real an action as preceived external ones is to pose
the question in reverse. For how does one know external actions
but by a process of intellection? If there is anything to be examined,
it is the "reality" of externally perceived actions in comparison with
the action that ends in a knowledge of them.

The next point to be established is that there is a finality in the intelligence; that, in the processes of intellection which it performs, the intelligence strives towards some end.

Every judgment, argues Maréchal, entails the statement that there exists a conformity between an external reality and the conception which the intelligence has of it. But if the intelligence were completely passive, merely receiving the mental representation of the external object, it could not posit the opposition between judgment and external reality. The intelligence knows its passive impression of the external reality. It knows, too, the limitation of the external reality, but only after seeing the limitation of its own representation of this finite reality. This the intelligence can know only if it has somehow surpassed this limit. We might argue that the intelligence sees its judgment as limited because it knows the object as limited, because it can surpass the external limits of the external object. But this is impossible. We have just seen that the intelligence sees the object as limited only after realizing the limitation of its judgment, of its process of intellection concerning the object. The realization of the limitation must therefore depend on the intelligence's having surpassed the limit in the consciousness of an internal striving, an active tendency carrying it beyond the limited judgment at hand. As Maréchal sums it up:

> But how can one have a consciousness of a limit undergone if not in the consciousness of a condition which, virtually, surmounts that limit: more definitely, in the consciousness of an active tendency, at once controlled and specified by the limiting object? . . . the consciousness of an immanent limitation is but the consciousness of the limitation of an immanent action.[26]

The presence of this active tendency, this desire in the intellect to be active, signals the existence of a finality in the intelligence.

Maréchal now passes from the fact that there is a finality in the intelligence to proof of the fact that the intelligence has a last end. Finality could take the form of desire for a single last end or of a tendency towards mere activity, that is, towards an infinite series of secondary ends. As St. Thomas put it: "But in the action of every agent, a point can be reached beyond which the agent does not desire to go; or else the actions would tend to infinity, which is impossible . . . for the agent would never begin to act, because nothing moves toward what it cannot reach."[27]

In other words, secondary ends are desired only because of the desire for the last end to which they lead. Without this desire for the last end, there is no desire for secondary ends. Consequently, the finality of the intelligence, the active tendency, implies that it has a last end. Kant's objection that an infinite series may be possible on the level of phenomena is thereby avoided. By removing the argument from the phenomenal level, Maréchal does away with the difficulty. Instead of considering observed phenomena, he uses the fact of intellection itself.

His next step is to demonstrate that the last end of the intelligence is infinite and that it exists.

His argument concerning the infinity of the last end of the intelligence can be divided into two parts. It is intuitively obvious, he says, and few have contested it, that the formal object of the intelligence is being as such, abstraction from all limit. When one abstracts from an object all that differentiates it from others of its genus and from every other genus, one is left with the being as such.

The relationship of the formal object of a faculty to the last end of the faculty is clear. Both are determined by the nature of the faculty itself. But the intelligence, as we have seen, is by its nature in a constant state of striving. Now if the last end comprised less than the formal object of the intelligence, the intelligence would not seek after that part of the formal object which was not included in the last end. Such a seeking would be a tendency without an end. Thus, since the formal object includes no limit, neither does the last end. But the formal object of a faculty is a mental entity, an intellectual fabrication used to describe the nature of the faculty. On the other hand, the last end of a faculty must be an attainable reality: otherwise, there is no motivation. The last end of the intelligence must be concrete. Consequently, limitation in that last end cannot be removed by abstraction. For the last end, limitless and concrete, is the infinite being.

Again, in arguing from the natural striving of the intelligence, Maréchal has succeeded in avoiding a Kantian objection. By bringing us directly to the infinite being, he has bypassed the objection of Kant.

Once it has been shown that the natural last end of the intelligence is the infinite being, Maréchal's task would appear to be complete. From the fact that there is order in the Universe, it follows that no natural faculty can be doomed to frustration. Therefore, the last end of the intelligence must exist.

But Maréchal takes the argument one step further by showing that the proposition, "the infinite being does not exist," is contradictory. The concept of an infinite being is not, of itself, contradictory. The last end of a natural faculty in movement is not contradictory. If then, the subject of the atheistic proposition is not of itself contradictory, any difficulty there is will be found to lie in the proposition itself. But the proposition is contradictory because the infinite being includes, by definition, the perfection of complete existence. Taken in this light, the proposition is clearly contradictory. The predicate must be altered to fit the subject, which is not, of itself, contradictory. Therefore, the infinite being exists.

In *Le Point de Depart de la Metaphysique,* Maréchal mentions another type of argument for the existence of God, the argument from moral obligation. All men have a sense of this obligation, a feeling of responsibility to seek "good." But this implies a certain dependence on the part of the subject whose striving for the "good" can only reach its last end in the attainment of the infinite "good," God.

It seems that deLubac also is referring to a kind of implicit knowledge of God, similar to that described by Maréchal, when he speaks of "the affirmation of God." Before there can be any conscious knowledge of God, one must *affirm* that there is a God. In fact, it seems that the kind of knowledge of God that results from this affirmation gives a more accurate kind of knowledge than other knowledge of Him. It is really this affirmation of God that constitutes the fundamental, lived truth which the philosophical demonstrations lay bare. This would seem to be the "primordial existential" knowledge of God which Maritain speaks of, arrived at by means of another approach.

DeLubac's approach to God's existence seems to remove effectively all of Kant's great objections to the classic proofs.

Aspects of the Thomistic proofs for God's existence had come under fire long before the eighteenth century, but the doubts voiced at that time by Immanuel Kant were among the most serious.

Kant's first objection states that since metaphysical determinations and sensuous determinations differ by their very nature, starting from the data of sense observation, one cannot deduce metaphysical conclusions. Since in every syllogism, the terms must be used univocally, if the terms of the premises are taken from the sensuous level, the conclusion drawn from these premises is valid only for this level. In other words, if there is no metaphysics prior to induction, there is no metaphysics at all.

Kant's first difficulty was of a general nature, questioning the very possibility of arriving at the existence of God. The next objection is more particular and concerns the second of St. Thomas's Ways, the argument from the nature of efficient causes.

The argument of St. Thomas hinges on the contention that it is impossible for a series of efficient causes to continue to infinity. There is an order of efficient causes and nothing can be the efficient cause of itself. There can never be an infinite chain of efficient causes for, without a first efficient cause, there would be no effects. Consequently there must be a first efficient cause, God.

Kant claims that on the sense level, the infinite series is rejected simply because of the imagination. Although we cannot *imagine* a world supported by infinite chains of efficient causes on a phenomenal level, such may nevertheless be the case. Kant's attack on the impossibility of infinite series was directed primarily at St. Thomas's second Way but it also casts doubt on the first and third of the five Ways.

Although there may be as many specific differences in the experience as there are people experiencing it, the ways of finding God are generically one. It is in his description of the essential components of the discovery of God that deLubac tends to unite and summarize the thought of his predeccessors. To all appearances, Kant's first objection (the impossibility of arriving at the infinite from a purely finite starting point) is completely accepted in our century. Authors no longer speak of the logical process as terminating in the generation of a *new idea* of God: instead, as deLubac puts it, the discovery of God is a process of the *revelation* of an idea already present in man (though in latent form). We are no longer dealing with an attempt to reach the metaphysical from a sensuous starting point. Rather, the whole of metaphysics is present in us in primitive form from the first moment of life. Consequently, man must attempt to bring ideas he already possesses to full consciousness. As deLubac says, speaking of the existence of God: "But in order that we should recognize it, that which is at the base must appear at the summit."[28] Although the existence of God has often appeared to men to be known only after a conscious reasoning process, it is actually implicit possession of the idea in primitive form that makes the very process possible.

In their expression of this concept of pre-conscious possession of the idea of God, deLubac and Maréchal typify the modern approaches to God.

Man is led to uncover the idea of God from his observation of the finite reflections of God surrounding him. God reveals Himself continuously to man by imprinting His image upon him. DeLubac emphasizes the providential influence of God, Who leads man, by revelation and reason, to more explicit knowledge of Himself.

"No one can have any knowledge of God unless God teaches him."[29]

It is, however, interesting to note the importance which deLubac gives to testimony in convincing others of the existence of God.

Without intervention of God, man's reason is earthbound. He is freed only by infusion of the first principles and by revelation. And testimony is, for the ordinary man, the original contact with revelation.

DeLubac places great emphasis on Maréchal's approach, and in fact appears to have written his whole book, *The Discovery of God,* with its many paradoxes, in order to arouse the reader to *think,* the better to arrive at the reality of God through this activity.

As deLubac points out, however, *any* approach is valid, for the sublime and simple operation which leads to God remains fundamentally the same. The different techniques in perspective and presentation really do not affect the proof itself. The knowledge of God is very close at hand in man, because man is made for God, whether he is aware of it or not. If a man but desires that knowledge, he will arrive at it. In the meanwhile, God Himself leads man on to this knowledge, revealing Himself on a natural level through the "witness" of creation, and on a supernatural level through the witness of faith. It is He always Who has the initiative. When man finally becomes aware of the reality of God with unshakable certitude, the astounding thing is that he "recognizes" God, which he could not do unless he had implicitly known Him before.

Maréchal's analysis, which brings to light this implicit knowledge of God, is especially valuable when we reflect that it expresses what many thinkers of the past seemed to postulate inaccurately and artificially. Could it not be that St. Anselm's awareness of this natural, instinctive knowledge led him to try to prove God's existence in *a priori* fashion? Immanuel Kant, too, claimed that the existence of God could not be demonstrated but had to be postulated as the "unifying idea" of speculative reason. In doing so Kant seems to have seen the need for a radical principle to explain the very activity of the mind. Maréchal answers him by showing that the implicit affirmation of God is the constitutive condition of our knowledge of any particular object, and that there would be no knowledge at all if God did not exist and if He were not the root principle of the mind's activity.

Descartes' "innate idea," Malebranche's "intellectual intuition," Huxley's "phantasm of human imagination," all are inaccurate conclusions about something that is a *fact,* but which seems to elude man's attempts at conceptualizing it—the natural, prephilosophic knowledge of God.[30]

Such knowledge can be arrived at through various approaches: the notion of existence, the moral choice for good, poetic "intuition" or experience, and lastly the activity of the mind itself.

Maritain also suggests that we can come to God by the intuition of our own intellection. Every man experiences this intuition at some moment of his life. One minute he is steeped in pure thought; his consciousness has removed itself completely from the material level. But then it happens. Something brings him back and suddenly he is aware of his thought, aware that, in the process of intellection, he is above matter. How, then, is it possible that he was born? How can it be possible that, prior to his birth, there was nothing, where there is now a man capable of purely intellectual activity? I know from certain testimony that I was born. I know from intellection that, in some form, I have always existed. There is only one way to resolve the contradiction. I have always existed but in a "supra-personal" way, in God.

It is to be hoped that this study may make more clear the teaching of the Church concerning the fact of the possibility of arriving at a knowledge of God through reason, and how this knowledge is arrived at by many who are unaware of the formal proofs for the existence of God. Beyond doubt, there is a natural pre-philosophic awareness of God in man which seems to be the necessary, latent "matter" for the "form" of all the logical demonstrations for the existence of God.

THE TESTIMONY OF OTHERS

In completing his discussion of the ways of the practical intellect, Maritain, like deLubac, includes the testimony of the friends of God. Both men would seem to imply that, no matter what convictions a man has reached through his own efforts, some distrust remains. He is curious to know the feelings of his fellows, uncertain that his own conclusions are valid. Although they are certainly true insofar as he can determine, who is to say that his entire approach, his intellectual equipment, are not faulty? By the same token, having heard the testimony of his comrades, some doubt may remain. Who is to say that judgments of the entire human order have any objective validity?

Perhaps the answer lies in the very fact that man can have such doubts. As Maréchal put it, you cannot know a limit without surpassing it. Perhaps man's very striving for absolute objectivity, perhaps his very mistrust of the entire human order, signals the existence of the Divine.

NOTES

1. R. Guardini, *The Living God*, New York, Pantheon, 1957, pp. 72, 73.
2. Denzinger, *Enchiridion Symbolorum*, Friburgi Brisgoviae, Herder, 1937, #1785, 1806.
3. *Ibid.*, #2145.
4. Cf. R. de Journel, *Enchiridion Patristicum*, Barcelona, Herder, 1946, "Existentia Dei" of Topical Index, p. 762, #86, 87.
5. *Ibid.*, #746, p. 258.
6. *Ibid.*, #1392, p. 503.
7. *Nicene and Post-Nicene Fathers*, Vol. VII, Grand Rapids, Eerdmans, 1956, p. 400.
8. St. Thomas, *Summa Theologica*, New York, Benziger, 1947, I, 2, 1.
9. R. Jolivet, *The God of Reason*, New York, Hawthorn Books, 1960, p. 10, p. 45 ff.
10. J. Maritain, *Approaches to God*, New York, Harper, 1954, pp. 1–10.
11. J. Maritain, *The Range of Reason*, New York, Scribners, 1951.
12. Guardini, *op. cit.*, p. 78.

13. J. Maritain, *Existence and Existent,* New York, Pantheon, 1949, pp. 26–27. As Maritain says, our idea of being precedes the judgment of existence materially speaking, i.e., in the order of material subjective causality; but formally (i.e., in the order of formal causality), the judgment that it exists precedes the idea of being. Maritain outlines the steps of this intellectual activity as follows: first, there is the judgment (improperly so-called) of our external senses, of a sensible object, which is equal to saying, "This exists." Then, but really at the same time, the intellect and judgment are awakened and there follow both the formation of an idea ("this *being*" or "thing") and the judgment ("this being exists"). Finally the *idea* of existence is formed. "The intellect grasps the act of existing affirmed in the first judgment of existence, in order to make of it an object of thought; it makes unto itself a concept or notion of existence (*existentia ut significata*)." (p. 27).

14. K. Barth, *The Knowledge of God and the Service of God,* London, Hodder and Stoughton, 1949, pp. 19–22.

15. H. deLubac, *The Discovery of God,* New York, P. J. Kenedy and Sons, 1960, pp. 88–89.

16. J. Maritain, *Approaches to God,* pp. 84–97.

17. J. Maritain, *Situation de la Poésie,* Paris, Desclée de Brouwer, 1938, p. 104.

18. de Journel, *op. cit.,* #1315, p. 488.

19. St. Thomas, *De Veritate,* q. XXII, a. 2, ad i m (*Truth*), trans. by Robert W. Schmidt, Chicago, Regnery, 1954, p. 42, Vol. III.

20. *Le Point de Départ de la Métaphysique,* Vol. V., 2 Ed., Paris, Desclée de Brouwer, 1949. For an outline of Maréchal's approach, cf. the article by G. Isaye, "La Finalité de l'intelligence" in the *Revue Philosophique de Louvain,* Vol. 51, Feb. 1933, pp. 68–100.

21. *Le Point de Départ de la Métaphysique,* p. 219.

22. *Summa Theologica,* I, 13, 2c, cf. also J. F. Donceel, S.J., *Philosophical Psychology,* New York, Sheed and Ward, 1955, p. 228. Also Maréchal, *op. cit.,* p. 278.

23. Maréchal, *op. cit.,* p. 259.

24. *Ibid.,* p. 321.

25. *Ibid.,* p. 448.

26. *Ibid.,* p. 548. Cf. K. Foster, "Affirming God: an informal reflection, *Blackfriars* XL, 1959, pp. 17–22.

27. St. Thomas, *Contra Gentiles* III, 2, 3.

28. deLubac, *op. cit.,* pp. 39–60.

29. *Ibid.,* p. 68.

30. E. Gilson, *God and Philosophy,* New Haven, Yale University Press, 1941, pp. 117–118.

APPENDIX A

St. Anselm's Ontological Proof

TRULY there is a God, although the fool hath said in his heart, There is no God.

And so, Lord, do thou, who does give understanding to faith, give me, so far as thou knowest it to be profitable, to understand that thou art as we believe; and that thou art that which we believe. And, indeed, we believe that thou art a being than which nothing greater can be conceived. Or is there no such nature, since the fool hath said in his heart, there is no God? (Psalms xiv. I). But, at any rate, this very fool, when he hears of this being of which I speak— a being than which nothing greater can be conceived—understands what he hears, and what he understands is in his understanding; although he does not understand it to exist.

For, it is one thing for an object to be in the understanding, and another to understand that the object exists. When a painter first conceives of what he will afterwards perform he has it in his understanding, but he does not yet understand it to be, because he has not yet performed it. But after he has made the painting, he both has it in his understanding, and he understands that it exists, because he has made it.

Hence, even the fool is convinced that something exists in the understanding, at least, than which nothing greater can be conceived. For, when he hears of this, he understands it. And whatever is understood, exists in the understanding. And assuredly that, than which nothing greater can be conceived, cannot exist in the understanding alone. For, suppose it exists in the understanding alone: then it can be conceived to exist in reality; which is greater.

Therefore, if that, than which nothing greater can be conceived, exists in the understanding alone, the very being, than which nothing greater can be conceived, is one, than which a greater can be conceived. But obviously this is impossible. Hence, there is no doubt that there exists a being, than which nothing greater can be conceived, and it exists both in the understanding and in reality.

APPENDIX B

Augustinian Proofs for God's Existence

St. Augustine's proofs for God's existence aim not only at demonstrating that God exists but that He is the soul's highest good, the source and sum of man's happiness. His intention is not only to elicit from men an intellectual assent to this truth but to arouse in them as well an ardent desire to cling to the Truth itself, the Supreme God, the font of all human happiness.[1] In seeking God, the soul is seeking happiness. Since the whole man is to rejoice in the possession of God, it is with all man's powers that he must search for the evidences of His existence.

In the *City of God,* Augustine recalls how the neo-Platonists had described the highest Being and shows how the characteristics which they had ascribed to the highest Being relate to men. The Supreme God is the Maker of all created things, and the first principle of nature. He is the light by which all things are known, and in Him is the truth of doctrine. He is the Good, the model of all human goodness and therefore, the ultimate joy of life. These three aspects of God are discussed throughout Augustine's writings, especially in the passages pertaining to God's existence. He is the cause of existence, the principle of knowledge and the rule of life.[2]

Augustine's most complete proof is contained in his early work, *De Libero Arbitrio,* Book Two. It is the longest, most developed, and in it we find elaborated the three major themes, Being, Knowledge, Goodness, which appear in his other works in briefer, fragmentary form. Setting out with the avowed aim of establishing the existence of God and refuting those "fools" who say in their hearts there is no God, Augustine makes use of the dialogue, as borrowed from the philosophers, in the form of an account of discussions held in Rome with his friend, Evodius. If the whole has a highly personal character, it is because it records and synthesizes Augustine's own journey towards a reasoned belief in the True God.

Some have thought that because of Augustine's insistence upon the role of faith he neglected that of reason, playing down its capacity to reach a knowledge of God. Now while he certainly holds that faith in divine revelation gives us the highest and firmest certitude, he also argues that genuine certitude can come from reason. But the truth at which reason arrives, though certain, is only a feeble type of knowledge compared with that of faith. Well aware of the importance of reason in making credible the claims of faith, Augustine still knew from long experience the difficulty of arriving at a secure and clear knowledge of God without His gracious self-disclosure.[3]

In the *De Libero Arbitrio* faith is the starting point, for Evodius already believes in God's existence. Certain himself by faith that God exists, the question is: will he be able to use this faith to convince an unbeliever? The first proof is the proof from authority, but Augustine limits its use to those who have already felt the pull of God, men of manifest good will. When dealing with matters as serious as the existence of God, authority will not suffice with those who are half-hearted in their search, with the "crafty and obstinate." However, once the sincerity of the unbeliever is granted, the proof proceeds rapidly and terminates suddenly. If the inquirer is sincere he wishes his own good dispositions to be believed, even though he can offer no convincing proof of them. Should he not then be willing also to accept the testimony of the Scriptures, to believe men who have lived with the Son of God, who have borne witness to His revelation even with their blood?

Though Augustine will accept the truth of God's existence on the testimony of others, still he wishes to "know and understand" what is believed.

In the *De Libero Arbitrio* he quotes Isaias: "Unless you believe, you will not understand" (Is. 7, 9).

With this quotation he introduces a point somewhat puzzling to his commentators. Does Augustine mean that a rational proof of God's existence must be preceded by an act of faith, that a rational proof is not possible unless one already believes? According to Cayré, Augustine uses the phrase "to understand" with reference, not to the comprehension of a natural object, but to an intellectual penetration of supernatural truths.[4] That faith is not Augustine's starting point for arriving at a knowledge of God can be seen from the type of argument he proposes. It is rather from a moral point of view that Augustine sees the importance of believing in order to understand, for things are grasped more clearly by good men, understood better by those prepared to adhere to them and to live the truth in charity. This first disposition has thus an intimate bearing on the goal, the gift of the soul to God. Belief implies a willingness to submit to the truth once it is found, and only through possession of this initial readiness to bear witness will one be able to recognize truth when one confronts it. Augustine knew that it was his own longing for the truth, his steadfast search, which made him open for it when it came: "(God) speaks by the truth. . . . if the ears of the mind be ready."[5] In his work, *Against the Sceptics,* Augustine explains to a friend that truth can not be seen unless one has a passion for it that affects one's whole being. This he knew from experience, for while he was still unprepared to follow the divine and eternal law, he made only ineffectual gropings for that truth to which the law pointed.

"We are impelled toward knowledge by a two-fold force: authority and reason."[6] But a committed, an unchallenged faith by no means excuses reason from providing proofs for God's existence, for what is believed without being somehow known is not fully found. The method Augustine follows in *De Libero Arbitrio* is closely linked to the thought of the proof itself. Reason must discover that there exists a realm above it. Consequently, it must progress, seeing, step by step, what it knows, how it knows it, and what remains mysterious, transcendent, opaque.

GOD, CAUSE OF EXISTENCE

To reach the fact of God's existence we can begin quite simply with the fact of our own. Can we be certain that we exist? Augustine spends very little time with Evodius on this point, although the problem of the ability of the human mind to know truth, even the truth of one's own existence, had long been a source of personal torment in his own search for truth. Categorically, he states that we can be certain of our existence, for even if we are mistaken we would still have to exist in order to err. In either case, it is clear that we exist, for a thing cannot be and not be at the same time. Consequently, to be mistaken that one exists is an impossibility. This part of the proof, establishing the certitude of our existence, emphasizes the power of the mind to know, more than the fact of existence, although both facets are present. As a matter of fact, Augustine composed, in 386, an answer to those who denied that the mind could know truth. There he confessed that the Academicians had so influenced him with their doubts that he had lost all desire to search for what could not be found. The arguments against the skeptics are drawn from logic ("it cannot be both day and night"); from mathematics ("if there are one world and six worlds, it is clear that there are seven worlds, no matter how I may be affected"); and from the immutable truths of ethics ("it is most true that we ought to live justly").

The idea of existence itself as a sharing in God's existence, which is implied in *De Libero Arbitrio*, is amplified in *The City of God*, where Augustine speaks of God as the Supreme Existence," the One Who "supremely is." The things that He made "He empowered to be," communicating a limited existence to them, to some more, to others less. Since no created nature is contrary to the nature that created it "save that which does not exist," there can be no being contrary to God.

Plato had seen that God alone could be the "Author of nature, the intelligence and the kindler of love by which life becomes good."[7] And although the philosophers dispute concerning the causes, no one doubts that nature has "some cause, science some method, life some end and aim." We could not be the cause of our own nature, for we would then be able to teach ourselves and have no need of authority, and our own love would suffice for us, which experience tells us is not so of our nature. He must also be our Teacher, and the Giver of that unchanging love which alone will make us happy.

Limited existence is used again by Augustine to prove the Supreme existence from the fact of the constant love which all things have for existence. Without exception all creatures that exist have such love for their being that they would rather exist in misery, it would seem, than not exist at all.

We see the traces of God in all creaturedom because created realities could not "so much as exist or have a particular nature or follow any law unless they had been made by Him Who supremely is "and is supremely wise and supremely good."[8]

Augustine frequently uses the words of St. Paul urging that we go from visible things to the knowledge of the invisible, to Him Who made them. The whole universe proclaims that it has a Creator, its very limitations announcing that He is unlimited. This Creator has given to men a mind to see that living things are to be preferred to non-living, that those that have understanding are to be preferred to those that do not, and that the immortal is to be preferred to the mortal. Even the pagan philosophers grasped that no material thing could be God, and rising above matter, sought a spiritual God. Realizing that whatever is changeable is not God, they transcended every changeable body and spirit to seek—the Unchanging God. Since in changeable things the form which makes them what they are cannot come from themselves, it can come only from Him Who truly is, from Him Who is unchangeable. If we consider the world, order, or life, whether of the plant or animal kingdom, whether of that life which gives understanding as in man, or the life of the angels, we are forced to conclude that all can "only be through Him Who absolutely is." These three degrees of creation are from Him because He is One, and in Him, to live, to understand, and to be blessed are the same as to exist. From His unchangeableness and simplicity we understand that everything that is was made by Him, but that He Himself was not made by anyone.

In the *Confessions* the same theme occurs. Beholding the things that are below God, Augustine sees that they "neither altogether are" nor "altogether are not." Insofar as they are from Him, they are; but insofar as they are not He, they are not. Without exception, all owe their being to God and all are true insofar as they imitate His truth.[9]

GOD, CAUSE OF KNOWLEDGE

In *De Libero Arbitrio,* once Evodius admits that he exists, Augustine leads him to the realization that in order to know that he exists he must be alive, and that if he comprehends the fact of his own life then he must be possessed of understanding. Seeing that he has not only being, but life and understanding, Evodius is led to a study of the comparative worth of the three.

In order to establish the greatness of reason, an essential part of his proof, Augustine questions Evodius as to the activity of his reason, beginning at what is most easily perceived, so that by means of visible, created things he may rise to what are created but invisible, and thus to God.[10] From careful investigation of the bodily senses the following conclusions become evident: 1)Each sense has its own object. The eye sees in any bodily object, not its texture, but its color or size. Hardness or softness are reserved for the sense of touch, odors for the sense of smell, and so forth. 2)Some senses have objects in common; for example, both touch and sight can determine the shape of a thing. The care with which Augustine examines the activities of the senses and the knowledge which comes from them is dictated by his desire to formulate the law which he sees as governing all knowledge. Since the senses are obviously limited in their power, it would appear that it is not the sense itself which distinguishes its proper object. The eye does not know what is its proper object, yet it restricts itself to this object. Does reason, then, make this distinction? Evodius thinks not, for beasts have the power to seek or to avoid what the senses report. Since animals lack reason, this perception must be something which we will call an inner sense. In a series of painstaking steps Augustine tries to convince Evodius of the distinction which exists between color, the seeing of color, the possession of a faculty by which we see color, and finally the perception that we have of sight; and similarly in the case of the other senses. He concludes that we know bodily things by a bodily sense, but it is a sense which cannot be perceived by itself. The inner sense perceives the activity of the outer senses, all is then made known by reason and grasped by knowledge.

What is the value of these three degrees of knowledge? By determining the value of the objects of outer sense, inner sense and reason, we can discover the relative worth of the knowledge which they bring us. The objects of the bodily senses—color, taste, and so on—are to be placed on the first rung of the ladder of creation: that is, among those things which merely exist. Since the sense itself, however, is on the second rung, among those things which not only exist but live, then the sense is superior to the object sensed. In what class then is the inner sense? Evodius has said that the inner sense is superior to the bodily sense, yet he places both on the same level, among those things which have existence and life, but are without understanding. If they are on the same level, what is it that distinguishes the one from the other?

Evodius replies that the inner sense is better than the outer sense because it controls and judges the outer, supplying what is wanting in the outer, and being able to tell the outer what should be done and what is needed in each case. The inner sense judges the outer sense in the same way that the outer sense judges the bodily object. The word "judge" here does not have its ordinary significance but means simply that one thing has active influence over another, and this implies dependence of the one upon the other.[11] What judges the inner sense? Obviously, there must be something above it, for we have already judged it by stating that it is higher than the bodily sense. It is clear that reason, which is the highest part of man's nature, is what judges the inner sense. The element of law discoverable in the activity of the senses points implicitly to a law-giver; God is guiding through the natural law.

The principle of subordination found in the relationships among the three types of knowledge will also be found in the life of the mind itself and will be used again by Augustine. For the present, he has established that the inner man, or mind, knows by the ministry of the outer man or sense. This theme, however, is found again in the *Confessions* where the supremacy of reason is shown as a means to reach God. Looking within himself, Augustine sees soul and body. In which should he seek God? The answer lies in the fact that the "better is the inner." It receives the message of the outer man, reporting the things of heaven and earth, and it tells them that they are not God, but that He made them.[12]

The next step in the journey of discovery will be to investigate if there is anything which exists and which is above reason. If any such being does exist, Augustine believes that it must be God, since reason is so exalted as to contain within itself all the other degrees of perfection. He then sets out to prove that the only thing above reason is unchangeable and eternal and therefore must be God. From this point on the search for the immutable becomes the characteristic of the proof. The very notion of an unchangeable being implies all that is understood by the Supreme Being since all the things around us, and we ourselves, are changing, limited, contingent, imperfect. Either this higher being is God, or if there is something higher, then *it* is God. "If you find there is nothing above reason except the eternal and unchangeable, will you hesitate to call this God?"[13]

Although reason is the most noble of our faculties by virtue of its control over the senses, it is, of course, not unchangeable. Observing the devious paths of our own reason we find that while sometimes it seeks the truth passionately, sometimes it does not seek it at all. So reason itself cannot be God. As bodily things change, so does the mind. Yet reason, by its own power, unaided by the senses, can discover something beyond it, nobler, unchanging—and that is God.

Augustine, using the senses as a means of comparisons, begins to come to the more essential part of his argument. There are certain things which are our own and certain things which we hold in common. For example, it is plain that each of us has his own bodily senses, seeing and hearing what others neither see nor hear. It is also clear that each of us has his own inner sense, judging what we see and hear, and each of us has his own reason. But, among all the objects of the senses, some are perceived in common and some are perceived separately. The objects of the sense of hearing, for instance, are wholly perceived by all who hear them. Sound is thus in a different category from the objects of touch and taste which cannot be shared wholly by two persons at the same time in the same way that two persons can hear the whole of the word simultaneously. There is a difference also on the part of the objects. We do not alter, by hearing, the objects of this sense, as we do with the objects of taste. The former are a common possession; they do not become private or changed in our contact with them. Augustine concludes that the faculties are distinct and that the objects are distinct from the faculties although they are often common to some.

Besides the knowledge obtained from the senses there is a higher knowledge not gained in this manner. Augustine, wishing now to show that there are absolute and unchanging truths, asks with regard to the objects of reason, if there is anything which all know in common and which does not change, whether seen or unseen? And he replies: yes, the "law of truth of numbers."[14] This is seen by all who have reason. When we see it we do not change it. It is impressed on our minds by its own nature. But the objection is made: could not this law come from the contact of the senses with visible things? To this Augustine has four answers.

First, the bodily senses cannot know the meaning of division or addition of numbers.

Second, the numbers which are present in visible things will not last longer than the things themselves. But the law of numbers is eternal and immutable. Seven and three have always been, and will always be, ten.

Third, no bodily thing is truly one, although we can say that it is imperfectly one by its resemblance to perfect oneness. No matter how small a material thing, it will always have parts. Yet we have a notion of perfect oneness or else we would not know that these things were not perfectly one. Therefore, if we do not receive the notion of one through the senses, we do not receive any number through the senses.

Fourth, the bodily senses could not know all numbers because by our stable laws of multiplication we can extend numbers beyond the reach of the senses. Numbers must somehow exist everlastingly since they do not change. They can be known by all, even though some understand them better than others, but they are not changed by our knowing them. Still, since we cannot see all numbers, how do we know that this law will always be true? Augustine concludes that we know this only by an inner light, unknown to the bodily senses.

What Augustine means by the inner light and its connection with the truth is not entirely clear from his writings. But we do know that he was influenced by the doctrines of Plotinus on this point when he said that rational souls derive the light of truth from God, the true Light. The neo-Platonists saw God as the "Sun of the intelligible world," according to St. Augustine, and he agrees with them that God gives the light by which the soul sees the truth. In *On the Trinity,* he says that the mind sees intelligible things "in a certain incorporeal light . . . . just as the corporeal eye sees adjacent objects in the corporeal light."[15]

Some have felt that God gives the light in the same way that the "agent intellect" of Aristotelian philosophy draws from created things the knowledge of their essences. The difficulty in interpreting

Augustine's theory of illumination can be seen from this question: "Is the inner light, this incorporeal Sun, God Himself?" At the end of the argument, Augustine says that if there is nothing more excellent than truth, then truth itself is God. Since he does not show us anything more excellent, it would appear that truth is God. If it is this eternal truth of which he speaks when comparing the ability of a healthy eye to look at the sun with that of a healthy mental gaze to look at the truth itself, it would mean that one can see God in this life directly, by seeing the truth directly. That Augustine does not hold this is the general opinion of his commentators, for then there would have been no need of his proof for God's existence.[16] But the explanations vary as to the precise meaning of this illumination.

Although we do not see directly the sun which gives light, but see it indirectly and inadequately, in the same way we see the Creator, not directly, but as cause of all that is. The lack of agreement among Augustine's commentators on his theory of knowledge, so closely linked to the proof, means that they also disagree as to the validity of the proof for God's existence.[17] Augustine limits himself to saying that there are eternal truths, for example, numbers, and that they are not derived from changeable things. Reason recognizes them, by a power higher than the senses, but does not cause them.

Gilson thinks that the doctrine of the internal light, or the interior teacher, is proposed as an explanation of the guarantee of the *truth* and consistency of the *judgments* involved, rather than an explanation of the manner of obtaining knowledge.

It is certainly not possible to understand Augustinian illumination as pantheism, ontologism, the reminiscence theory of Plato (pre-existence of the soul) or some kind of natural illuminism. What the illumination seems to be is an indirect view of God, an obscure intuition of Him as the foundation for the absolute unchanging character of the judgment of truth. These fundamental truths enlightening the mind do not come from the mind itself but are a created participation in the Perfect Truth which is

God.[18] Apparently the truth which is God Himself is reached by seeing created truths which do not have their reason for being in themselves. God is seen through seeing what He has made. Such a created participation in the Perfect Truth would be a natural presence of God in the soul and this presence has the effect of illumination because man possesses reason.

In addition to the truth of numbers, Augustine wishes to establish, in the *De Libero Arbitrio,* the unchangeable character of wisdom. Is there one wisdom, open to all, or does each man have his own wisdom? Since many seek different goals and still consider themselves wise, it is hard to see what wisdom is. Augustine holds that it is "the truth in which we distinguish and grasp the Supreme Good."[19]

It follows that, if one seeks what is not good, one departs from the truth and is in error. Even before we are happy, the idea of happiness is in our minds. But we need wisdom in order to reach this happiness because wisdom shows us the good which will make us happy. But we have an idea of wisdom because we have an idea of the good.

Is wisdom the same for all? It is, if the Supreme Good is the same for all, but since men take pleasure in different goods, it would appear that wisdom is not the same for all. But even if the goods are not the same for all, wisdom can be the same for all because it can be as the sun which enlightens many objects even though in itself it remains the same.

To discover whether this wisdom is common to all, it is well to examine in what manner men see it. We know with certainty that men wish to be happy, and we also know with certainty that wise men exist. Do men know these facts in the same way that they know their own thought? Or do they know them in such a way that they are simultaneously perceptible to all, so that they immediately know them to be true? If the latter is the case, even if one does not wish someone else to see them, one cannot prevent their being seen. Therefore, they are common to all. Other truths common to all are: every man should be given his due, the better should be preferred to the worse, and so on.

As soon as we admit a truth common to all, we are admitting that it is unchangeable and present to all who see it. The truths already mentioned are concerned with living a good life and are eternally, universally true and unchangeable. Therefore, they are concerned with wisdom.

Plato had held that the final good was to live according to virtue, that the only one who can do this is the man who knows God and also imitates Him, and that this knowledge and imitation are the cause of happiness. In his work *On the Trinity* Augustine expands this concept to show how one can grasp God in seeing created goodness. Speaking of the goodness of earth, of health, of cheerfulness, of righteousness, he says that each has its own goodness, but that if we could remove the thing that is good from the goodness itself then we would be able to see unparticipated good. We would see something that is good, not by some other good, but by the "good of all good." We could never say that one thing is better than another, with a true judgment, unless we had a conception of universal good. The good which we seek for the soul is not a good found by judging, but one that is found by loving. And this can only be God. To prove that in seeking God we are not seeking a good "something" but a "good good," Augustine looks at the two words: "good mind." The thing to be noticed is that there are two concepts, good and mind. The mind has no part in making itself good, because before it existed it had nothing by which to make itself anything. It is the will which makes the mind good, by turning it towards the good. A mind is not called good until there has been the action of the will upon it.

Augustine used this same argument to prove that all things are good, but not sovereignly good. Things can be corrupted, and are corrupted. But corruption impoverishes, that is, diminishes things in goodness. But if things were not good they could not be corrupted; if they were completely corrupted they would cease to be. Therefore, as long as a thing is, it is good, although deficiently so.

What is the relationship of this wisdom to our minds? Does it share the nature of the mind? Augustine holds that it does not. The soul is neither the Truth nor a part of the Truth. Just as the objects of sight and hearing are distinct from the senses and do not share their nature, so the objects of the mind are distinct from the mind and do not share its nature. Is it then lower, equal to, or higher than our minds? If it were lower, we would make judgments about it, but we do not. We merely say that seven and three are ten, not that they should be ten. And if it were equal to our minds, it would be changeable, since the mind is changeable. But wisdom is not changeable. Even though we sometimes see the truth less clearly than at other times, the truth itself is not changing. Therefore, if it is neither lower than our minds, nor equal to our minds, it must be higher, transcendent, unchanging and sovereign—God Himself.

We have therefore found something that is higher than our minds, the thing for which we have been searching. "If there is anything more excellent it is this which is God, but if there is nothing more excellent, then truth itself is God".[20]

Having discovered this truth, Augustine urges Evodius to "embrace it if you can, and enjoy it." He offers it to him for his happiness, for what more does he need to be happy than to contemplate the firm, unchangeable, most excellent truth, absolute truth? He cannot be happy, nor be truly free, unless he enjoys something securely, without fear of losing it, without fear of its being changed. Such a good he possesses when he possesses indefectible truth.

Augustine never denied the reality of this world but he emphasized that there are higher realities. In the writings of Plato, the world that we see is only the shadow of the real world. In the real world there exist unchangeable and eternal ideas of greatness, beauty, justice and similar concepts as well as ideas of corporeal things. For Augustine, the world of Ideas in the thought of Plato became the "Wisdom of God, the Eternal Thoughts of the Creator."

The Christians had found in Plato a valuable spiritual philosophy to aid them in counteracting the current materialistic philosophies. But it was the works of Plotinus which had the most influence on Augustine, for they had taught him to search for "incorporeal truth." In his proof in *De Libero Arbitrio* the element of progress is stressed; the progress from the world of individual things to that of the eternal and unchangeable. In Plotinus's philosophy there is the possibility that the soul, freeing itself from the individual body, can rise to the Universal Soul and thence to the Divine Mind. This sense of passing beyond created things manifests itself in other works of Augustine, particularly in the *Confessions*. There he describes his search for God as passing "from bodies to the soul," to its "inward faculty" and finally to reason. But finding reason to be variable, he searched further until he had arrived at "That Which is." But where Plotinus attributed intelligence to man because his soul came from the world soul, Augustine said that man possesses eternal truths because he is created by God and reflects the perfections of the Divine Intelligence Who naturally illuminates his mind.

In Plato, the One was an impersonal absolute; in Augustine, it is the most active of realities. In Plato, there are intermediaries in the creation of the world; in Augustine, God is absolutely transcendent yet touches each of us directly, drawing and illuminating us. In Plato the world is drawn from the substance of the One; in Augustine the world is the work of the One. No created being is divine in the proper sense. And although creation is known by revelation, this does not mean that a sound intellect could not discover God as Creator.

Augustine's theory of illumination, by means of which the soul has knowledge of God's existence, is similar in some points to that of Plotinus. But Augustine always had in mind the illumination which comes from the Light, as St. John recorded, in the words of Christ concerning Himself. Augustine's proof derives from a mind already enlightened by faith and is directed primarily to Christians who desire to strengthen their faith. Appealing to the universal desire to exist, to be wise and to be happy, he argued that these desires could only come from Him Who is Existence, Wisdom and Goodness itself and Who intends to fulfill what He has planted in man's nature.

Augustine undertook the proof in obedience to the Lord's command, so that the truth might be found by His teaching. The truth that he sought was not a speculative one, but the Truth which is also salvation. From the natural light of reason touched by the divine illumination he meant to lead man to the Eternal Light Who is also the Way, the Truth and the Life, Who seeks man before He is sought and Whom man unconsciously seeks in his every search for good.

NOTES

1. *St. Augustine. The Problem of Free Choice. De Libero Arbitrio* Translated and Annotated by Dom Mark Pontifex, Ancient Christian Writers Series, Westminster, Md., Newman, 1955, p. 121.
2. W. J. Oates, *Basic Writings of St. Augustine,* Vol. II, New York: Random House, 1948.
 The City of God, tr. M. Dods, p. 110 (Book 8 ch. 9), cf. also F. Cayré, *Dieu présent dans la vie de l'Esprit,* Paris, Desclée DeBrouwer, 1951, p. 59.
3. A. C. Vega, O.S.A. *St. Augustine—His Philosophy,* Philadelphia: The Peter Reilly Co., 1931, p. 105.
4. Cayré, *op. cit.,* p. 114.
5. *The City of God, ed. cit.,* Book 2 ch. 1, p. 313.
6. D. J. Kavanagh, *Answer to Skeptics.* A translation of St. Augustine's Contra Academicos. New York, Cosmopolitan Art and Service Co., Inc., 1943, p. 227.
7. *The City of God. ed. cit.,* book 12 ch. 25, p. 180.
8. *Ibid.,* p. 171.
9. *The Confessions of St. Augustine.* Tr. E. Pusey, New York, Pocket Books, 1951, p. 118.
10. *The Problem of Free Choice. ed. cit.,* p. 82.
11. Cayré, *op. cit.,* p. 121.
12. cf also *St. Augustine-Essays.* New York, Meridian Books, 1957, M. C. D'Arcy, "The Philosophy of St. Augustine," p. 178.

13. *The Problem of Free Choice. ed. cit.*, p. 91.
14. *Ibid.*, p. 98.
15. *Basic writings of St. Augustine: On the Trinity,* Ed. W. J. Oates, New York, Random House, 1948, Tr. A. W. Haddan, Book 8, ch. 4, p. 777.
16. E. Gilson, *Introduction à l'étude de St. Augustin,* Paris, Vrin, p. 110.
17. R. Ackworth, "God and Human Knowledge in Augustine: The Theory of Illumination," Downside Review (75) 1957, pp. 207–221.
18. Cayré, *op. cit.*, p. 108.
19. *The Problem of Free Choice, ed. cit.*, p. 117.
20. *Ibid.*, p. 120.